AF380466

Wild, Wild Erie

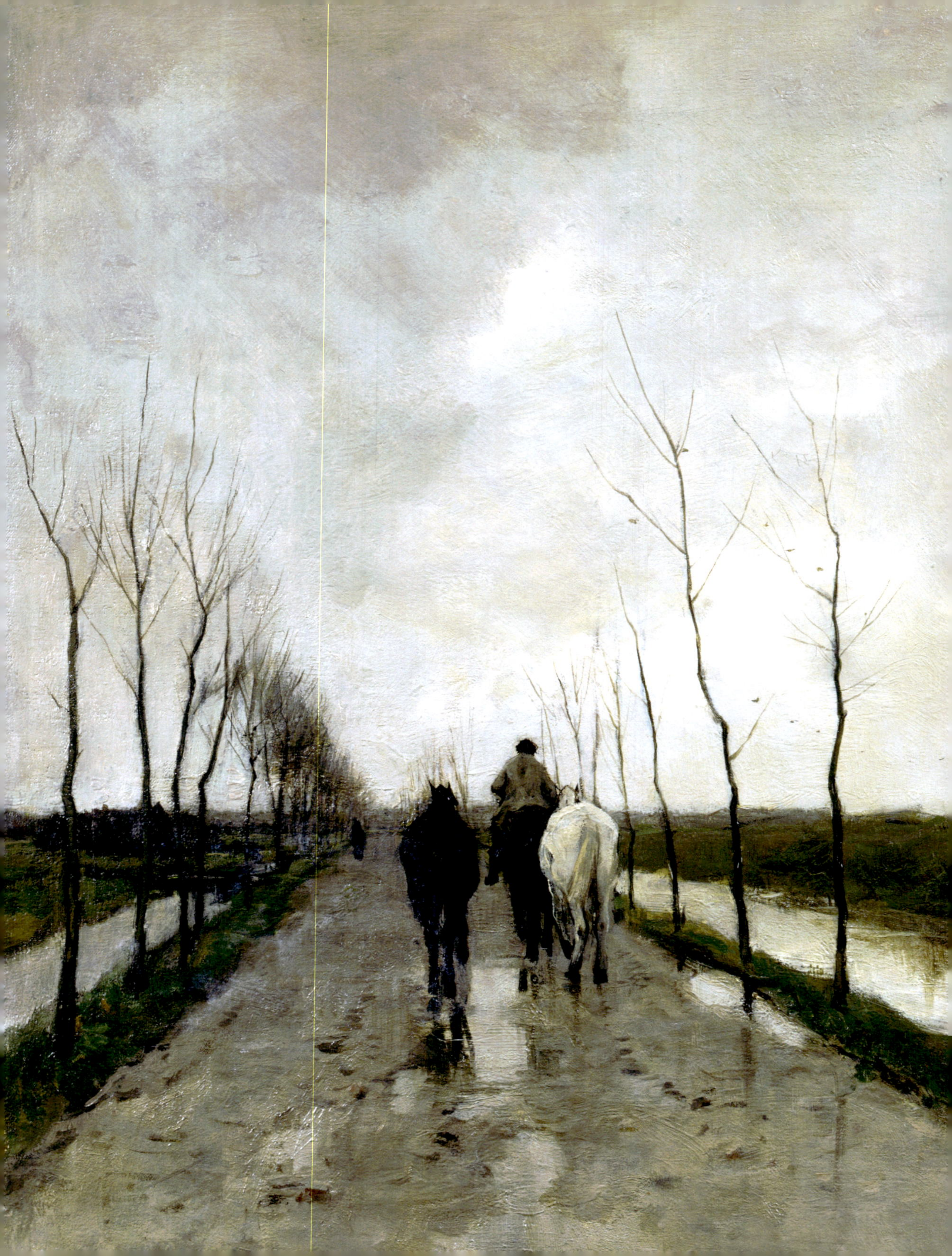

Paul Durcan

Wild, Wild Erie

POEMS INSPIRED BY WORKS OF ART IN THE
TOLEDO MUSEUM OF ART, OHIO

Toledo Museum of Art

TO

B. G. McCALL

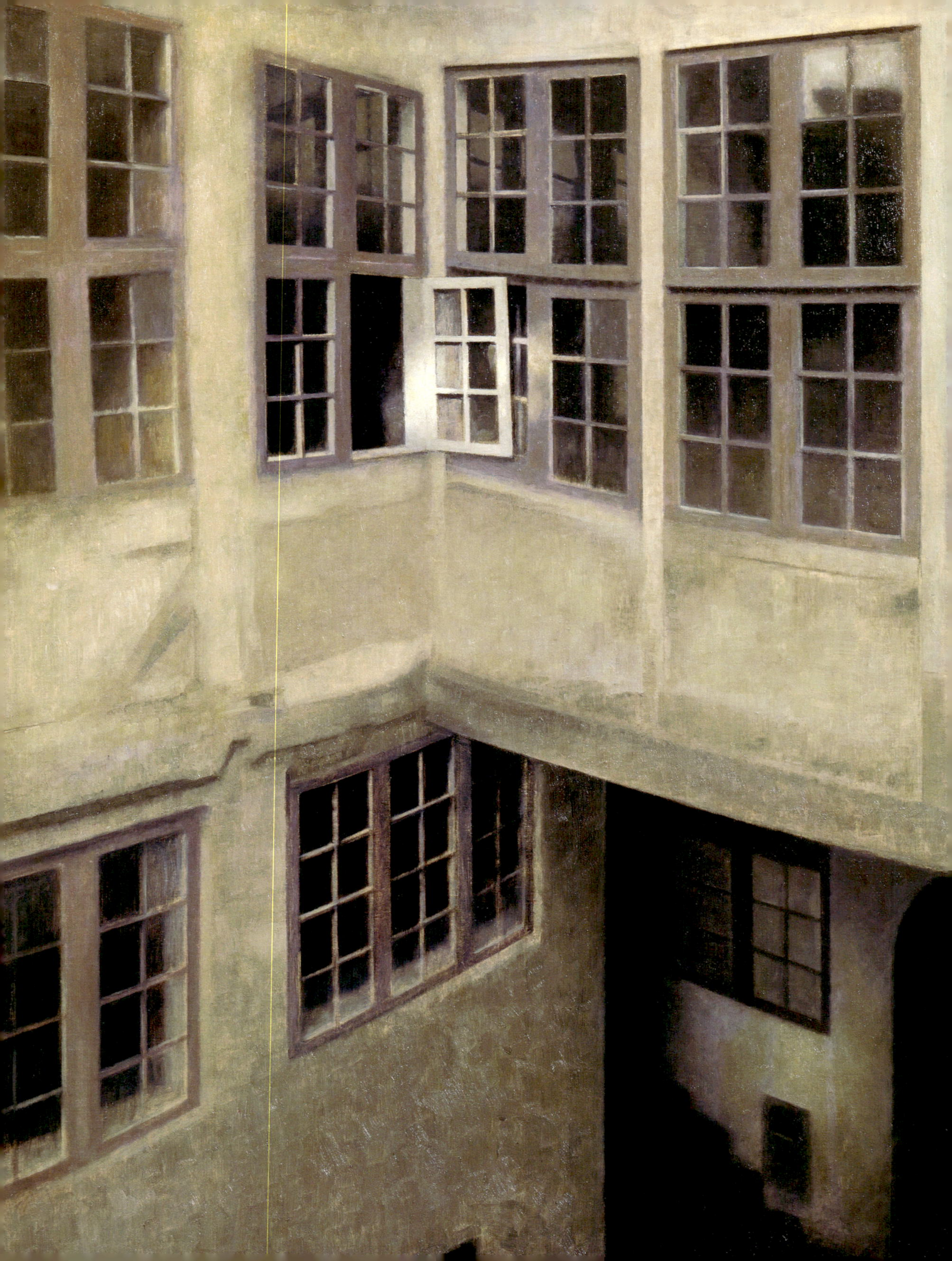

CONTENTS

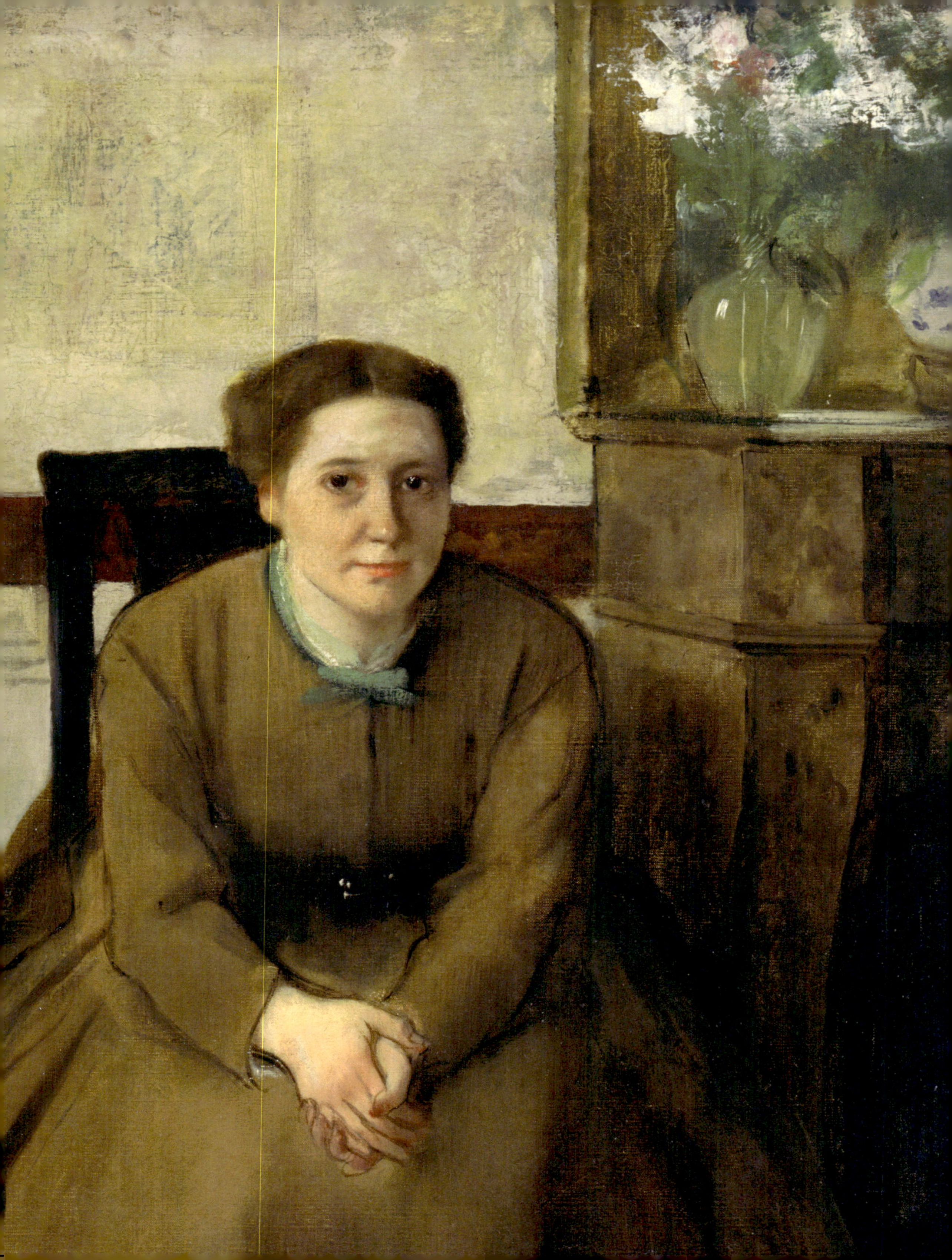

PAUL DURCAN will tell you that nothing gives him greater satisfaction as a poet than bathing in the pure enjoyment he experiences with works of visual art. Quite simply, he loves them. They bring out in him an artistry with words, at once playful and poignant. He is at home with them. His acclaimed art research projects, *Crazy About Women* at the National Gallery of Ireland, Dublin, in 1991, and *Give Me Your Hand* at the National Gallery, London, in 1994, are now joined by *Wild, Wild Erie,* his book of poems responding to works in the celebrated collection of the Toledo Museum of Art, to become a trinity of books of insightful, creative storytelling.

A collection of the caliber of the Toledo Museum of Art whets his erudition and powers of research, and he embraced the challenge thoroughly on intensive visits to Northwest Ohio. This Irish poet listens for word gems, nuggets, and pearls and for compelling turns of phrase, whether found in the works of art themselves, or in the utterances of museum staff and visitors. These he records carefully in handwritten notebooks where they become a lexicon to peruse when he composes his poems. It will be clear to the reader of *Wild, Wild Erie* that this singular poet has had a whale of a time in Toledo, Ohio.

Did Mr. and Mrs. Libbey—who feature prominently in this collection of poems—ever imagine that their outpouring of love for Toledo that led them to give to that city a museum so wonderful, would cause so many to continue to fund it, to support it, to champion it, and to make it ever more remarkable? When I proposed inviting Paul Durcan to weave his words in Toledo, Deke and Hope Welles, with Steve and Julie Taylor, happily said yes, we will help, recognizing that Paul's poems would be a literary treasure and would burnish and polish Toledo's gem of a museum. Paula Reich accepted the request to oversee the project and carried out her task with typical grace, becoming, in the word of our poet, his Maven. In *Wild, Wild Erie,* with surgical prowess and keen wisdom, Ireland's intelligent and fearless bard pokes and prods, claps and sings his way through a truly delightful gathering of poems. They demonstrate that vision creates empathy. A key role of art museums—one shared with the art of poetry—is to help communities become more tolerant and diverse. May these poems enrich your mind, warm your heart, and help you to celebrate our shared humanity.

BRIAN P. KENNEDY
President, Director & CEO, Toledo Museum of Art

ACKNOWLEDGMENTS

TWENTY-SIX YEARS AGO in Dublin, Spring 1990, I received a letter from a stranger—the then Assistant Director of the National Gallery of Ireland inviting me to lunch. It transpired he had but recently transferred from the Department of Finance in Government Buildings. He was a formally dressed young man exuding the energy of the techno-fiscal virtuoso; yet within less than twenty minutes I realised I was conversing with someone whose passion for Art was such as is rarely ever seen in anyone anywhere; a man for whom Art is as much the Bread of Life as Poetry, Music, Prayer. The man's name was Brian Kennedy and it is he who is the only begetter of this volume entitled *Wild, Wild Erie*: poems inspired by paintings and sculpture in the Toledo Museum of Art. It would be impossible to express adequately my gratitude to the man who is now the Director, CEO, and President of the Toledo Museum of Art.

I owe a similarly inexpressible debt of gratitude to Paula Reich, my in-house—in-museum!—editor, guide, mentor, shepherd, manager. Her art-historical expertise, her patriotic love of the Midwest and of Toledo, Ohio and of the Libbeys' great museum, her naturalist's ultra-sonic sensitivity, and her patience with an itinerant poet from Ireland, inspired as well as enabled me to compose our book.

Thirdly, I owe gratitude beyond words to Stephen D. Taylor of the TMA Board of Directors without whose 100% support, hospitality, and generosity the project could not have gone ahead.

To the entire team at the Toledo Museum of Art I bow my head in silent, affectionate, almost tearful, yet almost light-headed gratitude: "in energy alone is eternal delight."

PAUL DURCAN

The great cosmetic
Strangeness of the normal deep person.

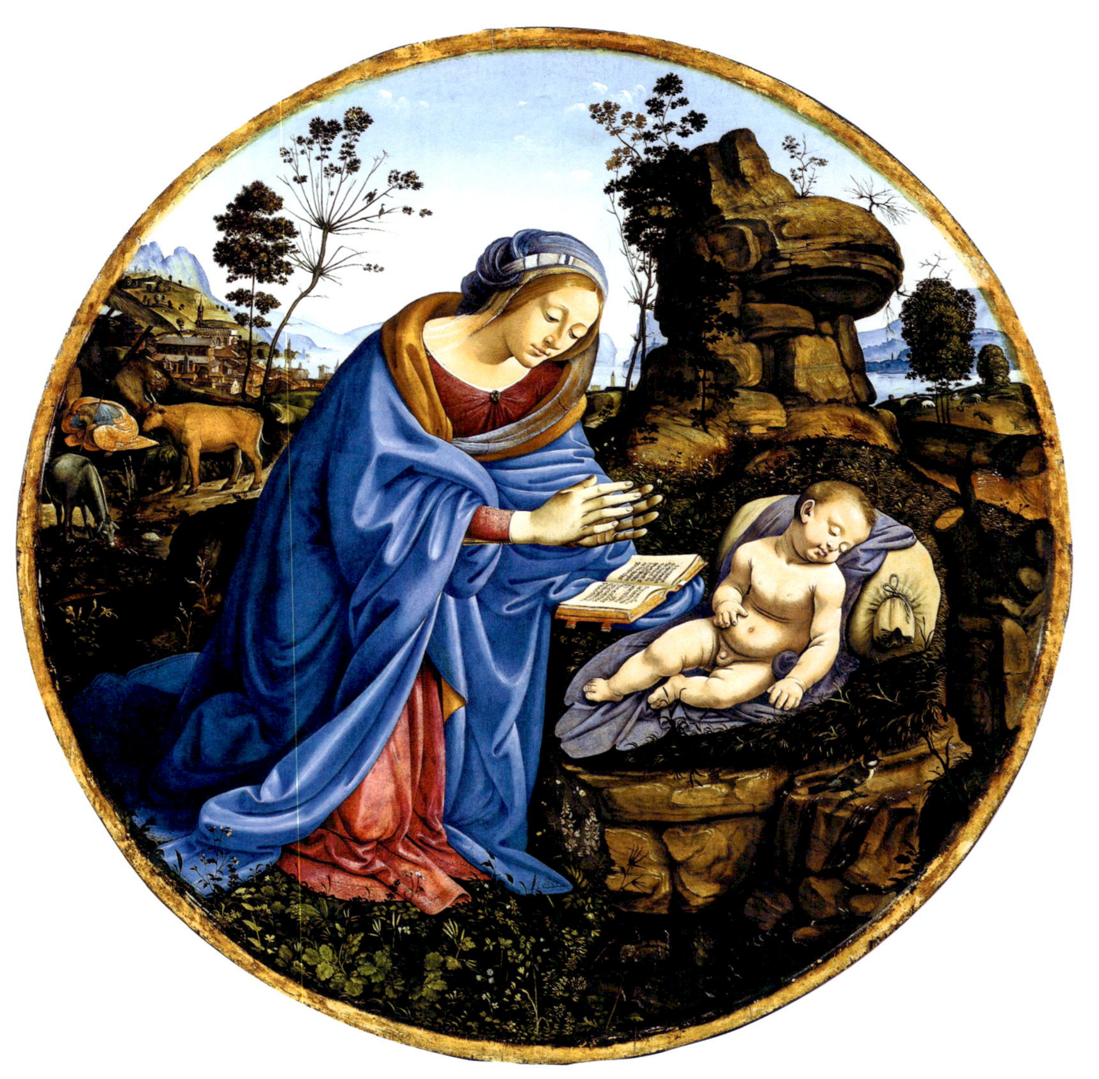

PIERO DI COSIMO

What's Baby Jesus up to?
Apart from not falling out of the cosmos
From his precipitous niche in the turning world
Baby Jesus is talking to his mother in his sleep:
"Ma, forgive me, but I am actually not in the raw:
Grandma got me a body-hugging outfit
In a Gymboree outlet in Westlake, Ohio:
It's a four-in-one: jump-suit; romper; body-suit; and one-piece.
The four-in-one shows off my body-and-soul to best advantage;
All my wrinkles, all my creases, all my puffiness crumpled-rumpled;
All my fatty, roundy body parts in finest flower;
My chubby bell-push compact penis; ditto my belly-button;
What a chubby little champ I am for a future gold medallist!
Best of all, it shows off how hale and hearty I am:
My great colour – my pale-gold champagne complexion;
If only I could describe my dreaming to you
But so far I'm only getting it out to the great tit
With the black head and the yellow breast!
Not to worry, Ma, I'll get my signal to you any minute now –
We'll have our song-line constructed in a jiffy.

Mother and Child slowly turning in the turning world,
Round and round, Clew Bay behind them spilling out of itself –
(Visitor, please stand back or you might get splashed and wet.)

Mary is reading that part of the gospel which annunciates
How crucial it is to sleep. Sleep, Baby, Sleep. Sleep, Man, Sleep.
Her spouse Joe is asleep in his Golden Bean-Bag,
One foot dangling – dangling out over the precipice
The other side of the stream from Mary – the ox
On the bridge is sniffing Joe – Joe is always and forever
Dozing and he likes being sniffed by oxen and – by Mary.

Another Joe – Joseph of Arimathea – the fastidious, conscientious auto dealer –
He's got the *Resurrection* franchise – he's getting everything ready
For Baby Jesus – the Sepulchre in the Rock.
Mary is a first-time unmarried mother adoring her baby boy.
(Real country-town girl – gorgeous red-head –
I glimpsed her once in a hospital in Damascus.)
The cosmos, after all, is spherical, so in his dreaming
Baby Jesus is spinning it, round and round
Until it lands on the rocky coastline of the Pleiades.
And to think!
The Great Mountains of the Reek and the Beautiful Town of Westport
Would all fall tumbling out of the cosmos were it not for one chubby small baby boy
And the courage of his mother and father – refugees on the run!
Be nice to your tadpoles!

". . . I am a living stone, rejected by human beings"
1 Peter 2: 1-5

I live with my parents on the right bank
In an upmarket suburb of Bassano Veneto.
My parents are respectable, upper-middle, middle-class.
Myself, as per usual, I am bored out of my mind
In my bedroom in our comfortable, hygienic villa
Fronting the river when suddenly gazing out the window
I glimpse a family of travellers on the far bank
On the stony hill under the high wood.
They're a notorious family of tramps – refugees –
Illegal immigrants – and WANTED.
Making a bee-line for Ashtabula, Ohio, I'd hazard.
Clandestinely, I have the highest admiration for them.
I can see the father, Old Joe, out front of his wife.
He's gripping a strong staff and he's tethered himself
    by rope
To a cute, prize-winning ass on which his young wife is riding
    side-saddle
With a new-born infant in her lap.
Good God! She must be half her husband's age!
How fortunate he is – Old Joe
To have such a sensationally alluring young *matrushka*

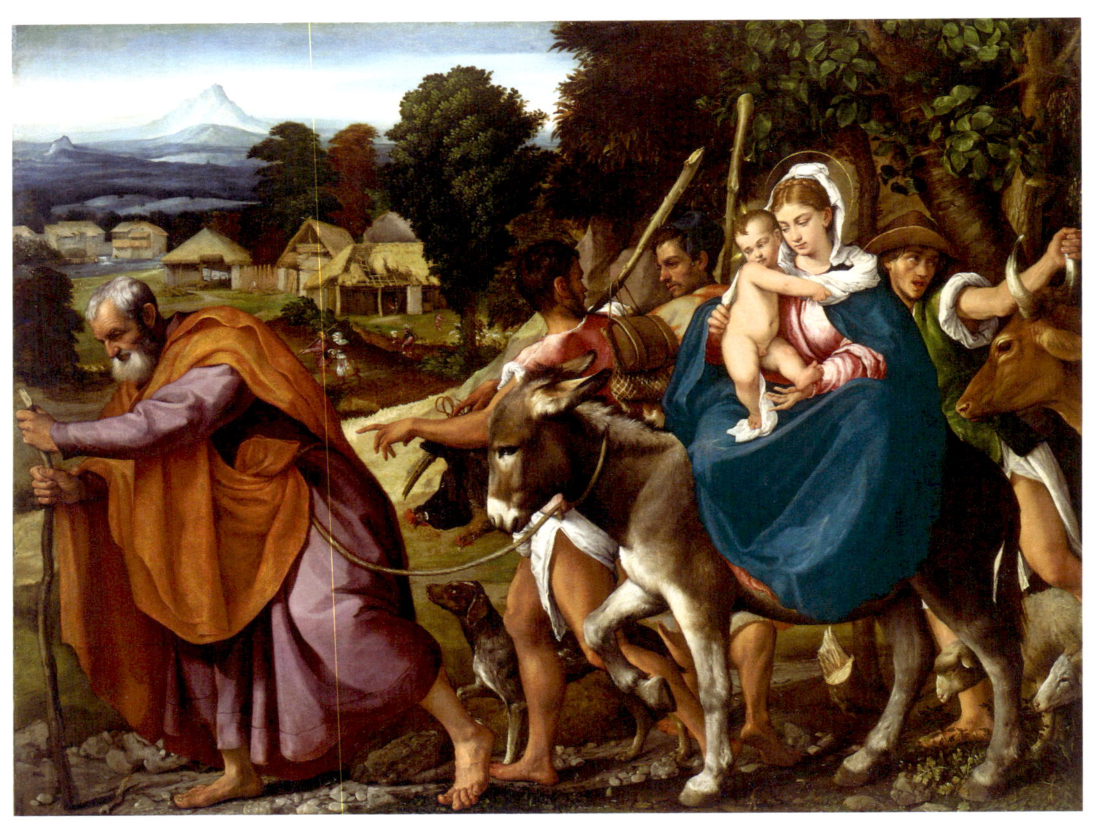

JACOPO DAL PONTE, CALLED JACOPO BASSANO

For his wife. No wonder
He is striding out so purposefully.
He's a king who does not know he is a king
But she is a queen and she does – in her frisbee halo.
She is the epitome of prettiness, of dignity, of wholesomeness;
Her red hair tied up in a braid across her head
But an itsy-bit – more than an itsy-bit – perplexed,
Possibly petrified; I wonder why.
I suspect it must be their constant predicament
Of being always on-the-run, always being WANTED,
Hunted creatures, and her infant male toddler boykins
Clinging to her and yet she's so surprisingly confident
In her casual hold of him.
They have at least three young male shepherds with them –
Members, I guess, of the extended family.
All these illegal immigrants have extended families.
But no! It is THEY who on this earth
Are the respectable people – the stars – the superstars – the Big Salt!
Comfortable, righteous people like me and my parents
Are bit-players, literally time-servers.
We are so uncool that we cannot see it
Whereas Joe, his girl, their baby boy and retinue are the Future of Cool.

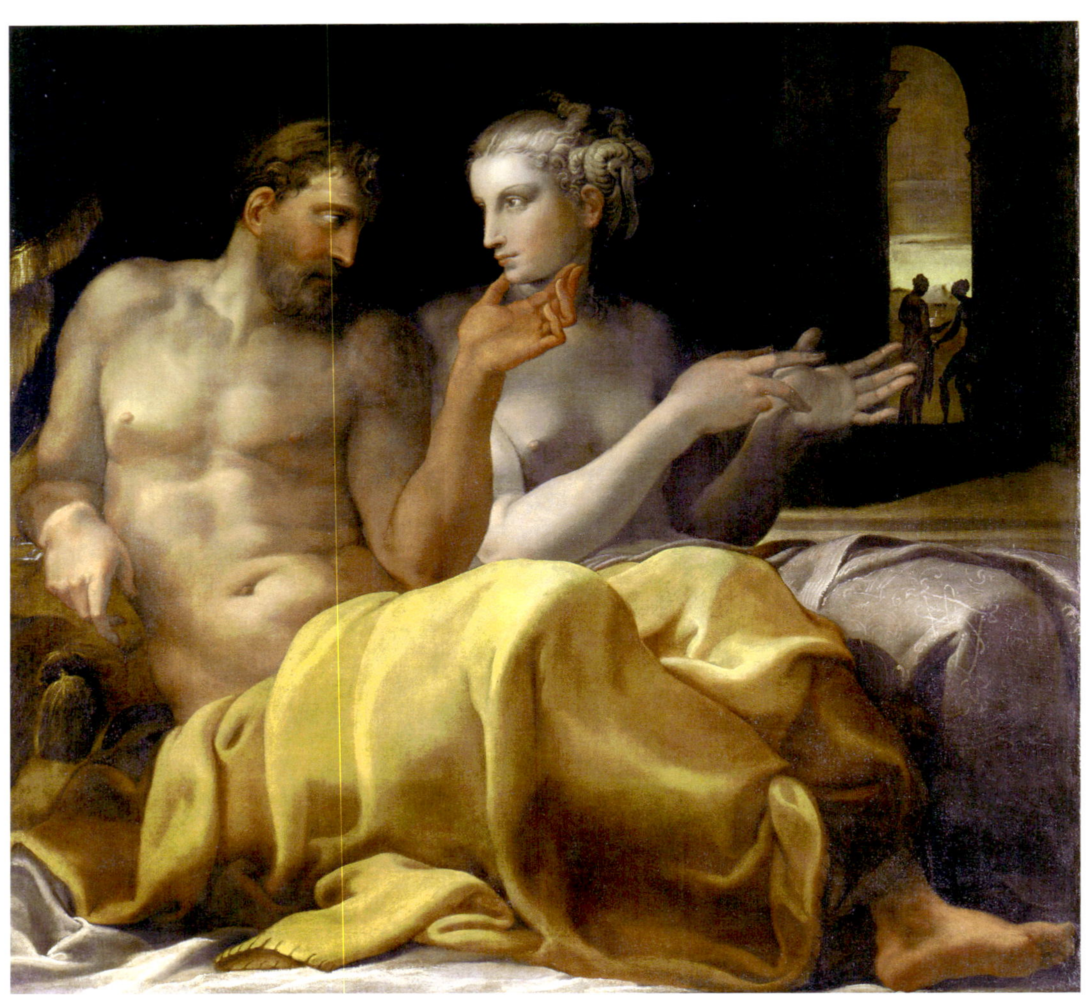

FRANCESCO PRIMATICCIO

I

My name is Edward Drummond Libbey and with my wife Florence Scott Libbey
I own this here Toledo Museum of Art in Ohio in the Midwest
And one winter's day that lovely little boy of ours in the Museum Store – Carlos –
Calls me over and tells me about a dude in Chicago
Called Primaticcio and he goes on to enlighten me –
So excited he can barely utter –
That this Primaticcio dude has painted a painting –
An oil on canvas –
Entitled *Ulysses and Penelope* and that – according to our Carlos –
It is the "greatest Love Painting ever painted"!

"Well, well, well" says I "Now here's 19 million bucks:
Take a Birmingham Limousine, thee Carlos, to Chicago this very minute
And bring back this Prima – whadya say his moniker is –
This Ticcio – with his 'greatest Love Painting ever painted' –
We could do with a touch of Ticcio in Toledo, Ohio."

II

What is the first thing a husband and wife do –
Who through no choice of their own get separated for twelve years –
In the long, dark night of their reunion?
Whose love and desire for one another burned even stronger

Through all those years of war, terror, carnage, seduction?
After nodding to their two North African slaves quietly to get lost
The first thing they do is pole-vault into bed
Performing an almighty get-together
And becoming *Uno Voce* again –
One act of love that prolongs itself
For twenty-four hours.
The second thing they do is to sit up in bed
And utter inaudible adoration of each other.
She counts her lovers on the fingers of both hands
As if reporting to him her losses on the Nikkei Index
Whilst – with her wren-like jawbone betwixt his thumb and forefinger –
Tearfully he confesses to his infidelities and his detours.
She asks: Y'ould rascal, would you like me to pour you a glass
          of 45% Proof?
He says: Sure thing, gal, sure thing.
Under the golden blanket and the dove-grey quilt –
You never know – except –
Peace, perfect peace.

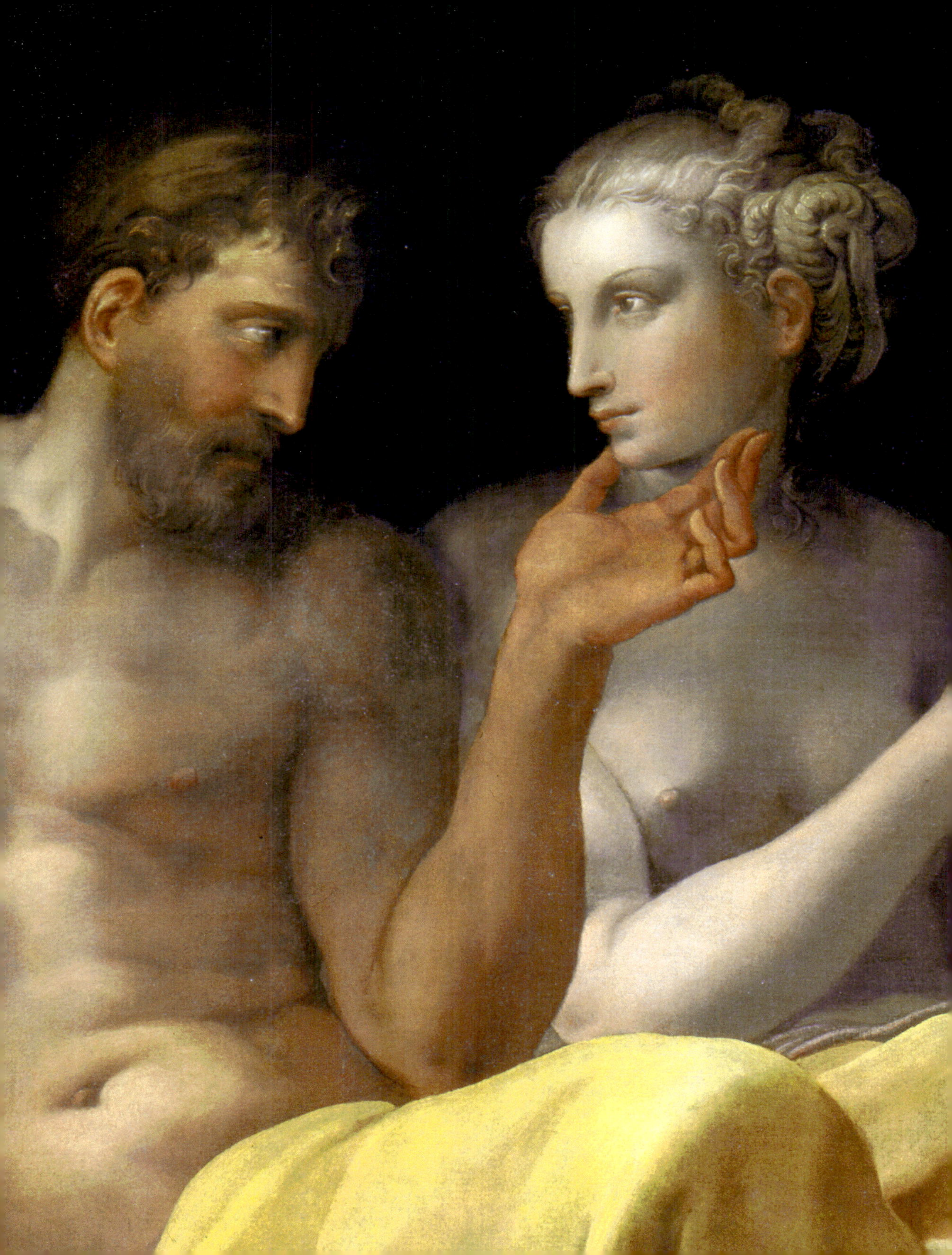

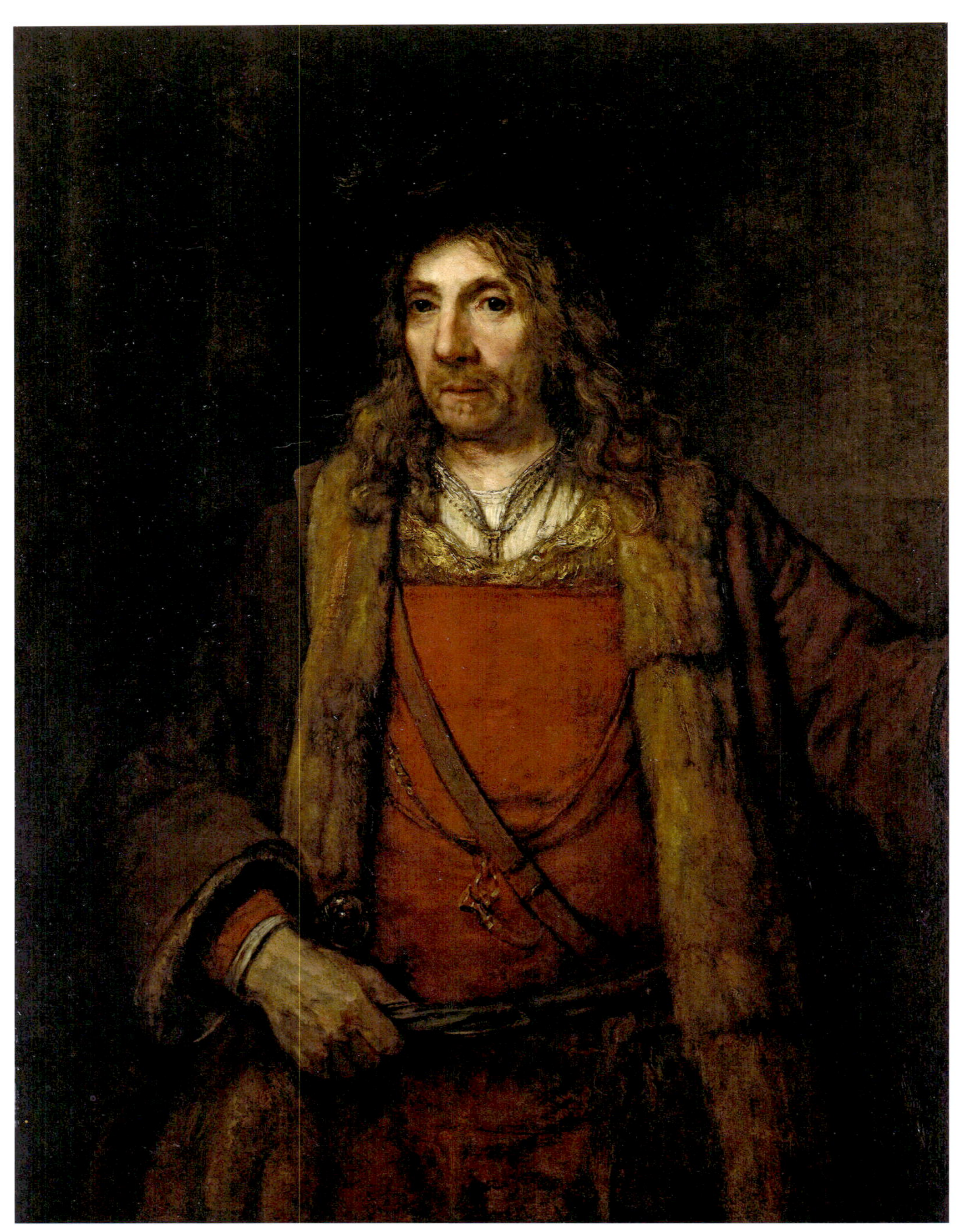

REMBRANDT HARMENSZ. VAN RIJN

I am a 17th-century Dutch Hollywood movie-star –
Sir Dirk Van Fine –
A celebrity, being above the law, I can do what I like –
The epitome of dissipation,
A champion of debauchery,
The idol of women and their ruin.
I like to quaff the Scotch Whisky by the bottle –
Two or three bottles a day.
As I peer out at you – kinda tricky to get my eyes open –
I am slitting your throat
Which after copulation is what I like to do
And pour you into a trash can.
Dirk the Ripper they call me
Or Dirk the Recycler.
The skirts adore my earring!
When I'm not working and I do work a darned heck of a lot –
13,000 movies, they reckon I've made –
You can view most of 'em on YOUTUBE –
I like to lounge at the street-corner sipping an Americano
With my toothpick between my lips, eyeing the Madonnas,
Sizing them up. I'm as dissolute a star
As you'll ever find in the Dutch Republic.
Have you ever seen a greedier mouth in your life?
A meaner, crueller, more sadistic pair of eyes?
Now trust me with your daughter and I'll do the necessary.

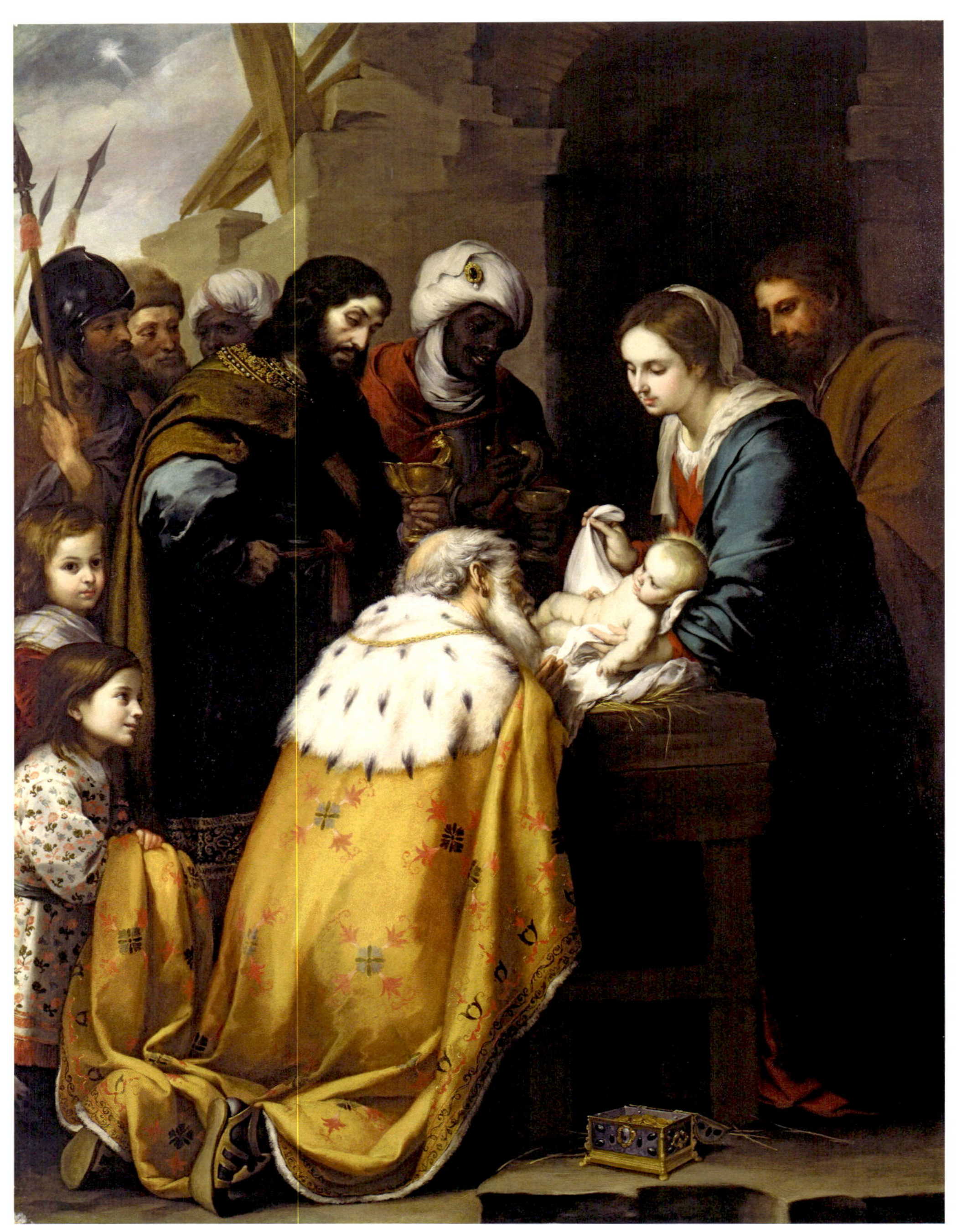

BARTOLOMÉ ESTEBAN MURILLO

I'm a bonny wee boy and my name it is Jesus

And I like you – old wise man –

'Cos you're cool

And 'cos you've got hairs in your nose and big bushy eyebrows;

I like you oodles

'Cos you've got smiling eyes so biggy-big

I could go to sleep in either of them.

May I tug your beard? And make you giggle?

I like it that just like my own papa

You don't wear a hat;

That's a cute ermine cape you've got on you

And where in Disneyland did you get that lavish golden cope

Or who gave it to you

Or did you nick it from one of those loaded old cardinals?

I LOVE the small boy holding up your cope –

Real, real pretty and you've obviously put a spell on him –

You wicked old magician!

And I love you too because I know

You're not going to kidnap me

And I'm chuffed that what Mama most wants to show off to you and your pals

       from Eritrea and Syria

Are my private parts – my chubby little thing-me-bob which is the soul of me;

I love doing pee-pee at sunrise and, of course, pooh-pooh too.

Joe my papa is a quiet guy –

Prefers the background – cannot stand limelight –
Prefers sleeping – or just leading the way –
Prefers his own company – it's not that other people are hell
Or anything but deffo they are purgatory.
PS: thanks a mill for the gold casket –
It'll help to pay the check for the Toledo-Maumee Holiday Inn
Which Ma and Papa have promised me for tonite! Have a good nice day, old man!

THE CLOISTER GALLERY
MID-12TH TO EARLY 15TH CENTURY

The Cloister is the hub – and, of course, the pearl –
Of the Monastery of the Toledo Museum of Art.
The Rule is Benedictine and, therefore, democratic:
Contemplating its medieval arcades
You are as likely to meet the Abbot
(Or the CEO as nowadays he or she is known) –
Greeting the infirm, the needy, the put-upon –
As a staff member of the Museum Café
Or a guard, a Docent, a volunteer, a cleaner, a curator, a Head
        Of Interpretive Projects, an archivist, an intern, a librarian
And the Abbot is as likely to be in shirt sleeves and loose-knotted polka-dot tie
As he is to be in his monastic, abbatial canonicals –
His cloak, his habit, his sandals, his cowl –
And of course a great many of the monks are women
And they are not all married monks, some are single – or singular – monks.

No pilgrimage to the Monastery of the Toledo Museum of Art
Is complete without an Epiphany in the Cloister:
My own personal Number One Epiphany in the Cloister
Occurred on a summer's day last year in 2015
When we were featuring PLAY TIME liturgy in the monastery
And as I was performing my Contemplation-Headstands in the Cloister
Two small boys – aged about 7 and 10 –
Were standing on tippy-toes at the font

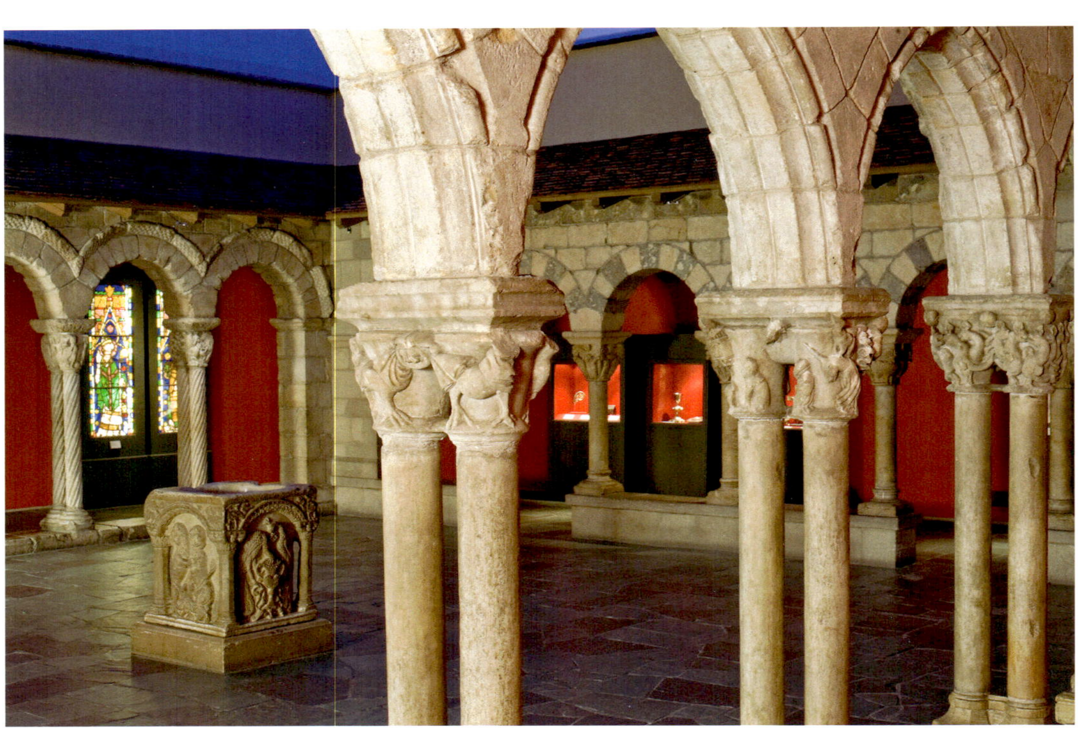

At the heart of the garth
When one of the guards – as kindly a retiree
As ever you'd meet on the shores of Lake Erie –
He pressed a switch and the ceiling above the cloister
Changed into a night sky –
All blue and void except for a few handfuls of stars –
The Pleiades and The Plough and Orion and Cassiopeia –
And the planet Jupiter.
The two boys were very shocked – as by a street-miracle –
A miracle, for God's sake! – which of course it was:
The miraculous coming together of technology and
          one man's charity.
The two boys asked the man: "Who are you? What are you?"
Gently, gently, kindly, kindly, beaming crinkles and wrinkles –
The old guard bowed down low into their ears:
 "I am Al Tennyson – the Cloister's Stellar Manipulator."

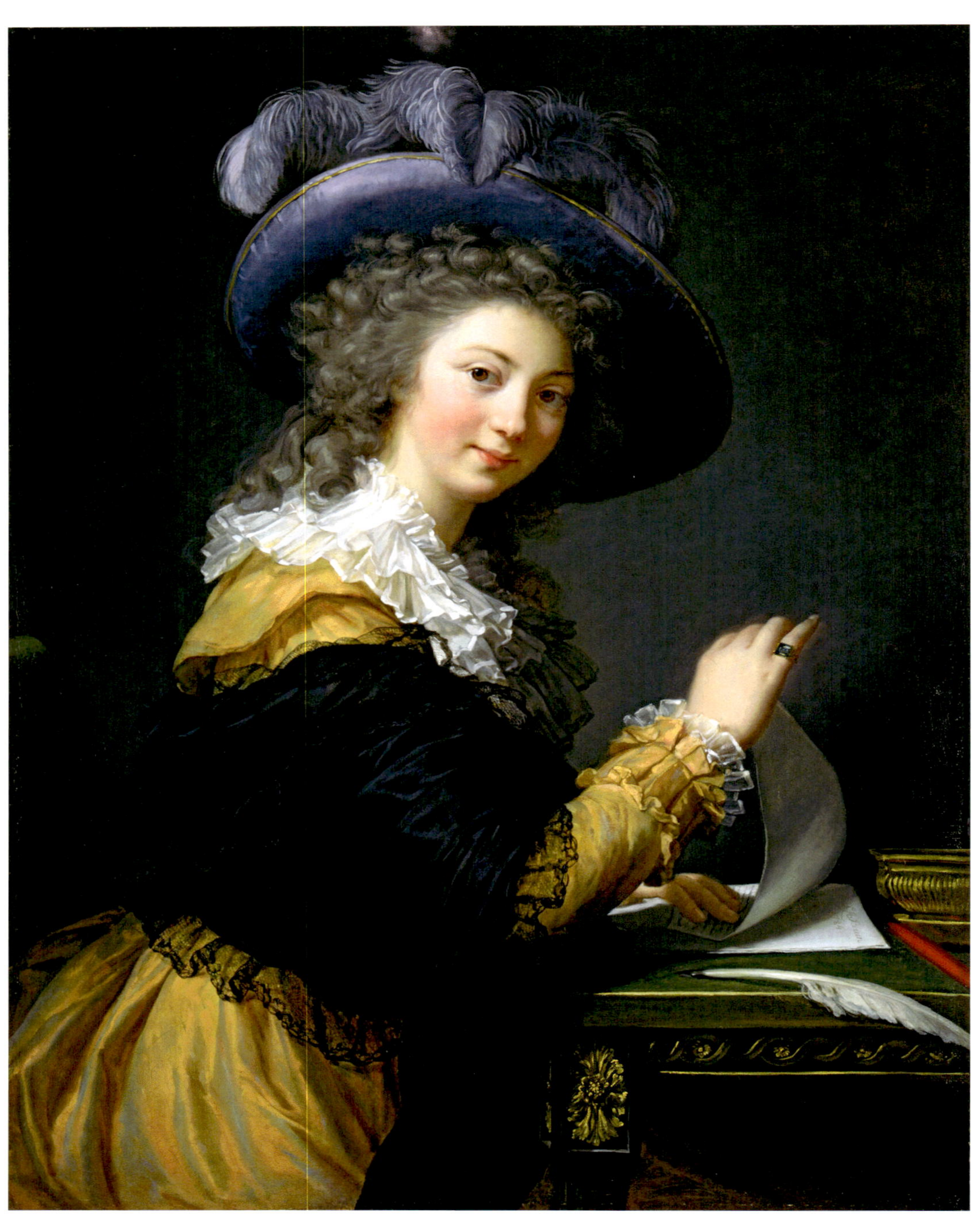

ÉLISABETH-LOUISE VIGÉE-LE BRUN

THE COMTESSE DE CÉRÈS
1784

I

Not only am I Professor of Macro Economics at *Sciences Po*
But I am also Head of Business Studies.
You can see Business Studies written all over my face
As well as the laws of Supply and Demand.
I demand that you visit me at home tonight
And that you supply me. Now be a good boy!

II

I wouldn't trust myself a millimetre, would you?
No, not a milli-milli-milli-milli-milli-milli millimetre.
I am far too busy pulling the wool over the eyes of powerful men –
An activity which I find immensely gratifying
To the pocket, the ego and – once in a blue moon –
A very blue, blue moon – my body and its appurtenances –
And preternaturally – no, supernaturally –
Ginormously satisfying to the inner *moi*.

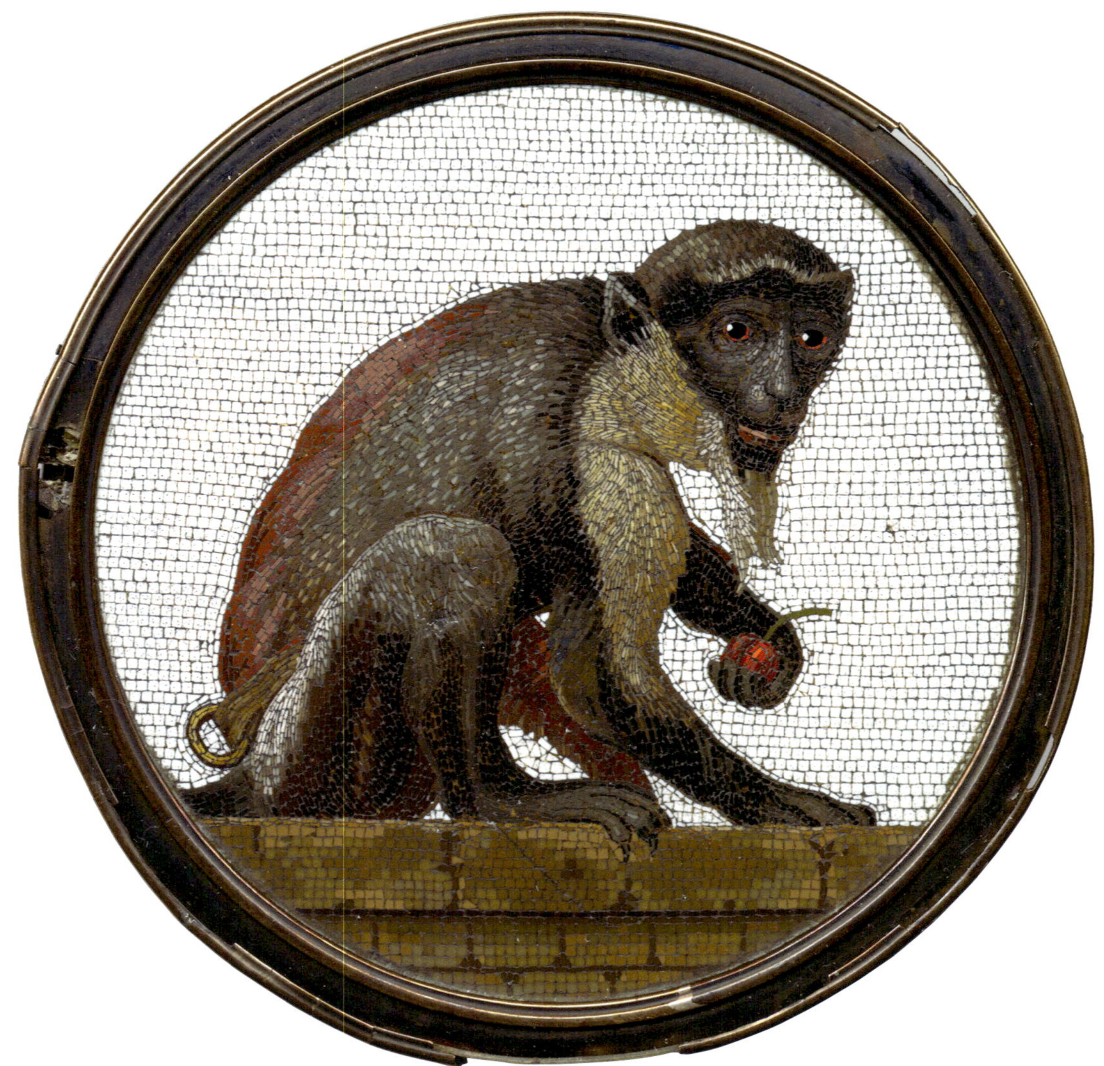

GIACOMO RAFFAELLI

MICROMOSAIC BOX WITH MONKEY
1794

---

to Roxann Brown

O my micromosaic monkey with your red cherry!
You are the mirror-image of my own ego.
As I am hooked on inhaling SNUFF
So too you are hooked on biting CHERRY.
There is a pair of us in it, you and I,
So much so that we are interchangeable:
Thou art a little old red-eyed man with his cherry;
I am a little old red-eyed monkey with my snuff – my perfumed tobacco
Without which I could not survive the day.
But – give me a bite of your cherry
And I will give you a pinch of my snuff:
Two micromosaic captives of a macromosaic day in Toledo, Ohio.

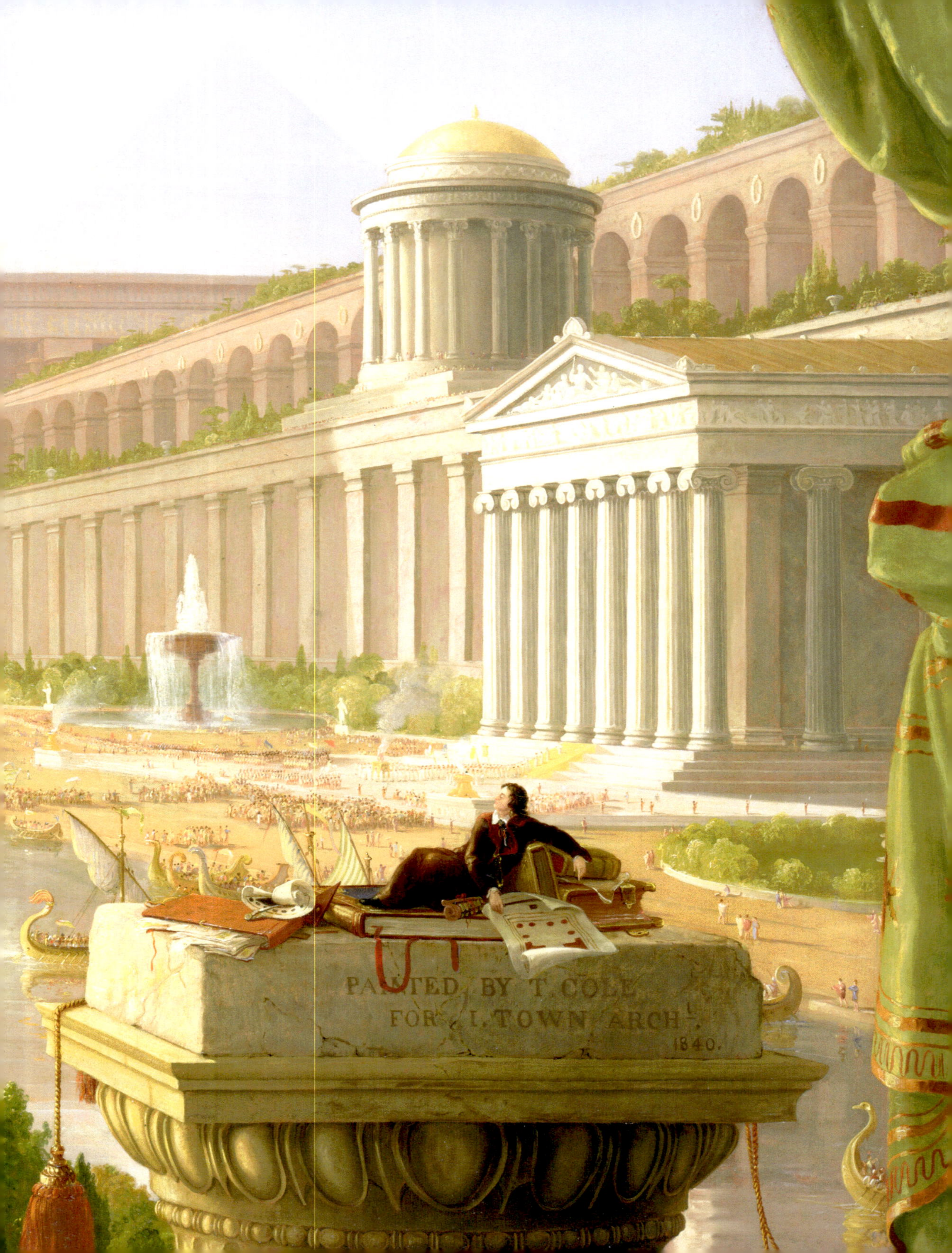

PAINTED BY T. COLE
FOR I. TOWN ARCH.
1840.

* * *

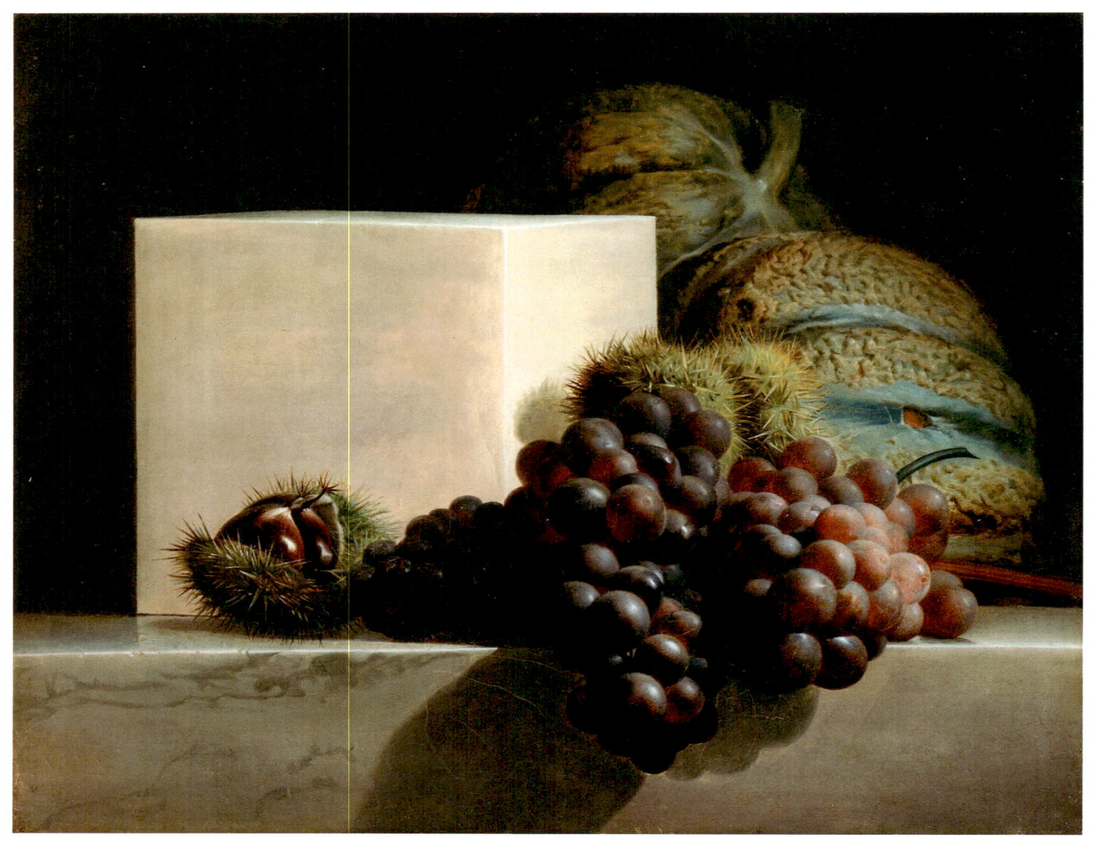

ANTOINE BERJON

STILL LIFE WITH GRAPES, CHESTNUTS, MELONS,
AND A MARBLE CUBE
ABOUT 1800–10

I

She came to me on a serene night of impassable snow
In Saskatoon on the Saskatchewan River.
Unzipping her thigh-high black leather boots
She threw down her mink greatcoat
On the floor of my library,
That reeking, mink greatcoat of hers
Almost as long as her raven black hair
Pooling around her moose feet.

In a tornado of smiles
Stilled only by her hushed laughter,
Letting slip her black jeans and her turquoise blouse,
She took my hands in hers
Silently saying: "These are yours" –
Three bunches of small red grapes,
Two enormous golden-green super-ripe melons,
Three spiky chestnut pods
One of which was already opening
To reveal its two perfect nuts
Meticulously burnished.

She asked: "Do you know why I have come?"
"No" – I replied, lying through my teeth –
"I do not know why you have come
And on a night like this
Of impassable snow!"

"I have come because not only
Are you a rare physicist
With eyesight as perfect as a bat
But you are a rare man!
I would like you to allow my melons
To crawl around your study,
Analyse their Gravitational Waves.
Then you must lie down on your own floor
And I will lie down beside you."
From her black shoulder bag
She took out a large white marble cube,
Placing it on the low wall of my soul.

II

And in the glassy night by the sheer wall down
    to the night sea
The old green otter with all his new red females
Under the Snow-White Palace of the Autumn Moon –
The hooves of La Grande Armée on the march!
Hypnosis, hypnosis, hypnosis, hypnosis, hypnosis:
And the One and the Many are free!

III

When the Toledo Art Museum Gallery Guard
Is not looking I pluck
The white marble cube from the wall of my soul,
Place it on my scorching-hot fevered forehead,
Hold it down long as I dare
Before placing it back into its frame,
Back into its own illuminating, illuminated night-life.
I dream of a child –
I dream of 1000s & 1000s & 1000s & 1000s
     & 1000s of children
          playing until Kingdom Come
For only a Still Life is never still!

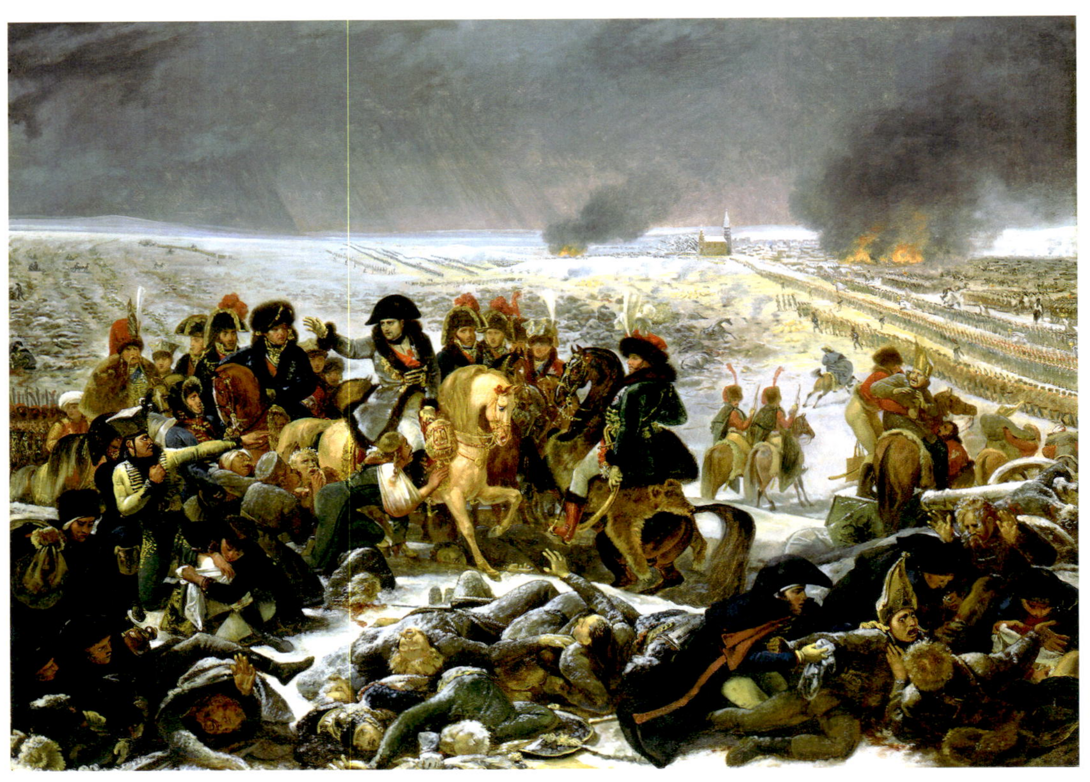

ANTOINE-JEAN GROS

NAPOLEON ON THE BATTLEFIELD OF EYLAU
1807

I

Carnage is merely the Introduction to the Fairytale.
Telling lies to your own people is the primary thing.

II

So here in his All-Pacifying and All-Enlightening Prance-About
Rides the Little Emperor George W. Bush around Damascus
With Rumsfeld, Cheney, Perle, Wolfowitz – his Comitatus –
After the Rape of Iraq.

III

Idiot Poet, when will you ever get it into your nut
That the narrative of history is digital?
Gros did not depict George W. Bush –
It was Her Excellency Antoinette Blair
That Gros depicted at Damascus
Riding the great pedigree grey stallion 'Marengo'.
Only the previous week, Her Excellency
Antoinette Blair had ridden the same stallion
At the Badminton Horse Three-Day Event,
Amused by the side-show
In the snow-and-sleet filigreed fields and hedgerows
Of prostrate suicides bleeding to death.
O this is what makes war so wizard, so jolly!
O Gros, Gros, Gros!
Thankee, high-fives, *danke, spasíba, shukran, tashakor, merci*!

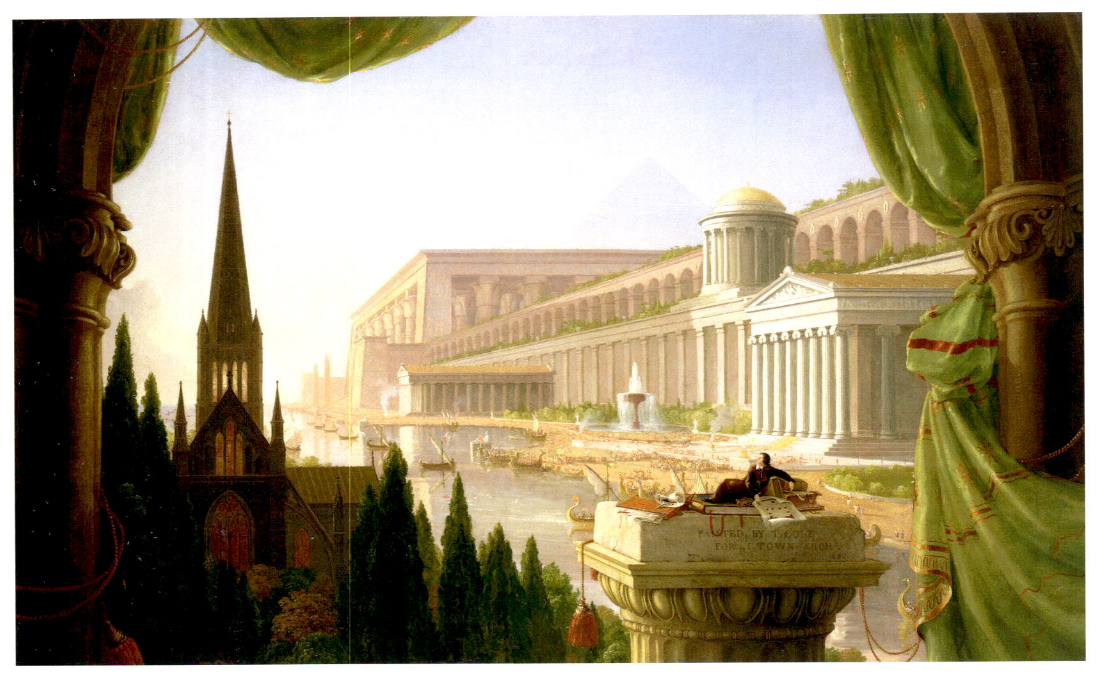

THOMAS COLE

THE ARCHITECT'S DREAM
1840

---

to Richard and Kristina Ford

I like to be at the centre of things – don't you?
At the centre of the drama, at the centre of the picture,
Or, as in your current spectacle, at the epicentre of the dream,
Day-dreaming. For day-dreaming as the poet Heaney had it –
Day-dreaming is the basis of all art:
Most especially of my own art, the art of architecture.
Close your eyes. Do not fear.
(Of course, what really I'd like to have been is a golfer.
In the Year of Grace 1840
Do any of you out there know what golf is?)

And anyway, so – the curtain goes up to expose me
In all my most casual but most artful finery:
My favourite black patent leather slippers,
My favourite velour dressing-gown of sherry-brown –
What I call to myself 'My Rory Gear'
(Sponsored by Perry & Co of Toledo, Ohio.)
Asleep upon a heap of tomes, atop Nelson's Column
Along with callipers, triangle, ruler, pencil.
(Liverpool? Or is it Bristol? But – no, no, no – of course not –
It's Boston!)

Dreaming of all my conquests, a vision of history,
And of Hollywood Epic and of all the great Casinos to be erected
In Monte Carlo and Cairo and Toledo, Ohio and Berlin and Rome
And of how in my minimalist, modest but not insignificant fashion
Out of barbarism created civilisation –
A little thing – but a thing, nevertheless.
Pyramid, temple, aqueduct, cathedral.
How Mark Twain, Walt Whitman, Sherwood Anderson would have not alone
Understood – but appreciated – my sense of humour
And the Freuds – Sigmund and Lucien – and Jung
My self-controlled submersion in nightmare
And Burke and Emerson my sublime sense of the Sublime.

What an eye for details, eh! Voluminous detail.
All these individual people in the crowds going up and down
Executed with but a few brush-strokes.
My smoking altars! My unspeakable sacrifices.
All my boats, all my skiffs, and bottom-right
My miniature prow with swan's neck, reptile head, dinosaur – *Diplodocus*!
And centre-stage, upfront, my scarlet tassel – dangling! Dong! Ding!

Ah me! Tom Cole! For all my bumps and bruises, ups and downs,
I was the lad to show ye the way!
Tom Cole!
The new Ohio Statehouse, 1839, Columbus, Ohio.
I was the lad to fling away my telescope –
To peer down my nose and close my eyes
And show ye all, Pilgrims, Natives, Slaves, the way.
Is this a golf ball that I see before me?

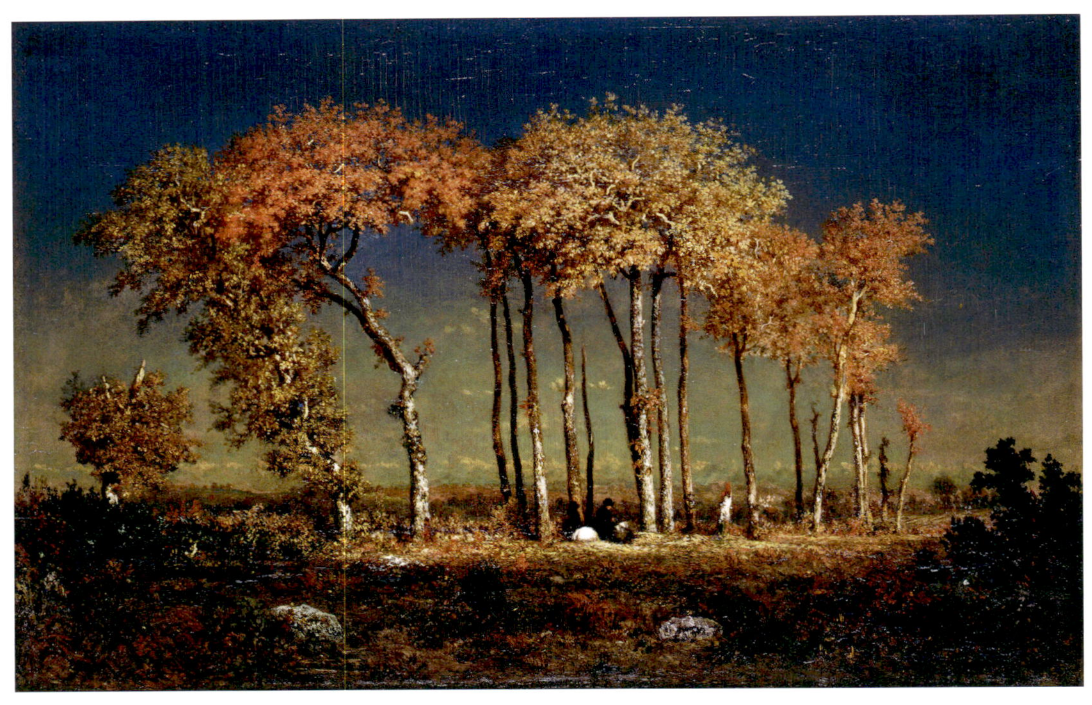

PIERRE-ÉTIENNE-THÉODORE ROUSSEAU

UNDER THE BIRCHES, EVENING
1842-43

How fortunate I am to have any parishioners –
I am thinking as I ride along of an autumn evening:
The blasts of winter not far away now –
No matter how agèd and sick they are,
How kind to me they are! Treating me as if I
Was someone special when in point of fact
All I am is their parish priest! Forty years ago
When I was ordained I made a special vow
To myself – that no matter how rough the road,
No matter how rough the weather,
I would always visit the agèd and the sick,
At the absolute least, once a week.

This evening, really, is not too bad
Riding along the back track to the parochial house.
Glad, all the same I donned my heavy overcoat
Although it is a shade too clerical.
Glancing back at the rump of my mare
I am surprised by how sunset shows up
To perfection what a snow-white rump she has –
My God, she could be the Mother of God –

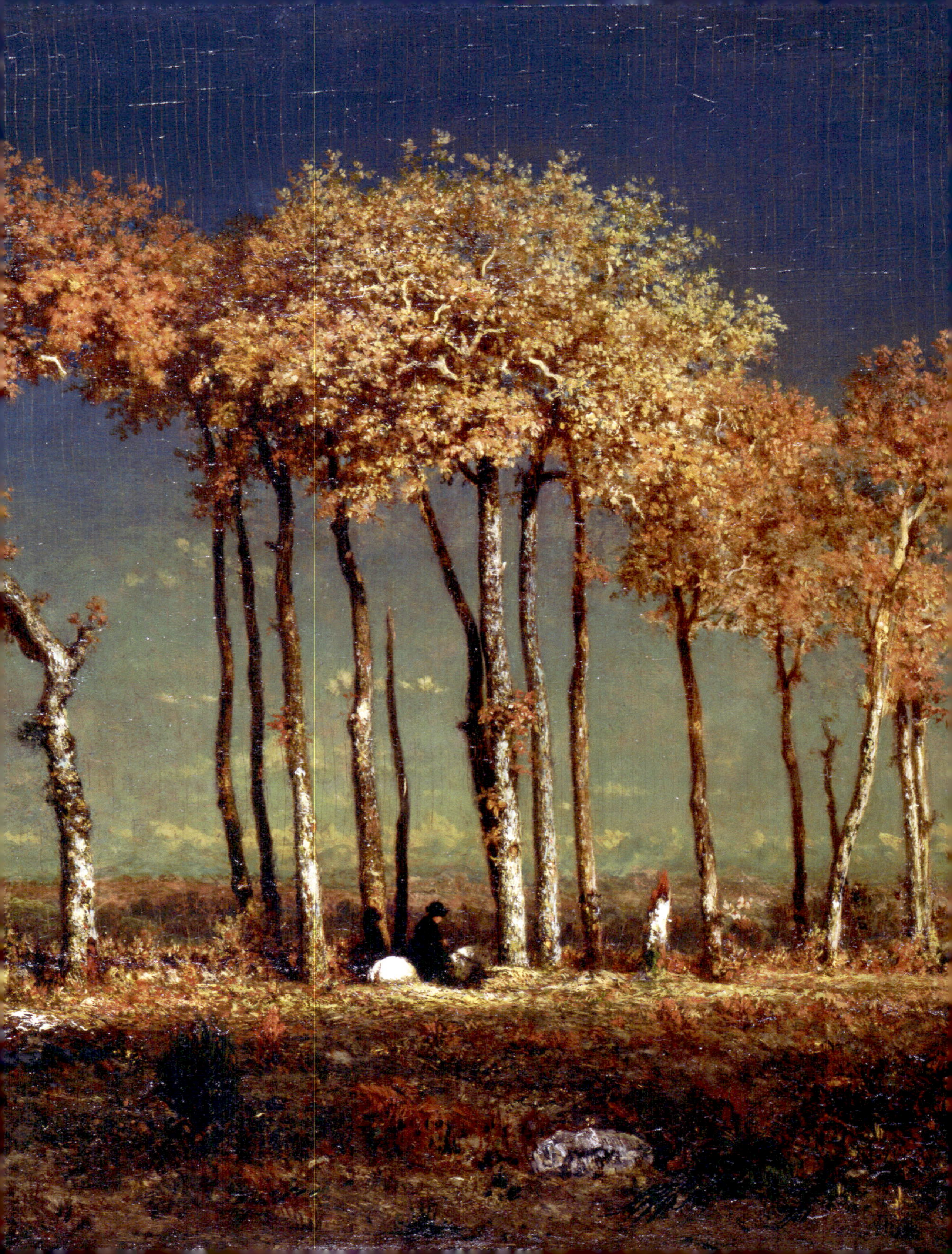

My holy mare! (Still, in my homily next Sunday
I had better employ more prudent language – a pity.)
But my God, also, these birch-trees
Have formed a guard of honour for my little mare!
And they are tossing about, high in the darkening sky,
Their heads of faded orange, caramel leaves –
Cheering on *Nôtre Dame*, my own mother, all of us!
O *Seigneur*, I am a mortal man but a thing of beauty!
A *curé* on his mare, I am a diamond of immortality!
Dearest, most beloved, cherished parishioners, pray for me.

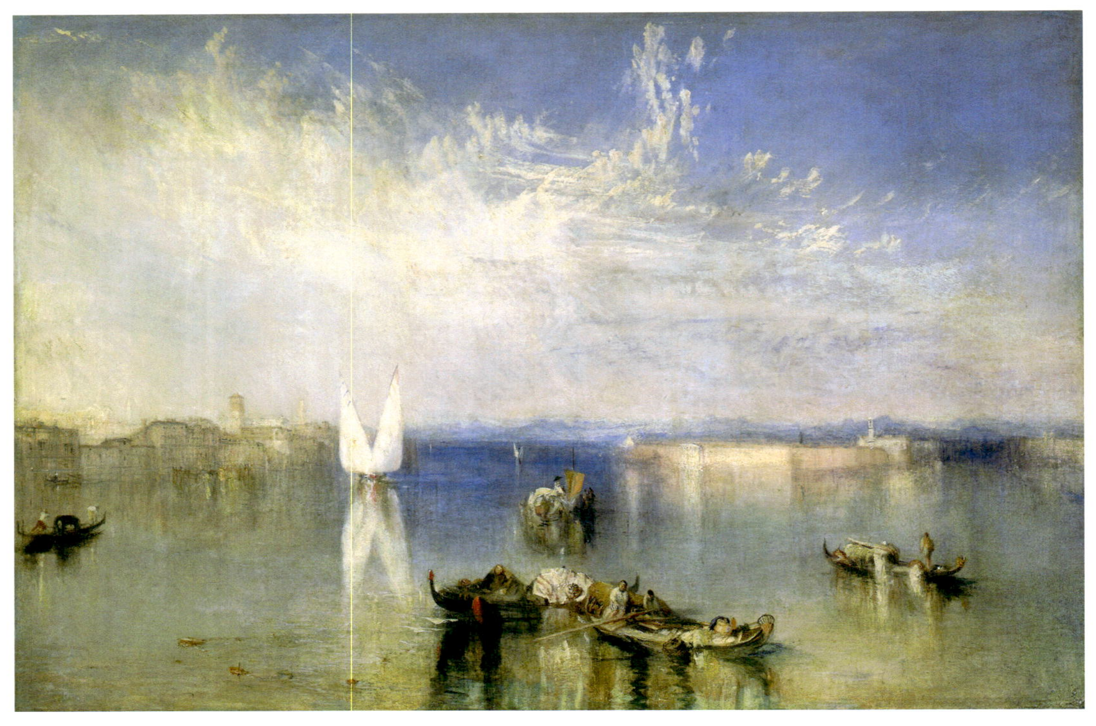

JOSEPH MALLORD WILLIAM TURNER

THE CAMPO SANTO, VENICE
1842

I have nowt to crap about my painting, oil on canvas,
'The Campo Santo, Venice' 1842
Except only – what a godlike work it is.
Never farted better!
The Sun is God!
My walls in the water and the sunshine on 'em!
Ever so slight feeling of 'appiness!

That German chappie Goethe
Recently had published his *Theory of Colour*
And mostly that morn in Venice lagoon
That's what I was at –
Making the odd lunge at the canvas, the odd swipe,
The odd smear, the odd elbow, the odd gouge, the odd spit.
But mostly browsing Goethe on colour and then
All of a sudden under his spell
I took off my boots and in my hairy bare feet
With uncut toenails I paced the quayside –
O God if only I had an old lady to pare my toenails!
Oh those paving-stones! What they can do
For a dying old bastard's stumps!
Seduce and assuage and embalm!
And what do I see but the Soul of the Poet before me –
The two great white sails of that American felucca

Whose accursed bloody black-listed moniker I can never recall,
That Archangel of a Poet from the Midwest –
Soul with the Wings of a Swan
With its back to ye!

('The Idaho Kid' – was that it? –
Or 'The Ohio Meteorite'? –)
And immediately I buried him – I buried him –
And where else but in the Campo Santo?
Where else but in the Campo Santo?

Oh Goethe on Yellow!
"Serene, gay, softly, exciting character of yella."
"What thou lov'st well shall not be reft from thee."
"Spontaneities that form their independent orbits."
No greater love hath a mother
Than in cheery-bye sunlight
To kneel down before her 71-year-old son
And to cut and to pare and to lard his toenails!
"The rain falls, the sun shines, the onions grow."

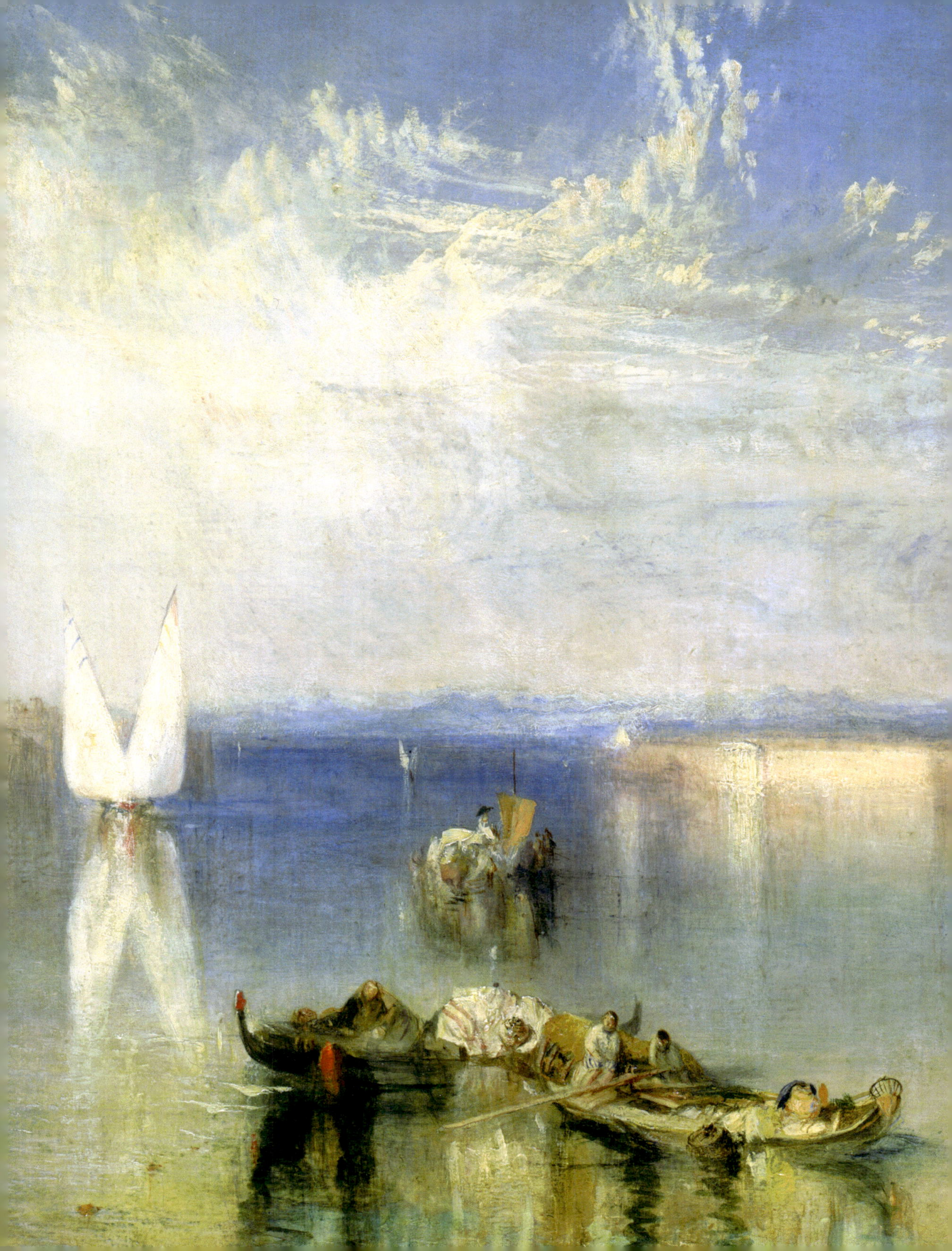

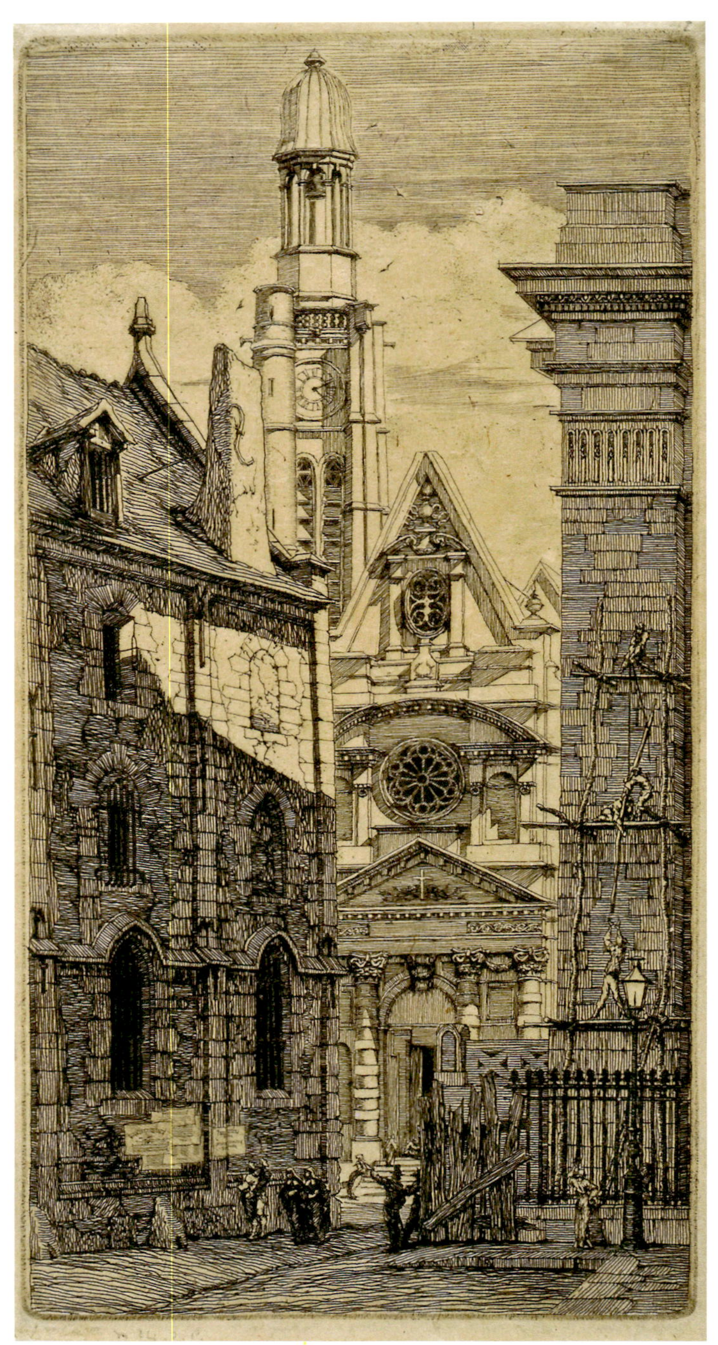

CHARLES MÉRYON

I

That year as a seminarian I spent in Paris
I spent most of it, particularly in the winter,
In the church of Saint-Étienne-du-Mont
High on the upper slopes of the Montagne Ste-Geneviève:
The original 5th–7th century city of Clovis and his mafia –
The Merovingian Long-Haired Kings of France
They had the gall – the gall! – to call themselves!
I'd been 'silenced' as Canon Law requires it
By the German Shepherd in Rome for preaching social justice,
Liberation theology, the option for the poor,
Equality of the sexes and/or same sex marriage:
Freedom for women as well as freedom for men.

My days were my own and I knew nobody –
And although I could read French I could not speak French
So every day I'd climb up the Montagne Ste-Geneviève
And sleep, sit or kneel in the church of Saint-Étienne-du-Mont
Either in the nave before the Rood Screen –
The most eloquently carved rood screen in medieval Europe –
Or in the chancel before the tabernacle and the sanctuary lamp

Or in the cloister with its medieval stained glass windows.
Although I was lonely beyond all telling
L'Église Saint-Étienne-du-Mont kept me human;
Its monumental façade transfigured by its humanity –
By the human hands that conceived and made it.
Always there'd be someone to whom to stutter *Bon – Bon – Bonjour –*
Sitting on the steps or slipping out the door.

When I could work up the courage I'd say the Stations of the Cross
In the name of Charles Méryon whose etching of Saint-Étienne-du-Mont
Is one of the epiphanies of French etching,
Primus inter pares among European printmakers,
Only to lose his mind, *le pauvre*, in his thirties.
But mostly I inhabited a pew, pleased, even comforted
If my mind became completely and easily empty
And I might even take a siesta in a side-chapel
Stretching out along a pew, lying on my side.

D'accord – I'd been silenced – so
I would meet silence with silence
Which is the story of my life.
In the Church of Saint-Étienne-du-Mont
I blew away silence with silence
And learned again to be kindred with men –

Even if those same men were my calumniators.
In Saint-Étienne-du-Mont I learned to say the Lord's Prayer:
'Our Father who art in heaven, hallowed be thy name . . .
And forgive us our trespasses
As we forgive those who trespass against us'
And always I'd think of my dear dead friend back in Ireland, Donal,
The young husband of 'The Dead',
Who used talk to me a lot about the Lord's Prayer:
"Just because we forgive them
Does not mean we have to like them!"

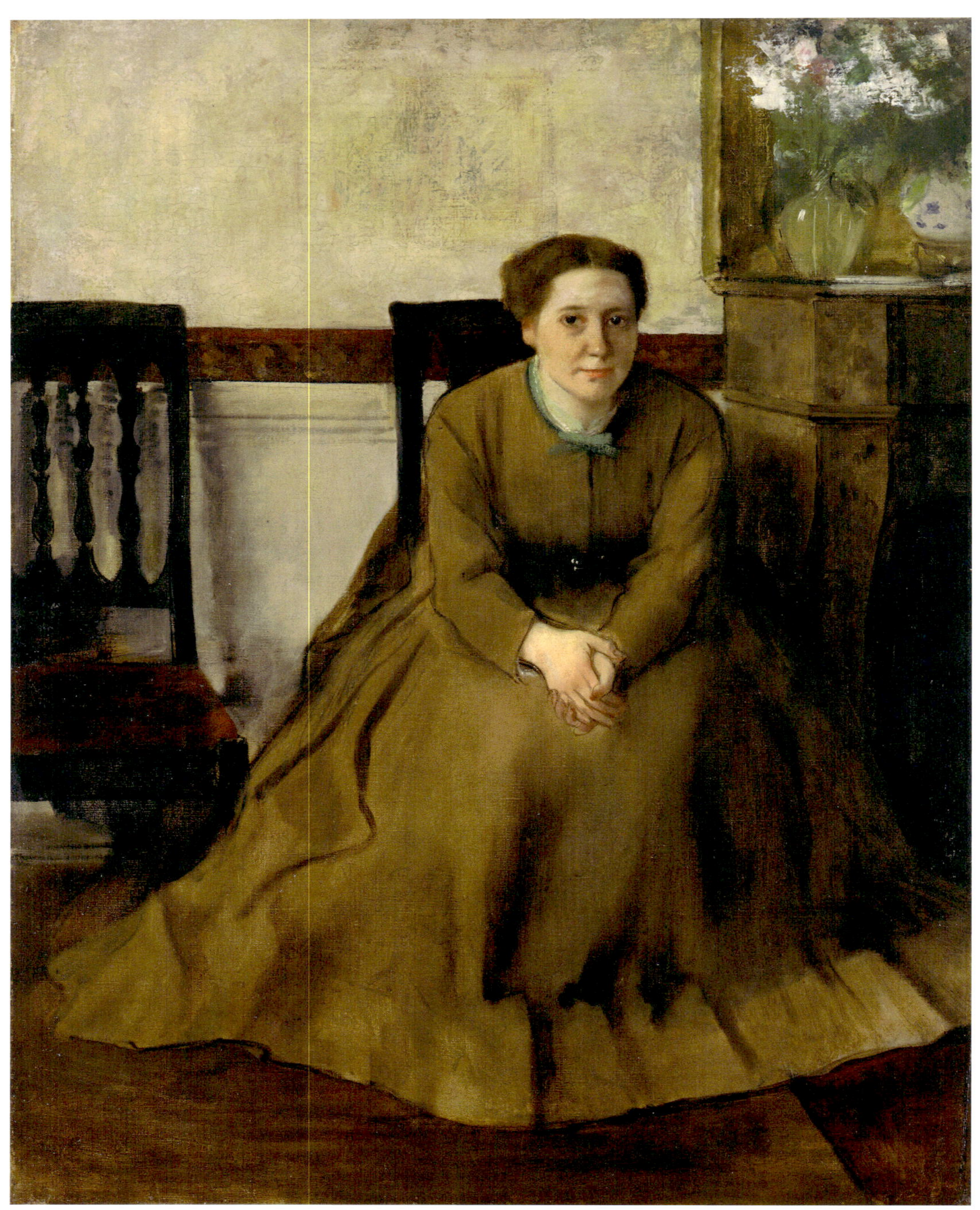

EDGAR DEGAS

VICTORIA DUBOURG

ABOUT 1868–69

---

to Eileen O'Mara Walsh

A beautiful woman – although still young
Already snared in early middle-age –
Her biological time-bomb ticking visibly.
The metamorphoses she yearns for – marriage, children –
Have eluded her and she is thirty-six.
I want to say to her but I cannot –
Such is the etiquette of our relationship –
Portrait painter to sitter –
I want to say to her "Victoria, may I?"
But I dare not.

It was she who chose to wear this absurdly,
Monumentally unfinished dress
And I did not demur. I invited her to sit down
In whatever chair she liked –
I had the usual selection –
And make herself comfortable and she sat down
On an upright chair
In the most uncomfortable pose of all, leaning forwards

With all the tension of her body in her lovely unwashed hands.
Unwashed? Yes, unwashed.
Her choice. I make no comment.
Her eyes bottomless lakes of tears unshed.
I make no comment.
Yet you think me a sadist for asking –
Is there anything more beautiful than
A young middle-aged woman's grief?

"In my unfinished dress, I am finished, no?"
She remarked lightly at the end of our seven weeks.
It's not often – in fact, it's seldom –
I meet a woman at once
More intelligent and more sensitive
Than myself, than
Almost any male – such
Was Mademoiselle Victoria Dubourg.
Accordingly, I asked if I might paint her
And being neither coy nor self-conscious
She accepted enthusiastically but matter-of-factly.
Of course, she herself was a painter, an authentic painter,
And as always a painter among women
Was a unique phenomenon, a rarity, almost unheard of.
At the end of our final sitting I asked her –

For we had surely by now become almost intimate friends –
I asked her if I might give her a new name
Which she and I would use only ever between ourselves –
It would be our secret. No one – but no one – else would ever know.
Yes – she instantly insisted – yes.

Amplitude – I named her – *Amplitude*.
She smiled for the first time in seven weeks.
She said: No. I said – not accustomed to being crossed –
I said: "What do you mean 'No'?"
She said: "Monsieur De Gas, you may call me *Plenitude*."
I said: "Mademoiselle Dubourg indeed, of course, your Divine
Name for now and for evermore – *Plenitude*."
I showed her out onto the street myself – *Plenitude* –
And hailed a cab and paid the cabbie and bowed down to her.
She whispered: "Monsieur De Gas, I do admire your bow-down."
Plenitude! Au Revoir! *Plenitude*!

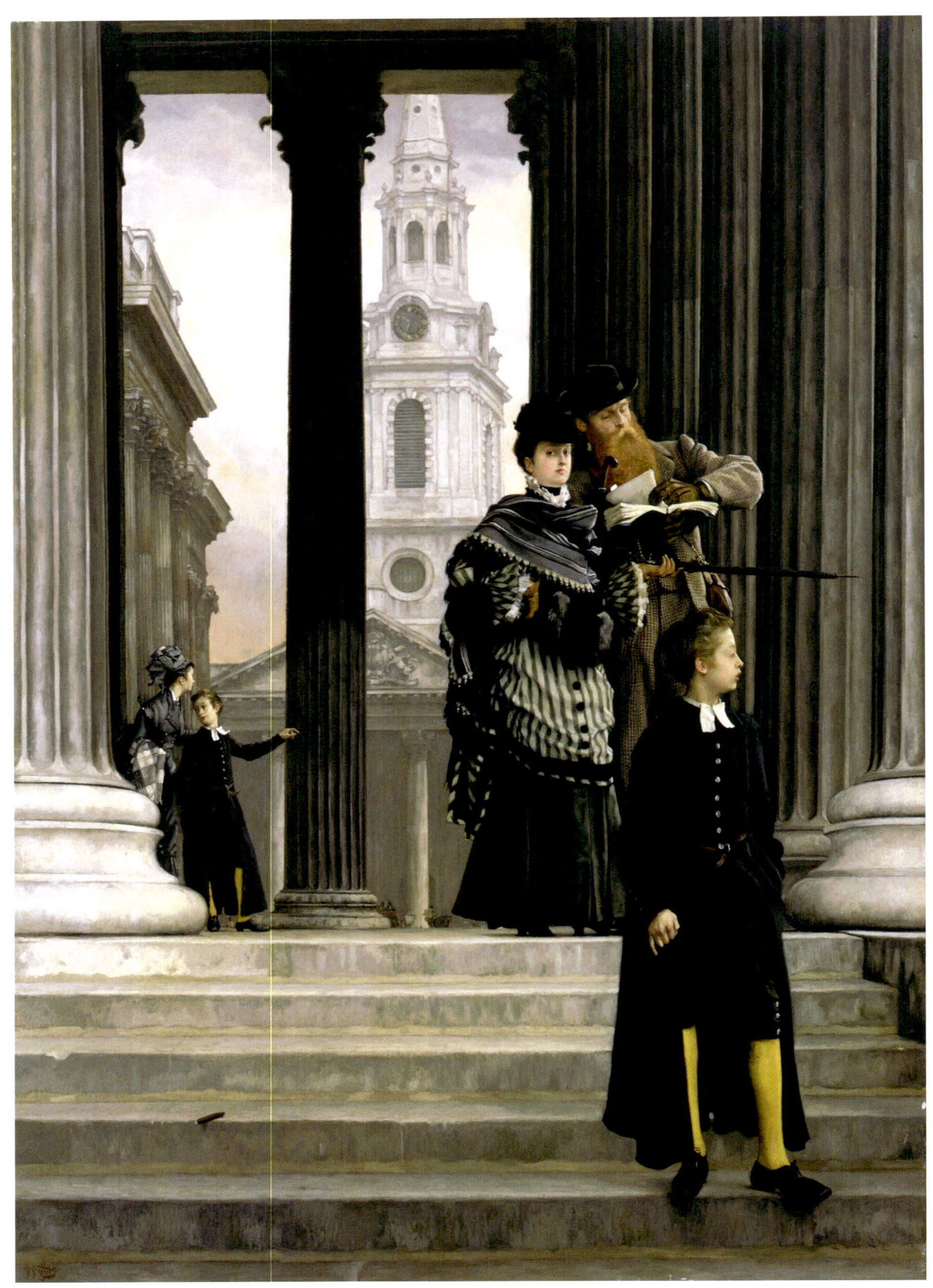

JAMES TISSOT

And to consider that you came all the way from Toledo, Ohio
To visit me! All the way to London, England
To visit plump little me! You ridiculous, arrogant, cigar-chewing American!
Plump little me – your very own equally ruthless English trollop!
Amn't I, Donald? Equally ruthless as you, even more so
Because like many men basically you are a coward at heel!
Well, then, look at me! I am eye-balling you!
I am giving you your orders, whipping you into line.
I will meet you – lethal umbrella to lethal umbrella –
Behind Nelson's – shall we call it his 'column'? –
Nelson's Column? –
In about 24 or 29 minutes – as soon as I can get rid
Of my silly old billy-goat of a husband which will be facile –
He being the fully equipped male tourist
Who knows everything and therefore nothing.
I will dispatch him down across the square to Whitehall –
To Downing Street – Number 10, of course –
And then he'll plunge on to Big Ben and the Houses of Parliament
And at 3 o'clock p.m. I'll meet up with him in Westminster Abbey
And together we will pray at the tomb of Donne
And then also share a silent pew in Poet's Corner
And at Poet's Corner we will say aloud Psalm 23
"The Lord is our shepherd; we shall not want."

So, Donald, I will meet you in 23 or 29 minutes,
At Horatio's Column after which, after I have caressed it –
Geology is what fundamentally preoccupies me –
We will shilly-shally arm in arm across Trafalgar Square
To the Charing Cross Hotel where hubby and I
Have a suite and for an hour or two – even three, depending –
Play poker-for-two
And with what eloquent double-talk you will undress me,
Naming each garment and its label and where it was purchased:
Pure architecture, darling!
My black silk satin corset with yellow silk ribbon,
Chemise and drawers of white cotton,
All my layers of petticoats, all my flounces,
My two-piece bustle dress, Worth & Pingat, Paris.

Don't be a bold boy now! Easy! Easy!
Did your Mama never teach you the word for Slowly?
Or for Gently? Slowly now, easy now, gently now,
Oh my very own American little Donald Duck!
Remember to close the door after you and to take your own brolly
And if you come back early tomorrow at the very same time
To the old entrance of the National Gallery in Trafalgar Square
Chewing your somewhat thin cigar
I will eye-ball you all over – all over – again.
But Oh my own little American Don (sure you're not Russian?)
"Thy rod and thy staff, they comfort me."

"She leadeth me beside the still waters . . ."
Huckleberry Finn sez it's fine so it must be fine!
Sez it's all part of the American Dream –
What can he mean?
That we're all Cherokee and Maumee
If we could only see it?
Look, Madeleine, look – concentrate
On your big sister, keep
Your eyes on Rosetta!

Rosetta in her blue jacket and striped tights!
Rosetta is waiting for you! Rosetta is expecting you!
Rosetta who 'all her life has had something' – the old folk say.
Rosetta our sister, our star, our navigator,
Our beautiful, generous, wholesome navigator.
Our golden girl, with her straw hat,
(O what would you not give for Rosetta's straw hat?)

Harry and Si, your two jacketed gallant brothers –
Each of us holding one of your hands
To negotiate you across the toppled tree.
Think of your dry boots – we're in our bare feet!
"Ma will kill me if I get my boots wet!"
Keep moving Madeleine, keep moving.

Come on, Madeleine, you can do it – of course, you can.
Do not stop for anything Madeleine, do not stop.
Keep moving, Madeleine, keep moving.
Feel the breeze in the leaves.
We're all innocent if we only knew it.
The Light of the Fall is upon our woods,
Our demesne, our stream, our stones.
"She restoreth my soul."

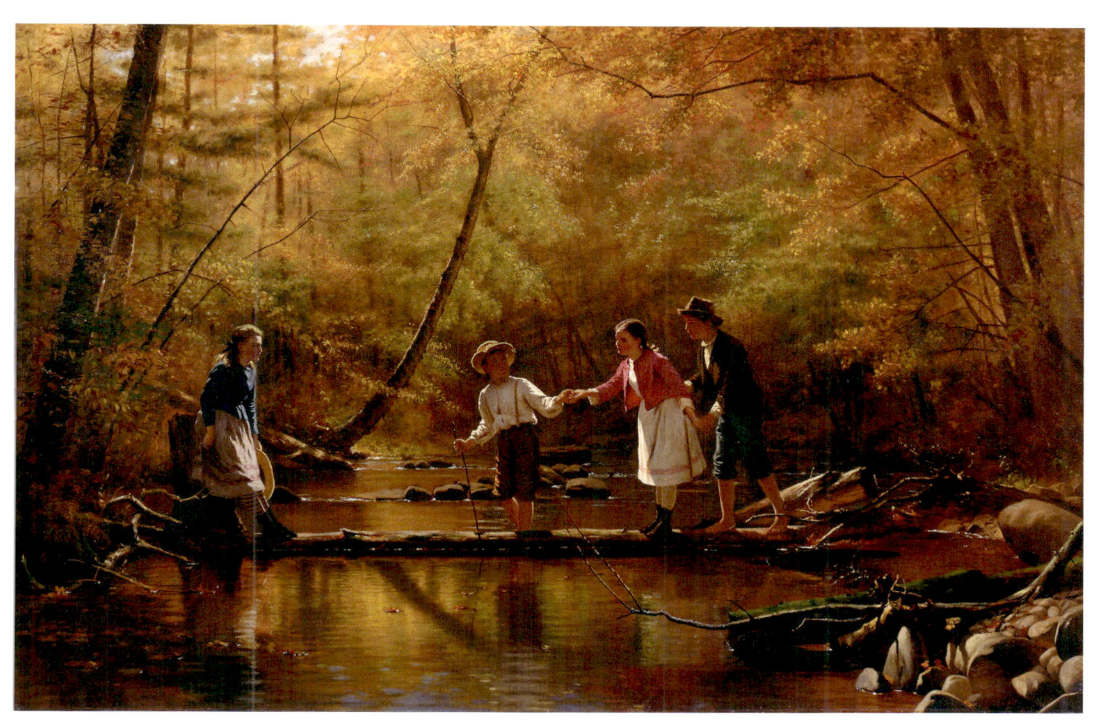

JOHN GEORGE BROWN

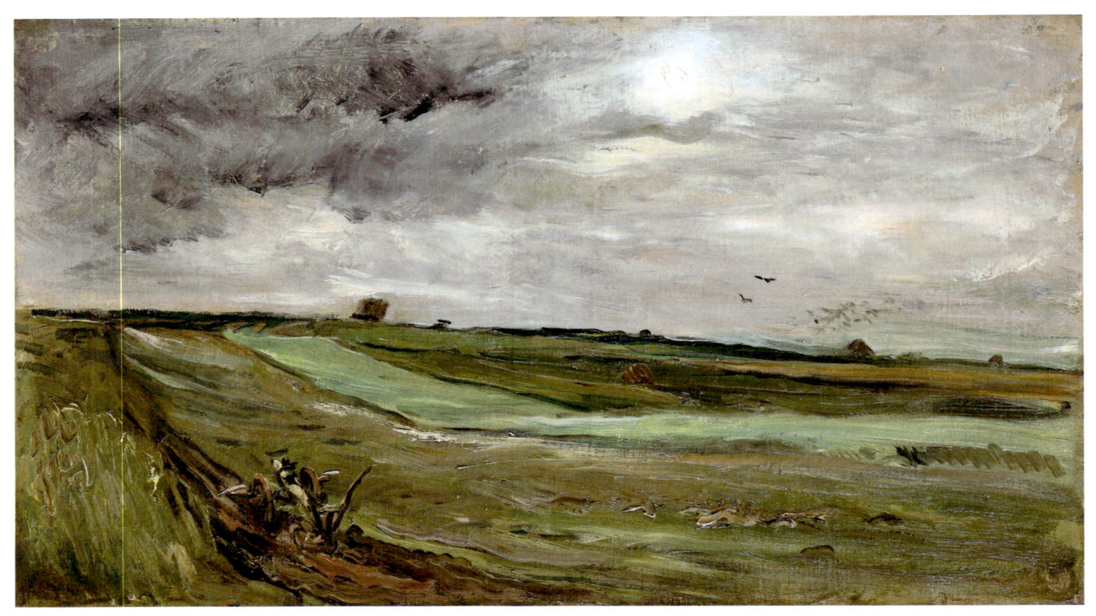

CHARLES-FRANÇOIS DAUBIGNY

to Larry Nichols

When the visitor on a day-trip to Auvers-sur-Oise –
A young bespectacled Ohioan woman at Art School in Paris –
(Is she near-sighted? He wonders)
Alights from the 9.56 a.m. train from the Gare du Nord –
The AUVERS DIRECT –
There to greet her on the windfurrowed, chilly platform
Of the small, empty, country railway-station
Is Old Man Charles-François Daubigny
Flagging her with a large smile on his small, wrinkled face –
(How agèd – darkly agèd – he has become!) –
The wryest smile you have just ever seen.

It is a damp black autumn day in Auvers, its wild sky gleaming.
"Welcome to Auvers-sur-Oise –
The Villefranche-sur-Champs de Blé of the North!"
He gurgles when she does not appreciate his witticism.
After a brief but not too brief visit to the Café –
A *crème* and a cognac for the old man;
A *café-au-lait* for the young woman –
Abruptly he announces: "Now we must go –
We have no time to lose –
Art is all about knowing when to go slow, when fast! –

We must climb up to the heart of Auvers
Which is not in Auvers but over it, above it
On the high plateau. *Vite! Vite! Rapidement! Rapidement!*"
Rapidly he crawls ahead of her, whirling
Like the clouds over their heads
His farmer's walking-stick.
Whacking the tops off weeds with it.
They pass under the east window of the Church of Auvers.
"Do you pray in church?" he inquires of her
But not waiting for an answer, adds:
"I pray with my paintbrush – at my easel!"
Out of breath he waits for her at the top
Surveying the vast fields – 'our Elysium' –
He calls it – and repeats the phrase – 'our Elysium'.
Without ado he staggers straight across the lane,
Stepping straight into the wet mud of a ploughed up field;
Scoops up a handful – no, a fistful – of wet earth
And proffers it to her, offering it to her
As the *Curé* offers up the Host at Mass in the church below.
Tentatively she dips her fingers:
"Non! Non, Non!" he cries "Non! Non, Non!"
He grips her other hand and plants it
Round her first hand already brimful of earth:
"Hold it, hold it, feel it, feel it.
Feel the pure, gritty filth of it.

Real life! For what is death?
Real life. Look, look at it.
Real life is real death!
God only knows what analysis your art teacher
Has stuffed into your exquisite
American head but it's all stuff!
What you hold in your hand
Is the essence of that painting of mine
He sent you out here to investigate:
Auvers, Landscape with Plough.
What you are holding in your porcelain hand
Is all of life, past, present and to come,
All of the earth, all of the earth
Including we creatures who inhabit it:
All that you eat, all that you digest,
All that nourishes you, all that you defecate:
Clay, worms, weeds, wildflowers, shit;
All that is green, green, green, green;
All that is black, black, black, black.
I call this painting of mine
Which you are analysing in Paris
With your fine fellow of a teacher
I call it my 'Green Black Masterpiece'.
Girl, look me in the eye,
Tell me if I lie!

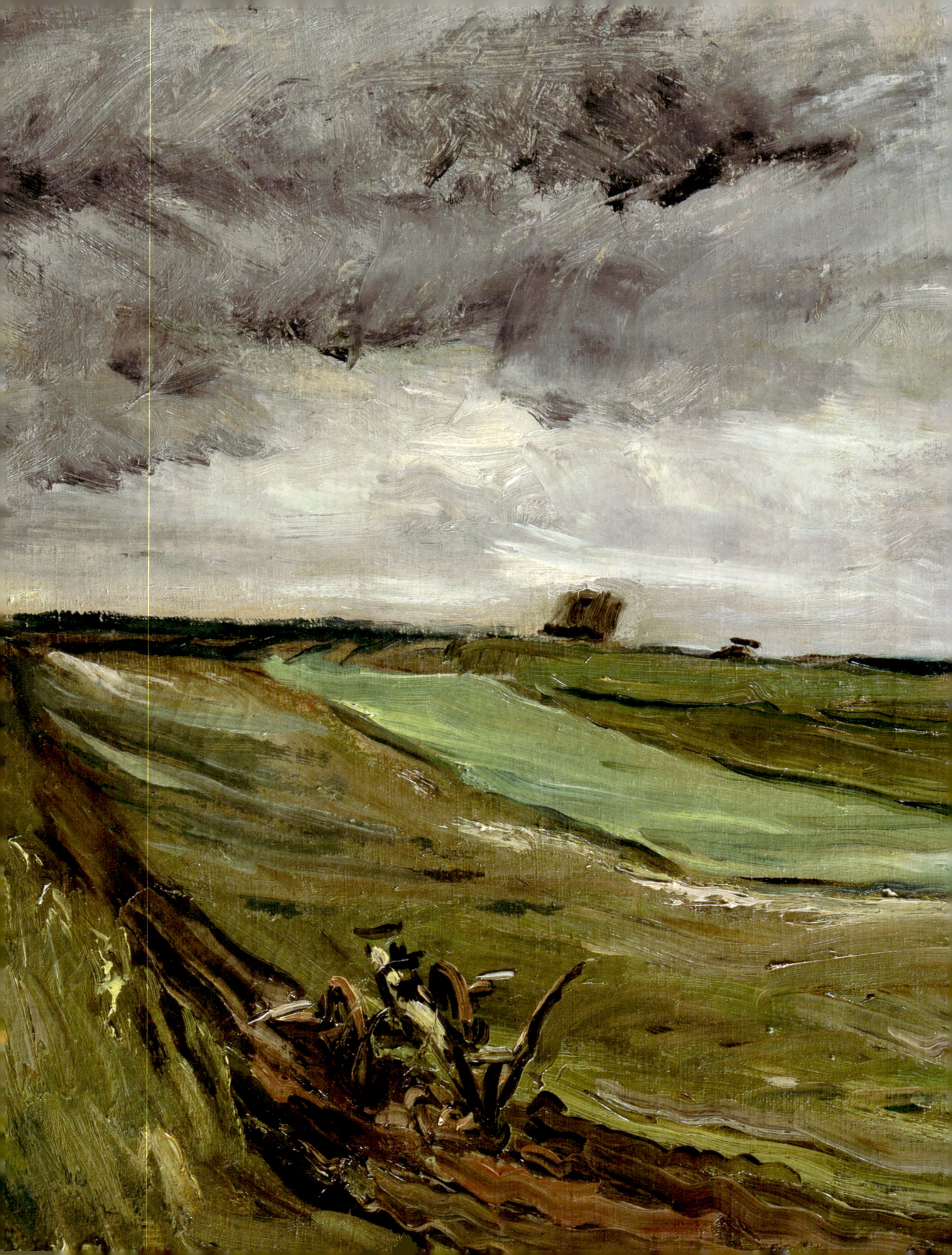

Old man that I am now and you but a girl
I can say with all the gaiety of authority –
All the inaudible laughter of authority –
You have here a great landscape painting by Daubigny –
Charles-François to his mother –
A painting which has that magic X
Which in Spain in Andalucía they call – *duende.*
From the loam of the earth, the angelic-demonic.
My painting of the low, long, sweeping fields,
Is singing – no, dancing with *duende.*
Brush strokes most formally, yet casually, done
In freedom, in the full knowledge of my approaching death.
I wager you 1000 francs that 138 years from this day
The paint on my canvas will be as wet as the day I applied it.
Such is *duende* – my *duende* – my painting life – my painting death –
An empty plough, a furrow, low grey-black skies on the charge
With a patch of blue too and a sunlight-discus and covens of crows.
We are the painters of the north, our fate to stay north.

And so now my dear young – dare I say – charming American daughter
Let us descend from the high plateau to the small village
Where you will break bread with me
And with le Patron in the café
Before I put you on the train for the Gare du Nord.
I hope you relish potatoes and cabbage and, ah, the soup!
I am the future – the future is me."

"*Et maintenant Messieurs et Mesdames* it is my honour, my privilege
On behalf of the Government of France
To propose that the plateau at Auvers-sur-Oise
Be sold, developed and converted
At a net profit of 690 million euro
Into the Two Premier Golf Courses of France!
The Van Gogh 36-Hole and the Daubigny 18-Hole.
Vive la France! Vive le Golf!"

---

to Clíona Ní Ríordáin

I

Just as Monsieur Antonin Proust is one of the primary sources
Of his life-long childhood friend Édouard Manet's life and work
Likewise Manet is one of the primary sources of Proust's life and work:
This audacious portrait of a French Republican is a painting about friendship:
About how, of all relationships, friendship
Is the primary relationship surpassing even love, marriage, family,
Tribe, club, gang, party, sect, salon, country.

II

Why did Monsieur Antonin Proust take his own life?
Manet by the wit and craft of this snapshot of his boyhood friend
In a frock coat with a flower in his lapel,
With his pigskin gloves,
With a silk handkerchief in his breast pocket.
With a diamond in his cravat,
With all the sensitivity of his technique,
With all its abundance of abandon,
In spite of being himself in the maw of a fatal illness,
Signals to us Proust's secret:

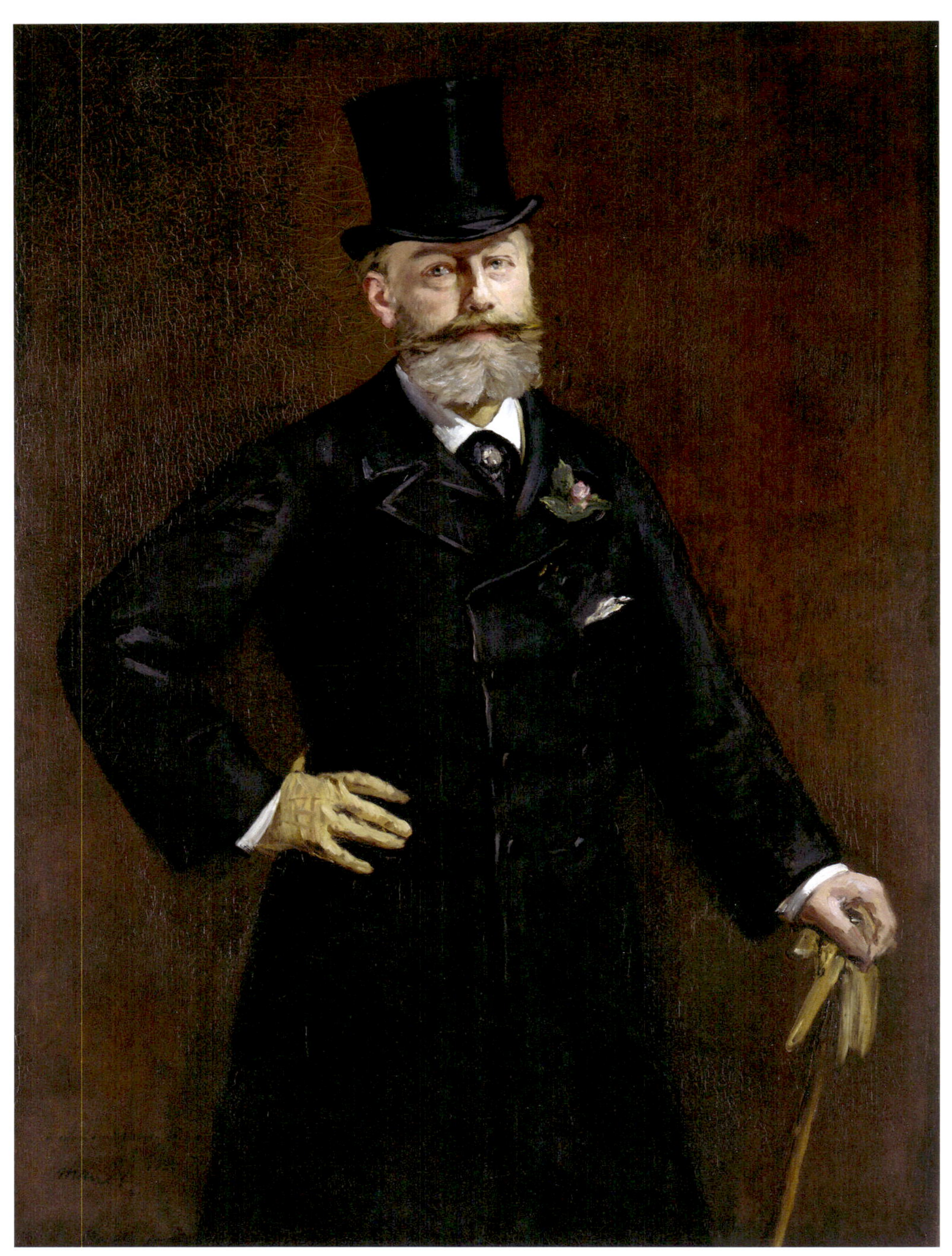

ÉDOUARD MANET

In the kindly, merry mischief of Proust's eyes we glimpse
The rock bottom depths of Proust's grief:
That sense of loss that for no well-known reason
A boy can know lifelong from the age of seven.

III

Every portrait is a theatre stage and every theatre stage has wings
And in the wings of Manet's one-sitting portrait of Proust –
'With three strokes – pique, pique, pique – it will be there' –
His defiant non-conformist portrait of the Republican Arts Minister
Who had been his soul-mate since childhood –
Stands Velázquez hands on hips and what is Velázquez doing?
Velázquez is serenading Manet's impertinence –
Proust wearing his top-hat tilted in his own portrait!
Well, I never!
As if at the Presidential Inauguration
The President were to appear in a biker's black leather jacket
Over a loose open-neck white blouse!
O the brazen, saucy cheek of him! The audacity of him!
L'Audace! Et encore de l'Audace! Et toujours de l'Audace!

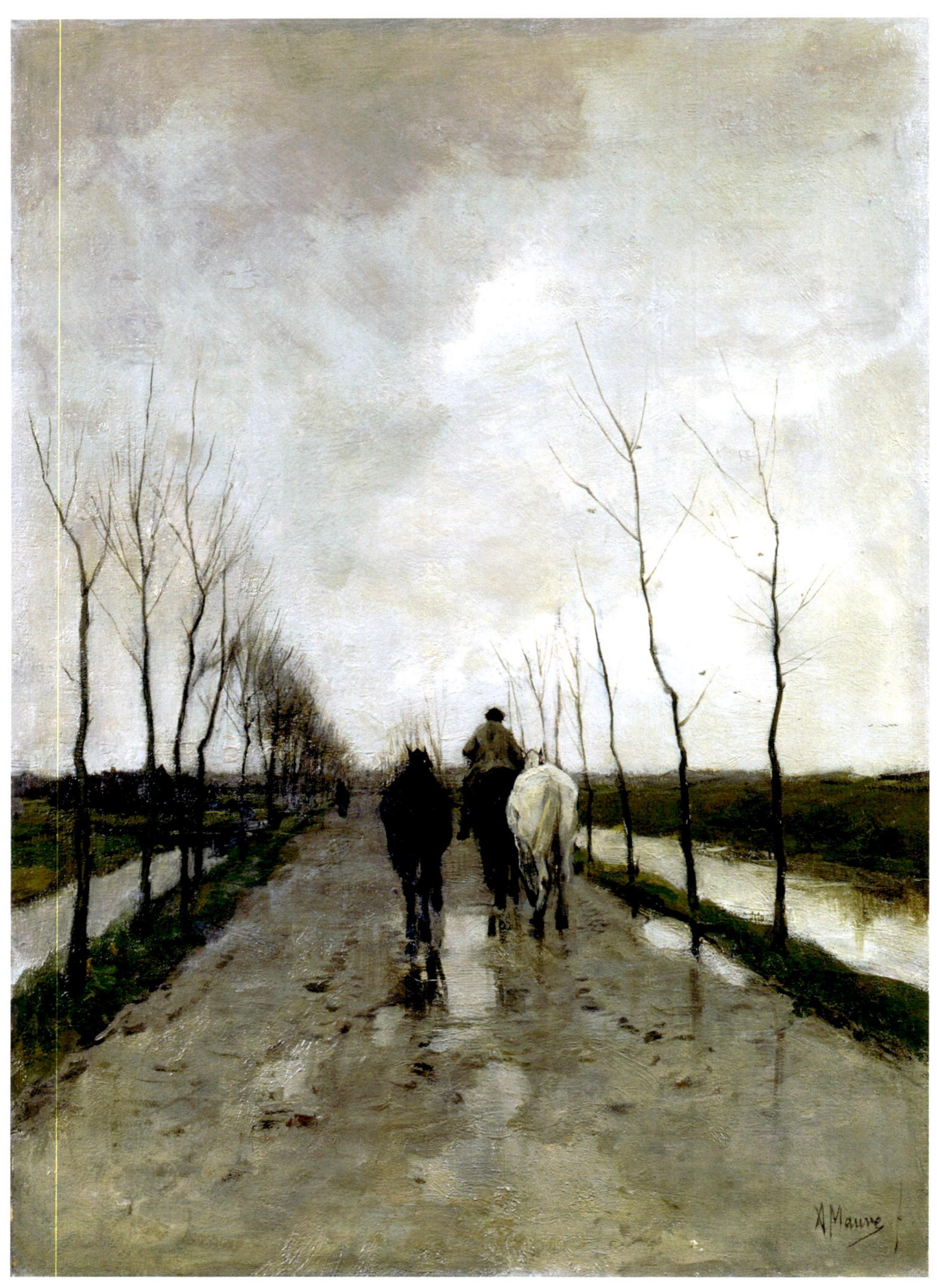

ANTON MAUVE

A DUTCH ROAD

ABOUT 1880

That life is a Dutch Road in Ohio –
The north road to Erie –
Which should be a tow-path –
Damn blast this water-sheeted aisle
Of spindly birches –
On an all-grey winter's day –
You know all too well:
How stoically, yet sensitively,
Even humorously,
Ploughing your cart-horses
All rump and tail;
Savouring the death of all,
Yet knowing in your soul
Prophetically
That Spring will come round again
And that your wife is still alive
And your creaking knees still function
And in summertime the grandchildren
Will come visit from Cincinnati
Wanting to try on your farmer's hat,
Demonstrating to Grandad
Their brand-new iPhones;
Pour small, grey metal cups
Of grey water through your knobbly fingers;
You are your horses' tails;
'*What cannot be cured love*
Has to be endured love
Forever headed to the North Pole Fair';
I am wild, wild Erie;
Mud Hen, Buckeye – of the Old Dutch Road.

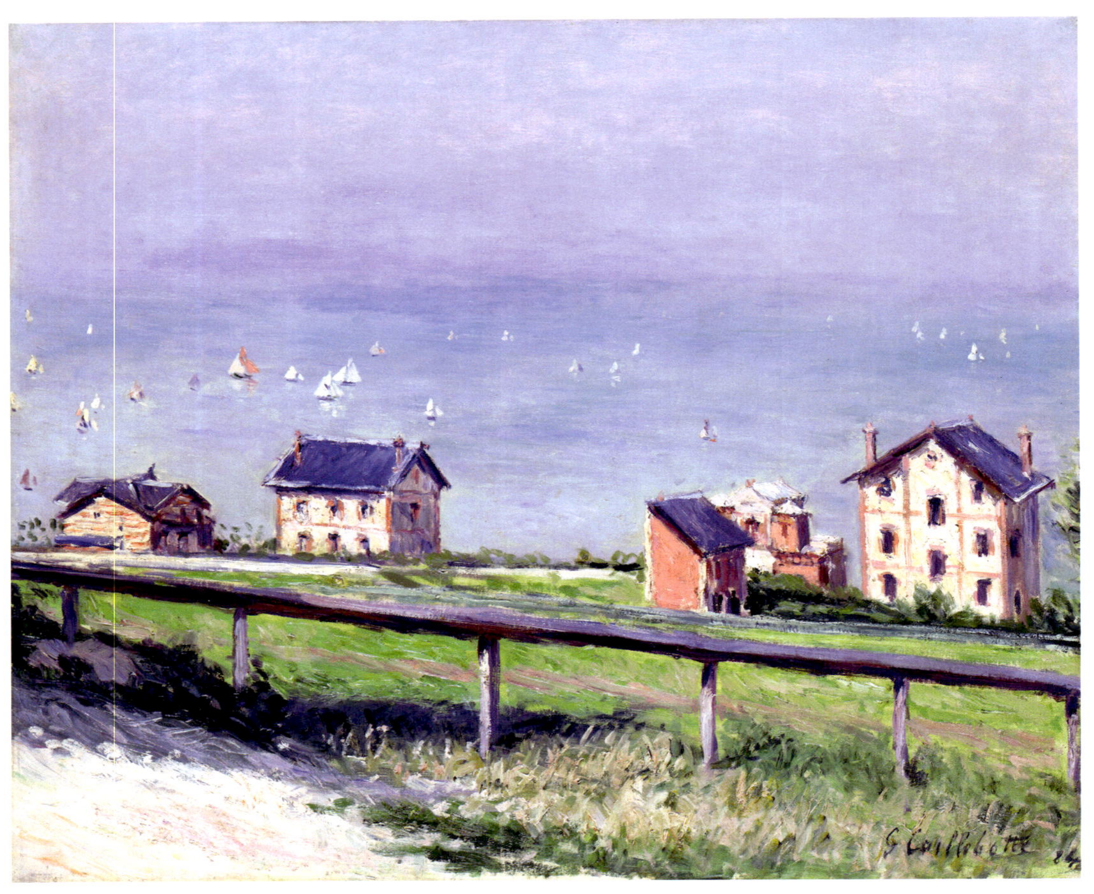

GUSTAVE CAILLEBOTTE

The gayest summer of my life –
I was only a fifteen years old boy –
Still a child, still a child –
My uncle Gustave Caillebotte
Invited me to stay in his summer villa –
His three-storey red-brick slated chalet
In Vaucottes on the coast near Trouville –
A line of self-made people's holiday homes
Constructed on open, common grassland on the cliff –
O the green, green uncut grass atop the blue-white sea!
Mostly notaries and their families from Lille and Paris,
A politician or two, a naval officer, a military man.

Uncle Gustave's was more of a chateau than a chalet
And its bare, spare rooms reflected my uncle –
His easy-going, casual kindness, his firm house-rules.
Sailing, of course, was his number one preoccupation
And passion – I often wondered why he had no wife
But, of course, it was his yacht he was wedded to.
He'd take me out in the yacht most days and he'd give me
The tiller to hold and he'd smile at me through his moustachioed lips
And no fifteen-year old boy ever felt more loved.

Rainy days – excursions to Fécamp and Étretat
To visit his friend Claude – Monet, I think, was the surname –
A real old weirdo whom Uncle Gustave adored –
But the BIG day was Regatta Day at Trouville:
Millions of sail boats out on the water – what fun –
Cool, really cool. Cool, cool, cool.
I stayed up on the cliff to watch
From my fourth storey attic bedroom window –
Taking a break only to look out the back window.

Only to see something I wish I had not seen –
Like Oliver in *Oliver Twist* seeing Sykes at the window –
A very sad-looking man, hands crossed as if in prayer,
With a woman who looked she was about to murder him;
The pair of them up against the wall of a strange, little house –
The narrow, shed-like one with the steep, steep roof –
The house known as Gangplank House.
And that was the year that Uncle Gustave won
In the yacht he had built himself. Late
Into the night Uncle Gustave fired rockets
Fore and aft such was his delight in victory
Up into the sky like a boy on his biggest high.

On my last night we visited the Benedictine monastery at Fécamp
Where the monks were in their heyday manufacturing '*Benedictine*' –
A sweet, scrumptious but savagely lethal liqueur.
How I laughed when Uncle Gustave poured it down my throat!
Learning to laugh at age 15! Yes –
For although my own father was a loving, affectionate papa
He was not a man given to laughter.
That night back at the chalet in Vaucottes
I laughed for eight hours until the sun came up
And we had *petit-déjeuner* and *café au lait*.
Oh those were the days with Uncle Gustave Caillebotte!
At *au revoir* time I wept and he cupped my head in his hands –
In his smooth, yet rough-hewn, salty, yacht-carpenter's hands.

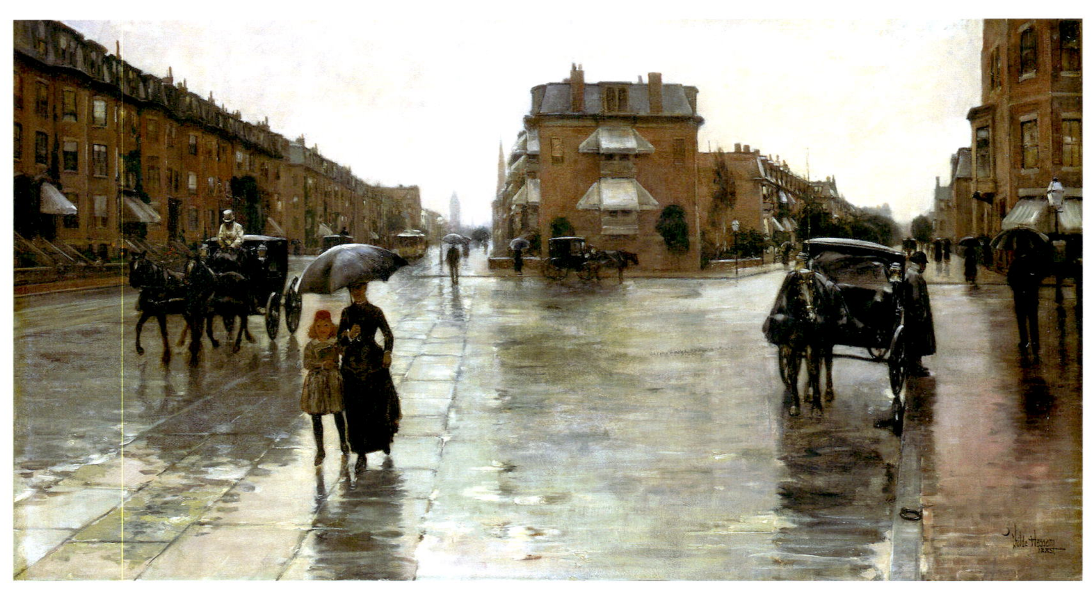

CHILDE HASSAM

RAINY DAY, BOSTON
1885

---

to David Rieff

So folks, what we're looking at now –
"I'm Abie Scattini, by the way, folks, senior Docent –
That is to say, your Volunteer Teacher and Guide –
What we're feasting our eyes on is *senza dubbio*
One of the most under-rated masterpieces, not only
Of Nineteenth-Century North American Art
But of Nineteenth-Century Art anywhere in the world
(The World including the Indigenous –
From the Ganges to the Volga to the Bulloo to the Maumee) –
I give you 'Rainy Day, Boston 1885' by Childe Hassam –
A New Englander prankster-genius
Known to family and friends as Child who, in spite of his super-abundant
Genius – he painted more than four thousand paintings –
Learned never to take himself too seriously.
"The only wisdom we can hope to acquire
Is the wisdom of humility" as Old Possum has it.
Look closely at his signature: note the crescent moon!
It amused him to pass himself off as Middle Eastern
Although he was as New Englander as you can be,
Descended as he was from the seventeenth-century Horshams
From West Sussex.

Hard to credit it but Hassam was only twenty-six
When he painted this very, very early masterpiece.
Not bad for a twenty-six year old, eh?
'Rainy Day, Boston' was inspired
By the young painter's recent brief sojourn in Paris;
Magisterially, he has taken his cue
From Gustave Caillebotte's 'Paris Street, Rainy Day'
A French masterwork painted in 1877 when Childe Hassam
Was barely seventeen years old –
(Happily – in the way of these serendipities –
The Caillebotte is now our neighbour in the Chicago Art Institute.)

Caillebotte's painting is an erotic dance of umbrella spokes
At the junction of five streets
Adjacent to the Gare du Nord in Paris in the 8th *arrondissement.*
n.b. – how although Hassam has immediately simplified the geography
By reducing his street-scape to three –
Columbus Avenue, Appleton Street and Canton Street –
He has purified Caillebotte's eroticism
By making his own depiction an homage to
And Celebration of Wetness –
180% wetness.

Look! Just even by my momentary glancing at the painting
I am soaked by Hassam's 'Wetness' – all that clammy wetness.
Standing here in the dry (!) gallery of the Toledo Museum of Art
I feel compelled to hitch up my pants ever so slightly
And save my Italian shoes from getting TOO wet –
Just like the young lady in the foreground
Under her taut, pricey, multi-spoked umbrella
In a chic, fitted black jacket,
Her white blouse, revealing just enough cuff and collar,
Hitching up her dress and her petticoats! You can hear her
Saying to herself – can't you – "my shoes have quite thin soles –
Hope all this wet rain doesn't ruin my shoes!"

Standing here in the Toledo Museum of Art
Knowing how dry it is out on Monroe and Collingwood –
Dry rain? –
The longer I gaze into Hassam's painting the wetter I get –
The rain belting down, swilling around,
What a rainy, rainy, rainy, rainy day in Boston!

All puddles and umbrellas and rain-gear
And yet where is all the light coming from?
The sun is high in the sky, not low;
The trees are green – full green.

A pair of very green silver birches on the corner.
Such understated attention to detail –
Awnings up, canopied oriel windows
All rendered so unobtrusively.

The young lady's chatting to her precocious nine-year old daughter –
Analysing this summer evening's meteorological predicament
But her daughter is gay with expectancy –
Clasping her music book with her right arm
And her free arm tucked into her mother's elbow –
Bouncing along in her black stockings,
Her cute red *fez* atop her golden locks! A genuine Hassam!

If Elgar – only two years older than Child(e) Hassam –
Had been another young Bostonian genius in the 1880s
He'd have composed a set of Hassam Variations
Chief among them a choral concerto
Entitled 'Rainy Day, Boston'– an Homage
To the Maestro of all working men –
The coachman, the cab-driver, the cabbie –
White top hat, black bowler –
Massed choirs of cabbies converging
On three great South End thoroughfares –
Columbus and Appleton and Canton –
Horses trotting or standing still
Rugg'd or waterproofed –

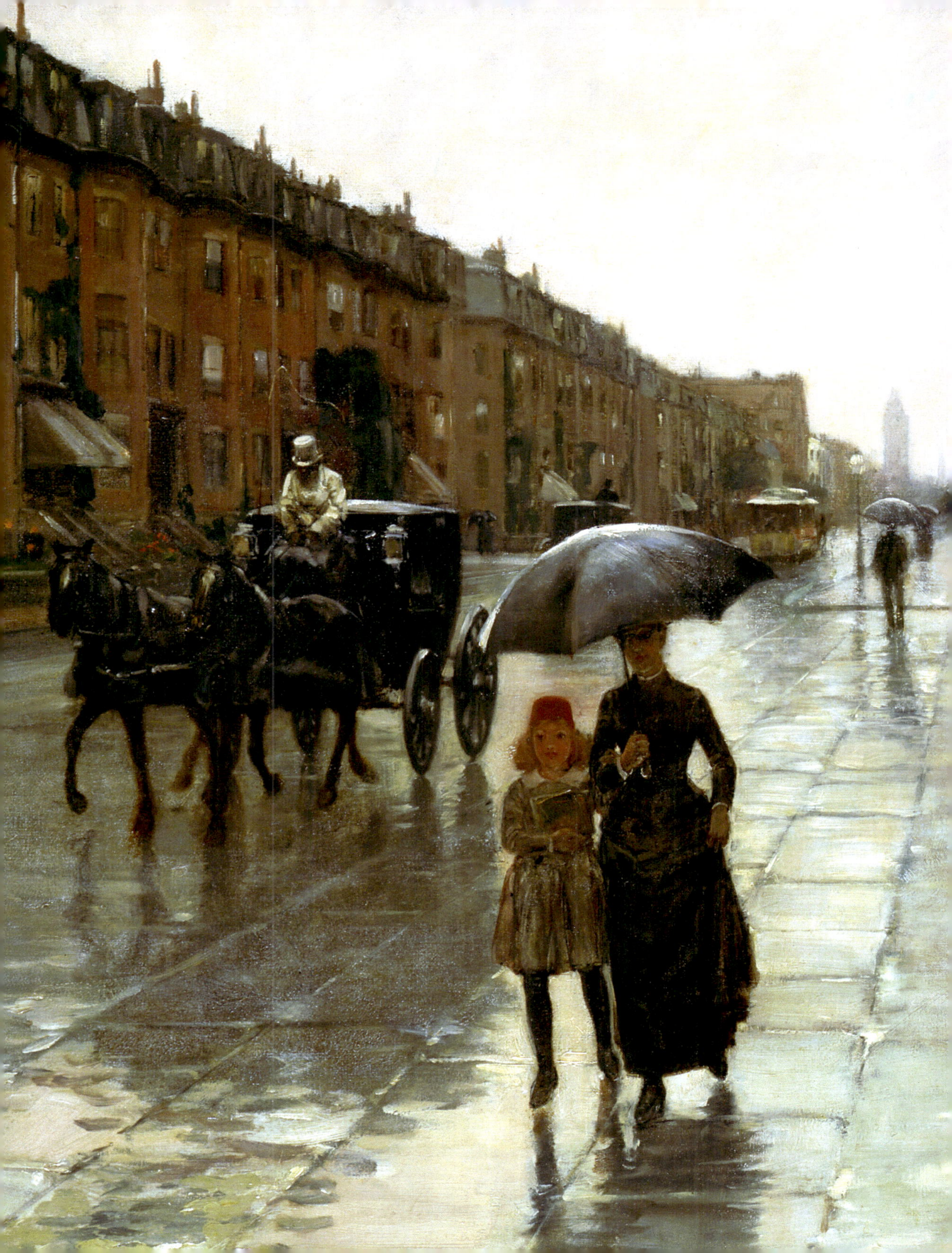

And all of these fronted by a single flute
Played by a nine year-old girl
With golden locks under a red *fez* –
Imagine –
"All art aspires to the condition of music"
And none more so than Childe Hassam's art
In 'Rainy Day, Boston'!

I want you all to exit the Toledo Museum of Art
Humming or whistling Elgar's Hassam Variation on Child(e).
Ciao! Have a nice trip around Lake Erie."

STILL LIFE WITH THE TOLEDO BLADE
1886

---

to Stephen and Julie Taylor

"I buy only one paper and it is not *The Blade*!" –
An Ohioan enchantress smiles gloatingly:
I return her cock-a-hoop grin with top-spin:
"I buy only one paper and it is not *Le Monde*!"

I

Often at evening when a boy
I'd carry home to Mother
From selling newspapers on the corner
An extra dollar for table food;
We were the Irish immigrant poor;
Father having died his actual death.

II

Father died by drowning in the local river
When I was but a year old.
As best I could, I supported Mother
For the rest of her days and nights
By painting Still Lives of actuality –
The actual shells of our mortal days:

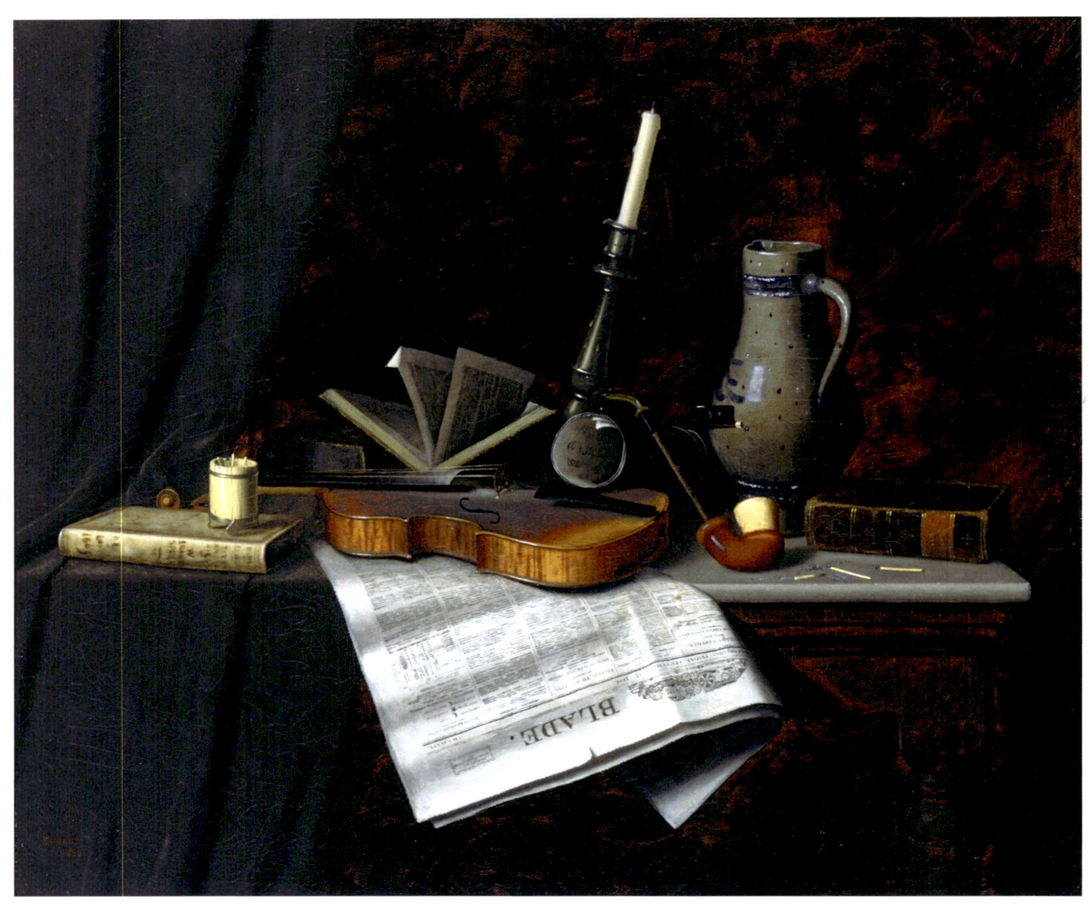

WILLIAM HARNETT

III

Jug, pipe, books, fiddle-and-bow –
'O Oft in the Stilly Night';
A folded newspaper, the *Toledo Blade*
For a friend in Toledo, Ohio; match-sticks;
A candle by which to read the small print
Upside-down, if necessary (a droll poet).

IV

Mother's life was a hard life
Rearing a family without husband or money;
She was miraculously hard-working and selfless,
Thinking nothing of her 14-hour day;
She had a wild colleen smile in her eyes,
Affectionate, devout, gently religious.

V

My Still Lives for Mother were shrines
Of objects and subjects of daily devotion
Such as my 'Still Life with the *Toledo Blade*'.
She died a good death the year before, at forty-four,
I died myself of womanlessness,
Melancholia, rheumatoid arthritis.

VI

I had no more reason to live.
My girlfriend could read the line on my spine.
My extraordinary mother from County Cork
Had crossed the bar into the next dream-field;
With her passing there was no more need
For any more pleasing 'Still Lives from William M. Harnett'.

VII

You might say after a glass or two –
Another 'actual' death at Algeciras:
'The heron-billed pale cattle-birds'
Over Cathedral Cemetery, Philadelphia –
Over the fresh grave of a small, lean man
Who was a prodigious poet of the art of painting.

VIII

They wrote that I painted 'bric-a-brac' –
'They' being the great critics, the great arbiters,
The great, furry know-alls of art
Who cannot even distinguish their bric from their brac.
I painted with dedication like Moore or Keats
That most sublime subject-matter of all – the ordinary.

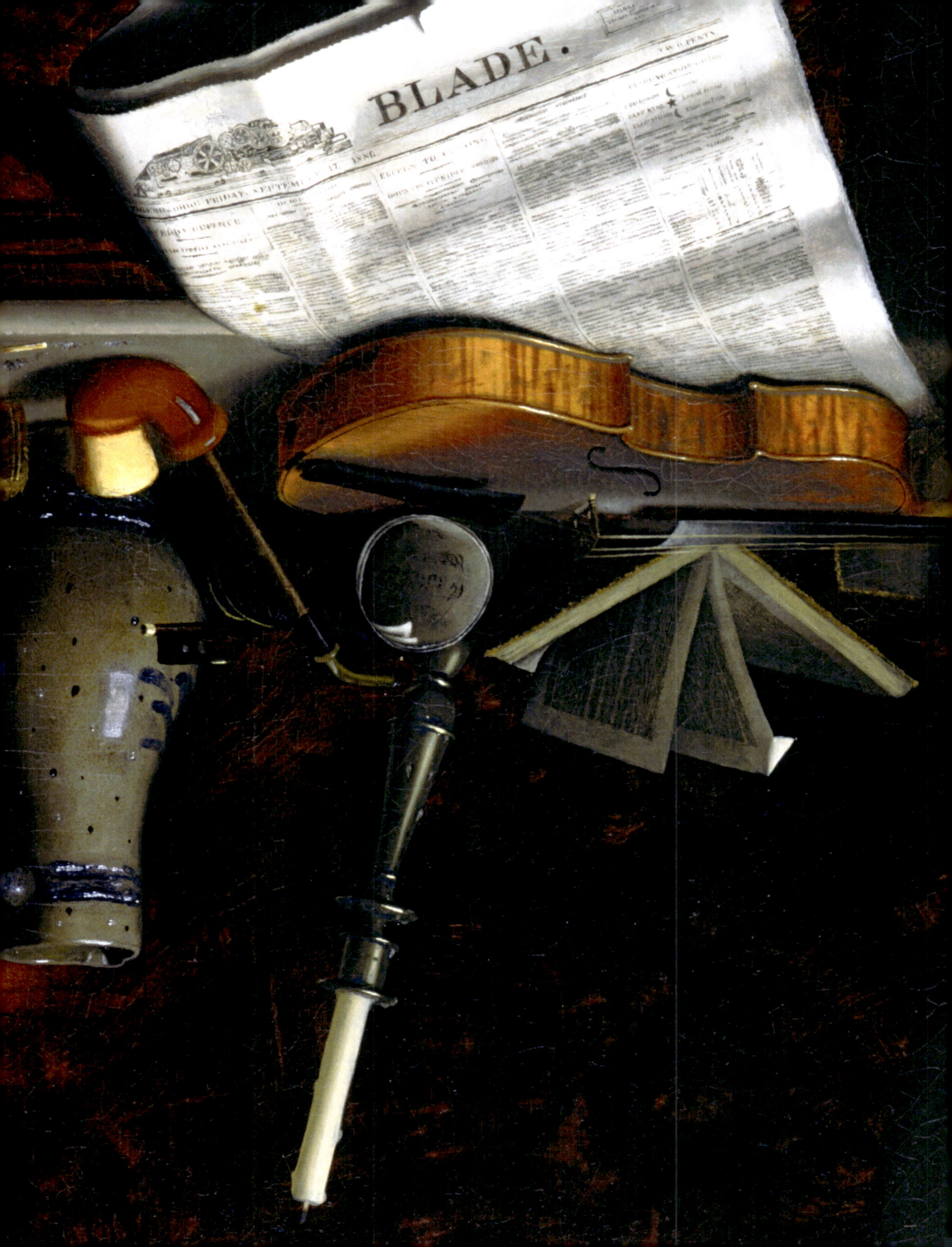
BLADE.
TWO CENTS
FRIDAY, SEPTEMBER 17, 1886.
PRICES TO CASH

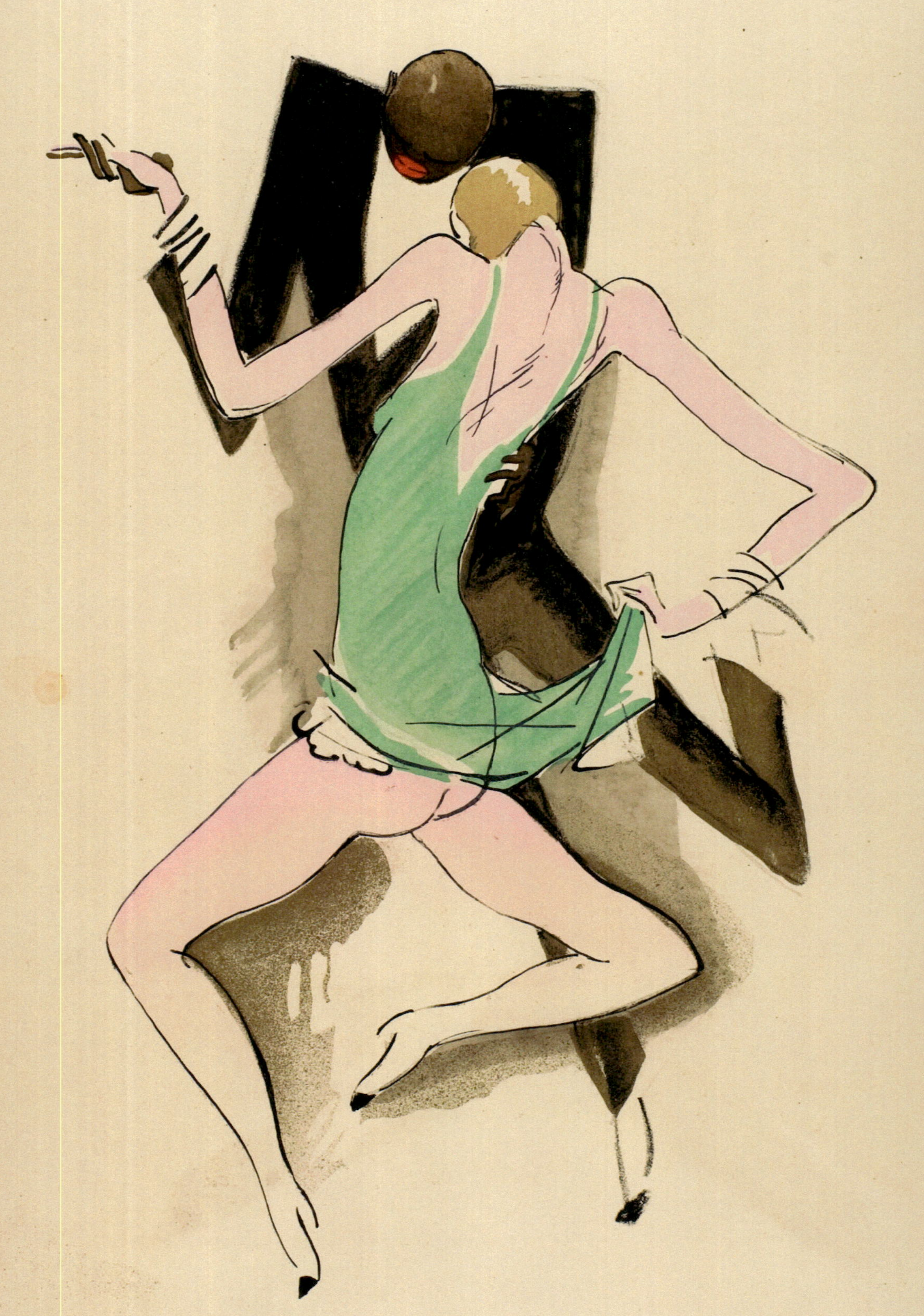

*   *   *

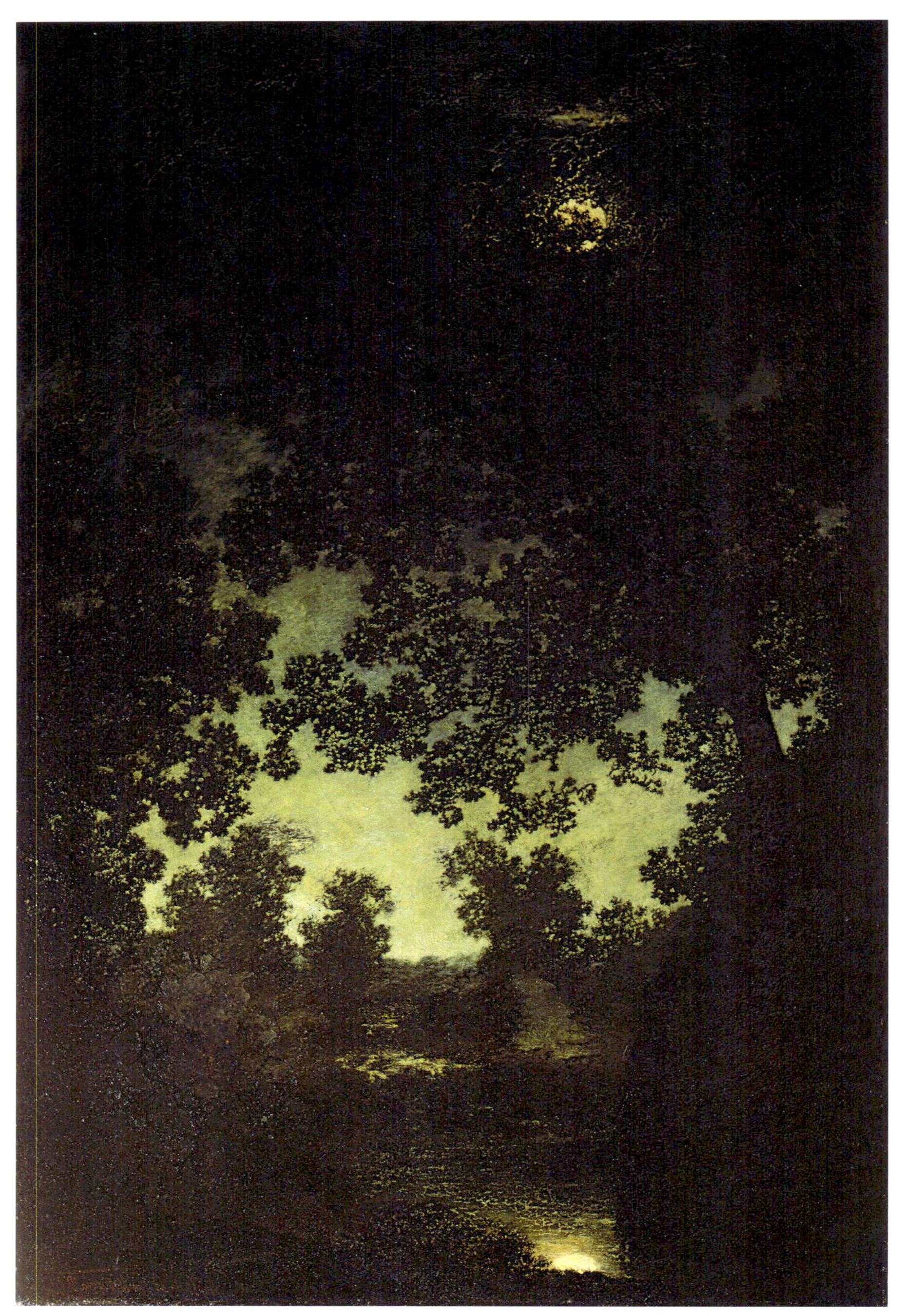

RALPH ALBERT BLAKELOCK

BROOK BY MOONLIGHT

BEFORE 1891

to Scott Boberg

Night in the forest can be a light into paradise
But equally it can be not a good place to be.
We're on sticky ground, so sticky, sticky.
With only a paintbrush in your hand
How do you keep away from Lobotomy Farm?
Dearest John Keats, Dearest Alfred Lord Tennyson,
Dearest Robert Lowell, Dearest Edgar Allan Poe,
Let there be no more romanticising of Melancholia.

All I can do is to try and paint myself out of it –
Year in, year out –
Layer upon layer upon layer upon layer of paint –
Out of the blackness in my mind –
Out of all of the mood-swings, out of all of the anxieties,
Out of all the obsessions, out of all the millennia of loneliness
Getting blacker and blacker and blacker and –
How *do* I paint myself out of it?
How *can* I paint myself out of it?

I go deep down into it, descending the stairs
Of Black Mountain until down at the base of it
I sit on a rock and with a sketchpad and pencil
I cry out to all my dead friends, dead, dead,
John, Brian, Mummy, Daddy, Seamus, Lizzie, Donal, Girly.
After what seems like hours – maybe 45 minutes –
I discern a brook by moonlight!
> *I come from haunts of coot and hern*
> *I make a sudden sally,*
> *And sparkle out among the fern,*
> *To bicker down a valley.*

O my full moon glimpsed through her lacy green eyes
Whilst far down beyond and far beyond nearby and out beyond
The pebbly lower reaches where in childhood paradise
We boys and girls played and we played until we dropped!
Such delicious frissons of excitement of groundless fear
Of shapes and sounds coming at us out of the dark!
Is that an ape? A badger? A vixen barking?
And the sumptuously sinister oak leaves – frilly cut-outs!
How many years have I been chained
To this rock in Black Mountain
And not seen the brook by moonlight,
Not even discerned it?
Discerned it as it is and

Humping the years that I do
I strip down to my t-shirt and my shorts,
Step secretively across fallen trees, shattered boughs,
Until I arrive at the brook
By whose curving banks I lie and curl up
With one hand – my painting hand –
Dangling down deep into the water
And I overhear myself whispering to her:
Brook, I am making love to you –
By moonlight – making love to you!

Back up in my studio for years and years
I am painting my dark, secret love – my Brook by Moonlight –
For years and years – painting over it and over it
Knowing that the day I complete it
Will be the day I die. . . . Yet I can say, may I not,
I am getting it so right, amn't I? Yet
I can never complete my Brook by Moonlight.
Listen to me singing my lines in my bath-tub:
'I can never complete my Brook by Moonlight!'
I am morally obligated never to finish my painting –
My great love-painting that I call 'Brook by Moonlight'!
So there you are, tender-hearted curator, gallery-tripper, art nerd, take care.
Watch your step. Thank you. I will think of thee always.

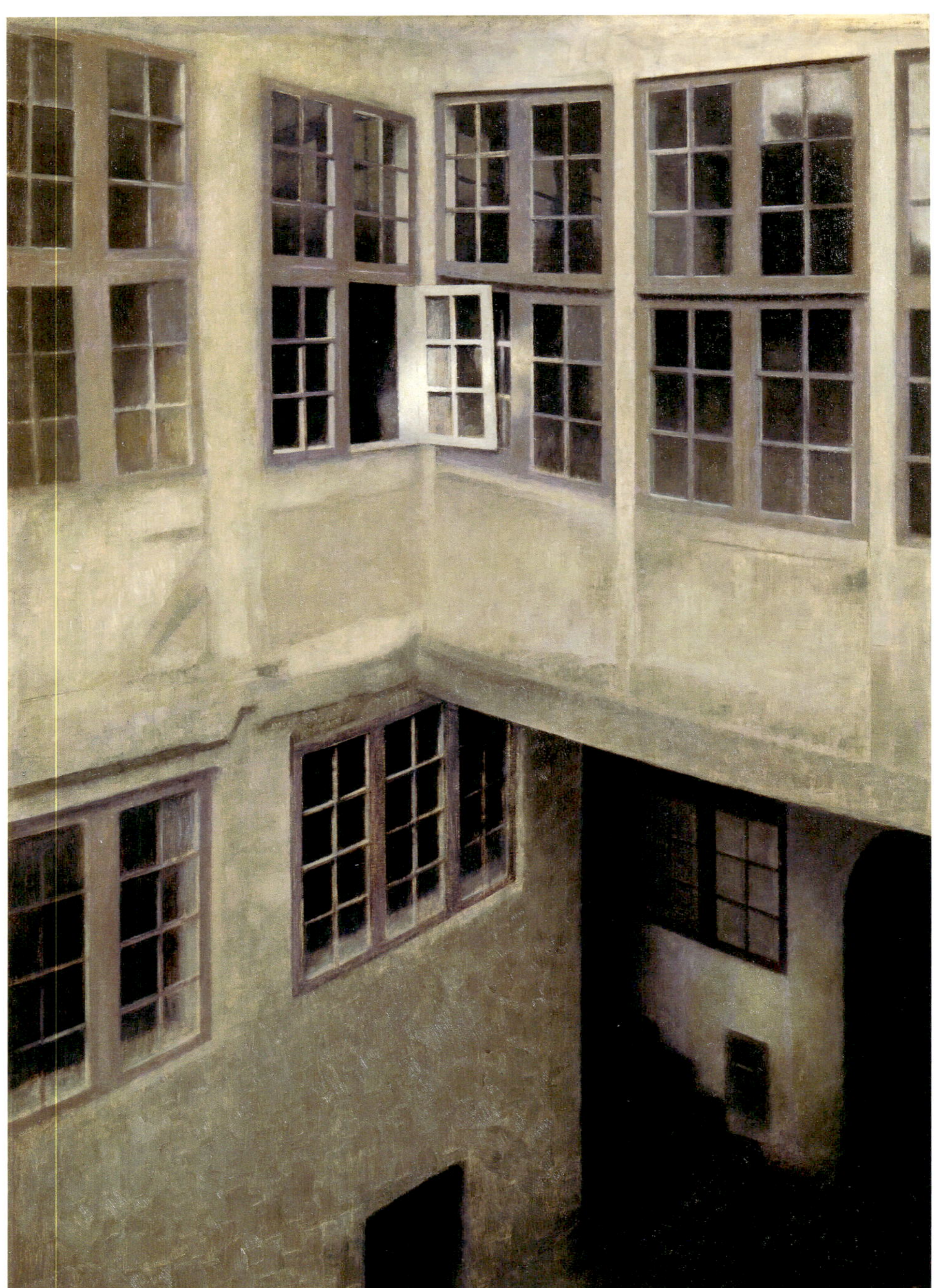

VILHELM HAMMERSHØI

Of all the women I have known it was with my grandmother
I was most in love, on whom I was most hung up,
Her open window, the secret of her three dark doorways.
Everyone else's window, men and women, was closed,
Hers alone remaining open;
Her private, secret darkness, her picture-framed groin
Alone attracting light
From such obscure corners as my small boy's soul,
A god-beam from the cranium between my appalled eyes.
All other adults were without light, inaccessible, tall.
Only she was small, reachable, palpable, forever young.
When my father would draw back his vast hairy-backed hand
To slap it across my face,
In her scented, embroidered, sugary, Persian kitchen apron
She would emerge scuttling across the courtyard
To stand between me and him.
Now, fifty-five years later, gazing up
At the black window of my own sweet death,
The mystery of my own three doorways,
I cry: Grandma, I want your black gown only, only yours
And you will take my hand in yours walking out along Sunnyside.

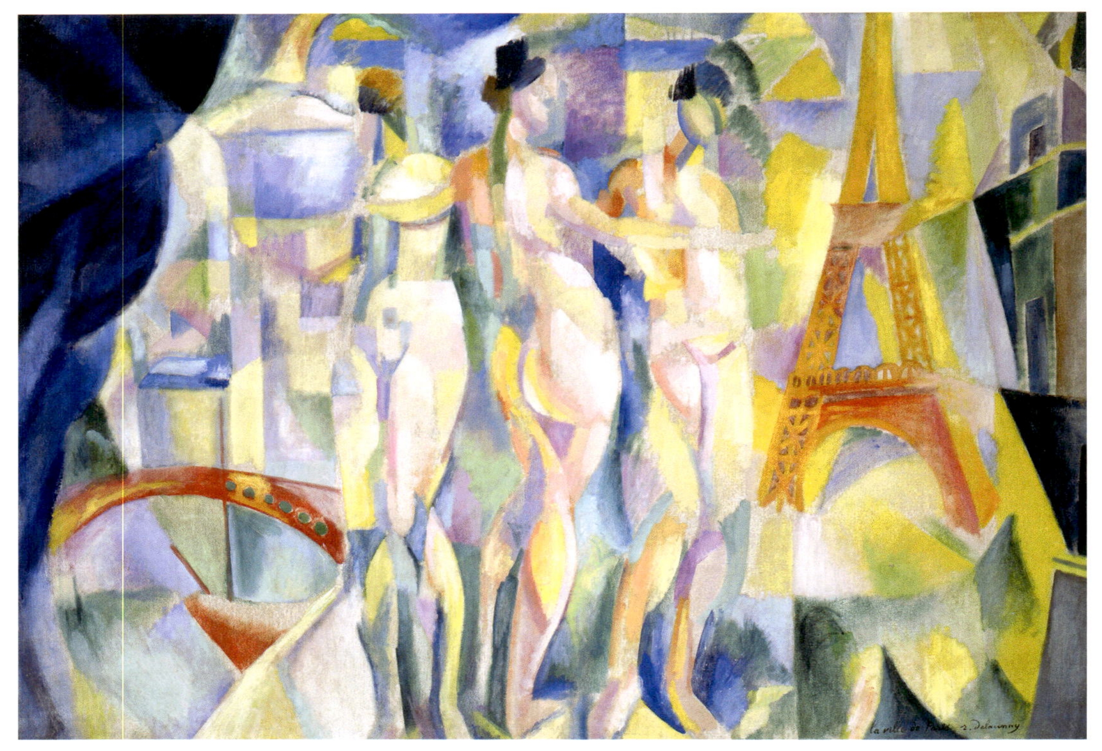

ROBERT DELAUNAY

When I was a nine-year-old boy the rocket of puberty
Landed on the moon of my innocence and behind
My grandmother's dressing-table I used peer out erect,
Naked in the sunlight and the blue sky –
She brushing and combing out her silver-grey hair
As she sat smiling in self-admiration before her looking-glass,
Regaling me with her Paris days in the early 1900s –
How she and the other two girls used undress in her boudoir
Behind her navy-blue satin bathroom curtains,
Fling off their chemises, fling their negligees up in the air,
Don their petite, toy, naughty, saucy black hats, perch on her balcony
Of their Passy apartment in the 16th *arrondisement*
Gazing across the river at Gustave Eiffel's even more mother-naked gazelle
With its 2,500,000 rivets!
The three girls used perform a secret game the winner of which
Put her arm out, elongating it until she got to play with
And hold Eiffel's Tower in her very own hands.
Grandmother confided in me: "I used close my eyes
CLASPING Eiffel's – well – *outré*, rather attractive tower in my own two hands.
Disentangling it, caressing it, drying the sopping rain off it.
Mon petit, it was *absolument* very heaven in 1911 to be a young woman *à Paris*."

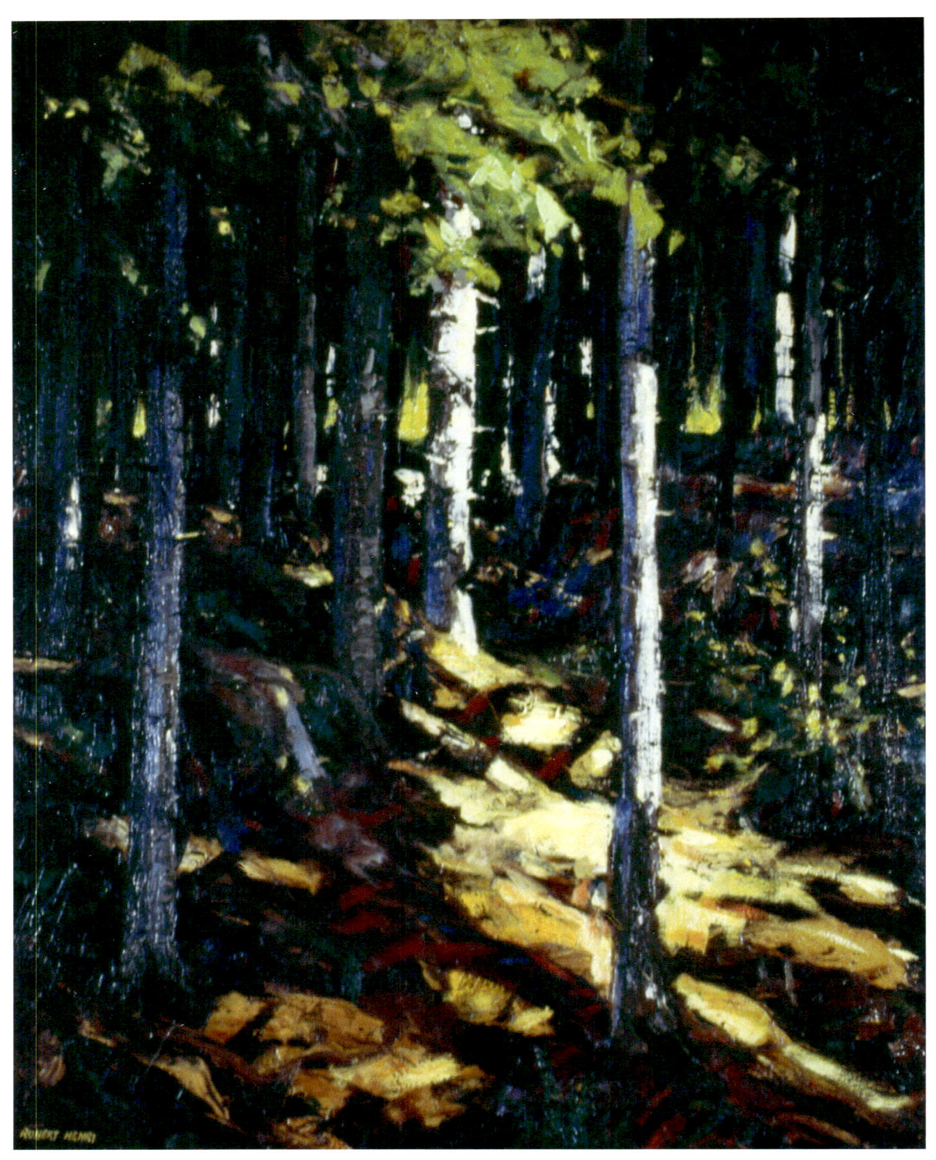

ROBERT HENRI

It was to Ohio the hills of home I always went back
And to Achill Island off the west coast of the island of Ireland.
But above all to Monhegan Island off Maine –
In the Cathedral Woods of Monhegan I painted trees as the Persons
Trees really are, the visceral spirituality of their Light and Shade.
And in Achill Island cliffs and portraits with my eyes closed –
Hundreds and hundreds of portraits of children and women –
And a lady – not a woman but a lady – named Kiddo Sheridan
And the odd old man.

But now that I am aged sixty-four and dying in New York City
Of prostate cancer in St. Luke's Hospital, Room 521 –
"Bob, you've run out of vim" cries my wife Marjorie Organ –
It is in my painting of the Cathedral Woods on Monhegan Island (1911)
That I see everything –
All I ever attempted in a painting
With oil on canvas – and – with that Palette – the Maratta Palette.
'Cathedral Woods' is one of my Vincent paintings that works –
Van Gogh.
Nick always said that despite appearances I had 'the Dutch thing' –
Only that my Dutch thing in 'Cathedral Woods' was calmer.

'Cathedral Woods' on Monhegan Island –
So what is it all about?
In these trees are all the people I have loved – but
Is not every island the same – every woods?

Light and Shade and – but only if you gaze lightly enough –
A woman's face – a woman sitting up against a tree,
Her red skirt, her blue blouse,
All I ever wanted to know of fleeting life and therefore eternity;
Of comradeship, of married love, of conversation, of memory.

In six weeks in the summer of 1911 on Monhegan Island
I painted 290 oils! Rumble, man, rumble!
Of course I had my new wife Marjorie Organ in my corner
But not exclusively;
All the women I adored in my life are there also
Along with "My People" – I called them –
The children, the thousands of children –
All, all of these in Cathedral Woods in silence
In light and shade – in shade and light.

And all with the Hardesty Maratta palette –
Now there's a story!
Let's walk over the mountain to Keel and Dooagh
And let me tell you about Hardesty G. Maratta
And his painstaking, miraculous palette
And after dinner back in Boycott's house –
(Imagine – I bought Captain Boycott's house
For a song – the infamous land agent's mansion –
Evicting tenant farmers was what gave him his kicks -
With my own dollars and dimes, for Maxim Gorky's sakes!)

But let me tell you about the greatest Yeats of them all –
Greater even than his two sons –
Greater even than Jack B. Yeats the painter or his poet brother William –
Their ancient, itinerant, painter-father John Butler Yeats with whom I spent
Many nights down the years when the years were apocalyptically young
In Petitpas's French Restaurant in Greenwich Village
With Good Man John Sloan and all the new Old Believers.

John Butler Yeats – 'The Prodigal Father'
William Michael Murphy, the scholar, named him –
The greatest ever speaker of the English language
And portrait painter *extraordinaire* . . .
All in 'Cathedral Woods'!
Cathedral Woods, indeed. Indeedio!
Not to mention that day back in Toledo, Ohio
That woman called Emma Goldman –
That wow of an anarchist –
Her lecture on Tolstoy in Toledo, Ohio –
There also was a prodigal woman –
Almost as great as John Butler Yeats, the Prodigal Father
Hiding out in New York City where now I lie dying 12th July 1929 –
The Eighth Man! –
Only fourteen days after my sixty-fourth birthday.
"A tumbler of water, *merci bien, ma chérie*, a tumbler of water!"
"De rien."

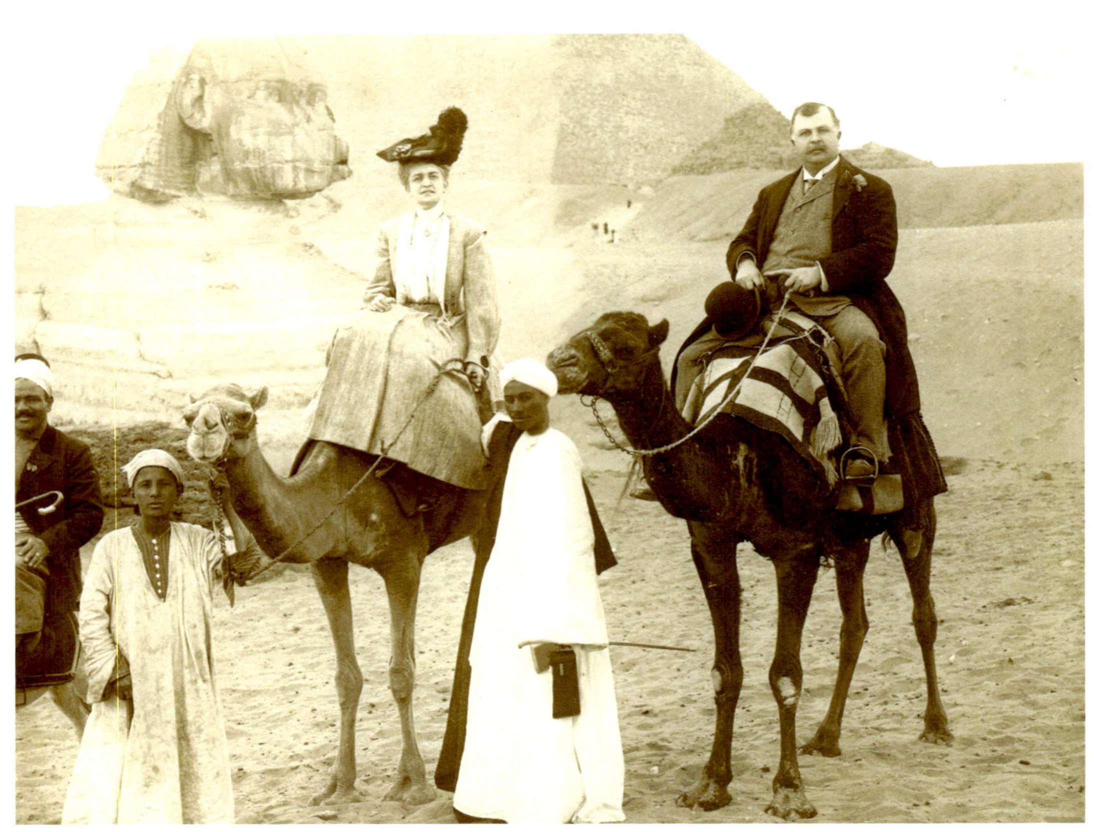

MR AND MRS LIBBEY, CAMEL-BACK, EGYPT
1906

I

In polite society in the early 1900s in North America
Egyptomania was in the air:
But Mr Edward Drummond Libbey, the Glass millionaire,
Did the only logical and practical thing –
Booked passage for himself and his wife to sunny Cairo
For the several months of the Toledo, Ohio winter.
Mrs Florence Scott Libbey kept her cool.

II

Side-saddle on my camel –
Like sitting in the centre
Of the balcony of the dress circle
At the Paris Opéra –
Sotto voce I whispered to the camel-herd
(So that Mr Libbey would not hear me)
"Hold my hand, dear man,"
And he did as he was bid –
As if he had known me
In a previous life
(I wonder – had he?)
His hand fitted me like a glove.
After having felt a mite –
Well – shall we say – apprehensive

I felt much more comfortable –
And comforted –
More at home in the universe
Than I had ever done
Since I was a five-year old small girl –
Ever, ever, ever, ever!
I felt at ease with myself –
I felt, dare I say it, loved!
I glanced over at my husband
Astride his own camel and he winked:
"Happy Cowboys!" he drawled.

Nothing would do him
But to ship home
All the way to Toledo, Ohio,
A camel especially for me.
You see, he was that kind of unusual husband,
Extraordinarily unpredictable, impetuous, generous.
He shipped over, also, of course, the camel-herd
Who really became a sort of spiritual therapist,
My advisor, my guru, my confidante
In our household in the West End of Toledo –
My very own camel-herd in his laundered
Snow-white robe and his snow-white turban –

So erect, so manly, so lean,
So strong, so dark, so prehensile.
In the springtime every morning around noon
An hour before luncheon
I'd ride across Monroe Street to our new *musée* –
The Toledo Museum of Art –
And such is the classical beauty of the façade –
Sixteen Ionic marble columns,
Our copper roof and *chéneau* of acanthus leaves –
My camel appeared to rejoice in each and every step
Magisterially making our way up to the front entrance.
You know, Nina, I began to suspect that my Egyptian camel
Had had a Greek education in the Socratic method:
A camel for sure but with a Greek sensitivity!

Passers-by would pause – often stop –
To behold and admire, even applaud,
Our minuscule, oriental procession
Across the vast granite terrace
Especially when at the top of the steps
(Oh that was what I liked best – ascending the steps –
Why I – I positively LUSTED after that moment – ASCENDING)
My camel-herd would help me
To dismount from my perch to *terra firma*:

How extra-delicately he held my hand,
How sensually he man-handled my skirts.
You know, Nina, there was something –
Something feminine about my camel-herd!
He became almost – well – a soul-mate –
Even something more than a soul-mate!

In bed at night my husband would bellow and roar:
"My Dear Florence but how you STINK of camel!
But how I do love dung, O my Flor, I love it.
You recall that night in the Tile Club
With the Men of Toledo when I agreed to bankroll
And incorporate a new Museum of Art –
That was the swellest night of my life
Listening to the bawdy applause and the laddish cheering
And Oh Yeah, the wild, wild merry-making
Of those men of the all-male, men-only Tile Club
But tonight inhaling the camel – pure camel –
From your night-dress – why my darlin' beloved
Tonight – tonight is the Happiest Night of my Life!"

Glamour-boy in trade-mark Panama, brand-new brown suit, white silk scarf
With my idle hands in my pockets, leaning up against the side
Of the entrance to the movie-house – tonight the feature movie
About to begin 'A ROMANCE OF THE HAREM';
All the guys and dolls – more dolls than guys.
Ye know what? Lotsa guys are as terrified of MOVIES
As they are of dolls!
Lining up on the side-walk in the piss-yellow spotlight –
The New York City spring night blacker than last night –
Daring themselves to – to – WOW – go to the MOVIES
And for Christ's sakes a movie with a goddamn Oriental name
'A ROMANCE OF THE HAREM'!
All that a Guy – but a Gal even more so – ever dreamed of
And you know what a Harem is?
A Harem, man, is where the Sultan keeps his women!
Right out front of me, in the midst of all,
Three little sisters laughing themselves sick
At the spectacle, the tallest teasing the youngest
"Baby sis, cool it" – Baby Sis is hollering!
Ain't never seen nothing like this in her little life before!
Why, she's catatonic! "Cool it, sis, cool it."

Myself, of course, I am sizing up the Form.
Under my nose two department store girls in their curvaceously
Tight dresses, ankle boots, red, gold and green fashion-hats,

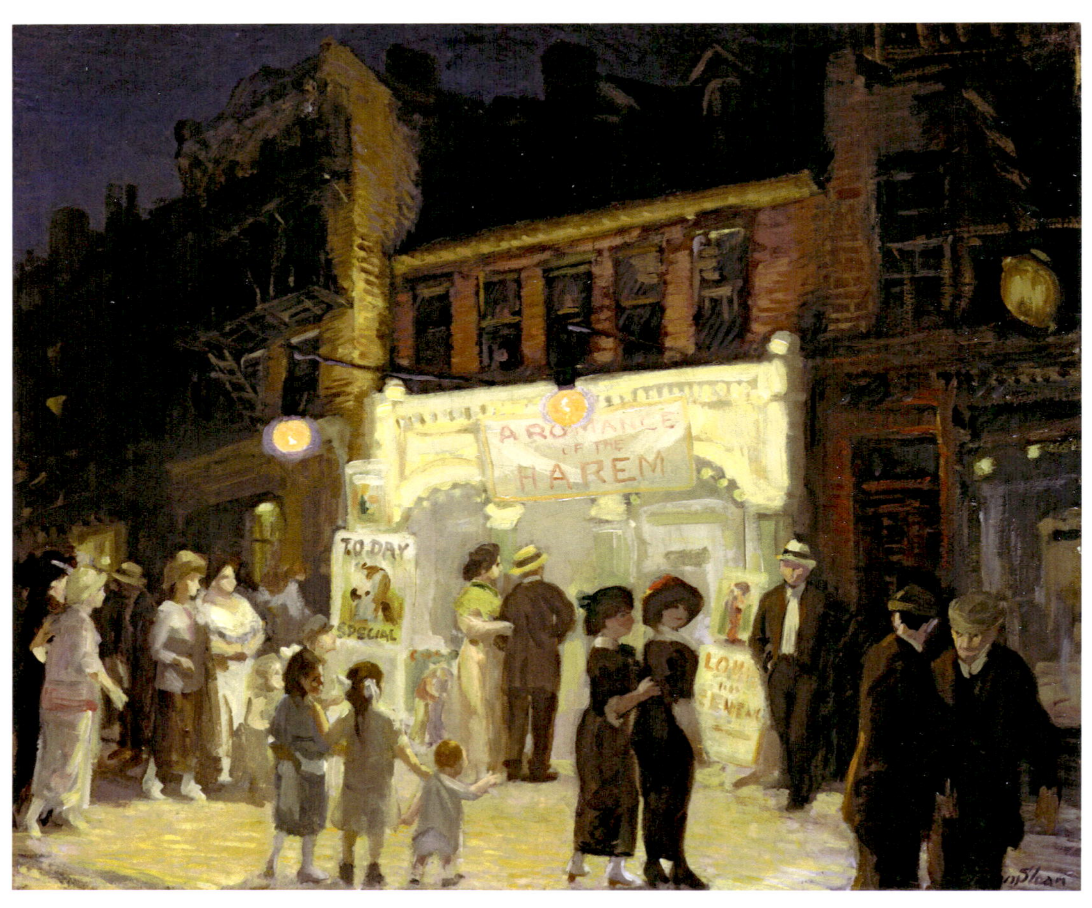

JOHN SLOAN

Detachable white collars over non-detachable bosoms.
The first one – the red hat – is trying to catch the eye –
I just can't guess why – of an ancient Irish – Jewish – maybe Italian geezer
In a rumpled peasant suit and he's taking the bait
And in about 20 seconds, you bet, he'll lumber back to her
Leaving his older brother marooned. What do I care?
Her friend, hand on her elbow, trying to restrain her
And point her in my direction 'cos she knows I'm the goods!

No use, I'm already hooked on the broad on the roadway:
This will be an odds-on battle for me to win but I have to –
I have already decided to pounce on the newest arrival
Stepping up off the roadway arm in arm
With her momma – the most gorgeous piece of stuff
I've seen in centuries – in a yellow hat and a pink and white floral
          gauzy outfit –
Women are so much cuter than men –
She's all dressed up, got out for tonight in Harem Gear!
I can see, too, she's got real class!
Real, goddamn, Upper East Side class.
It's 3 to 1 odds-on she'll turn me down
And worse she will employ not words but knives –
Knives of superior eyes – to stab me repeatedly but quickly
With knives of rejection and repudiation –

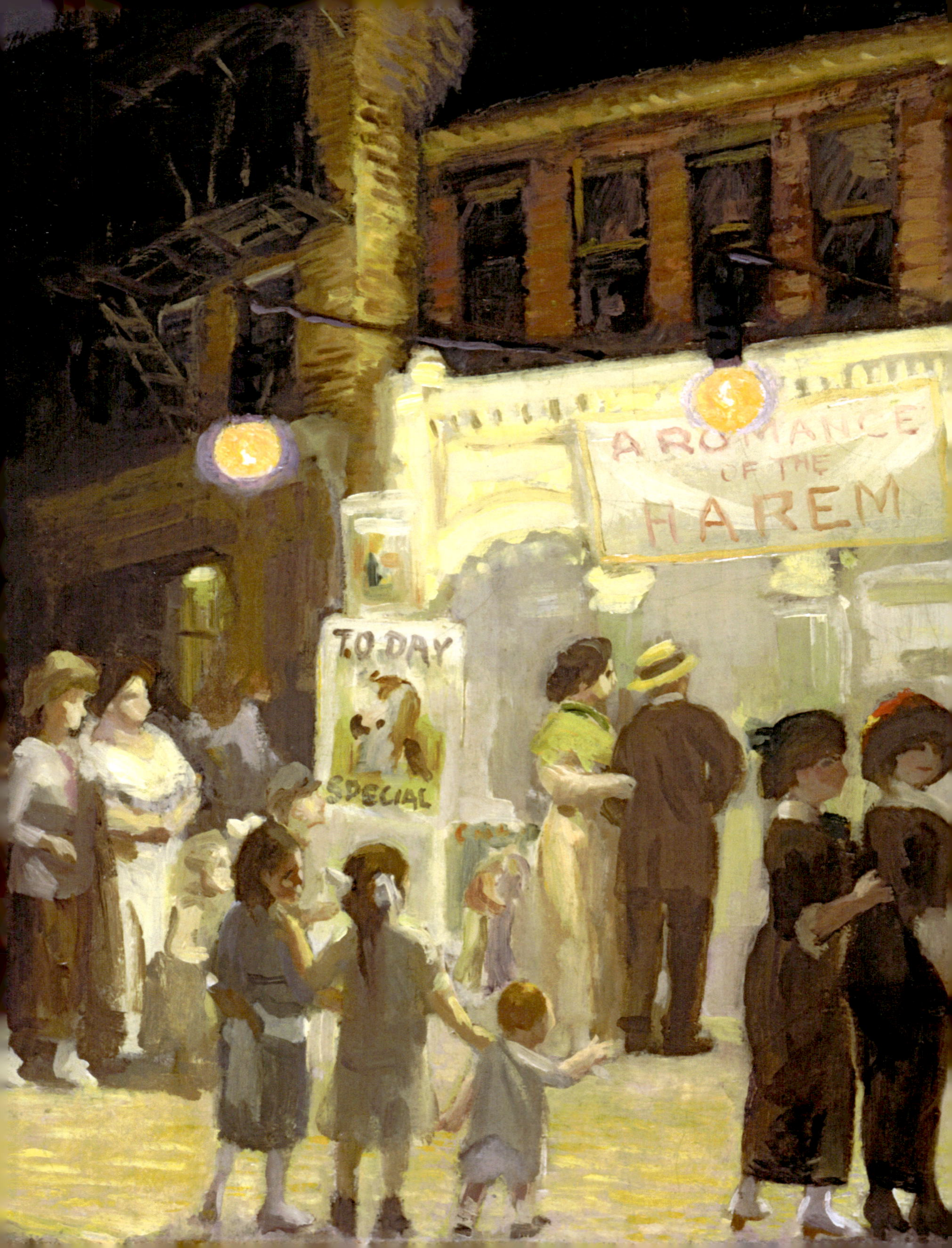
A ROMANCE
OF THE
HAREM
TO DAY
SPECIAL

Worse than being kicked in the Garibaldis!
From being cock o' the walk
I'll slink away down the Lower East Side
To an empty dive and perch alone on a high bar-stool
Watching the most boring movie ever made –
The goddamn movie of my sole, solitary, superman personality.
Glamour-boy, my ass – I am a top-of-the range ass-hole.

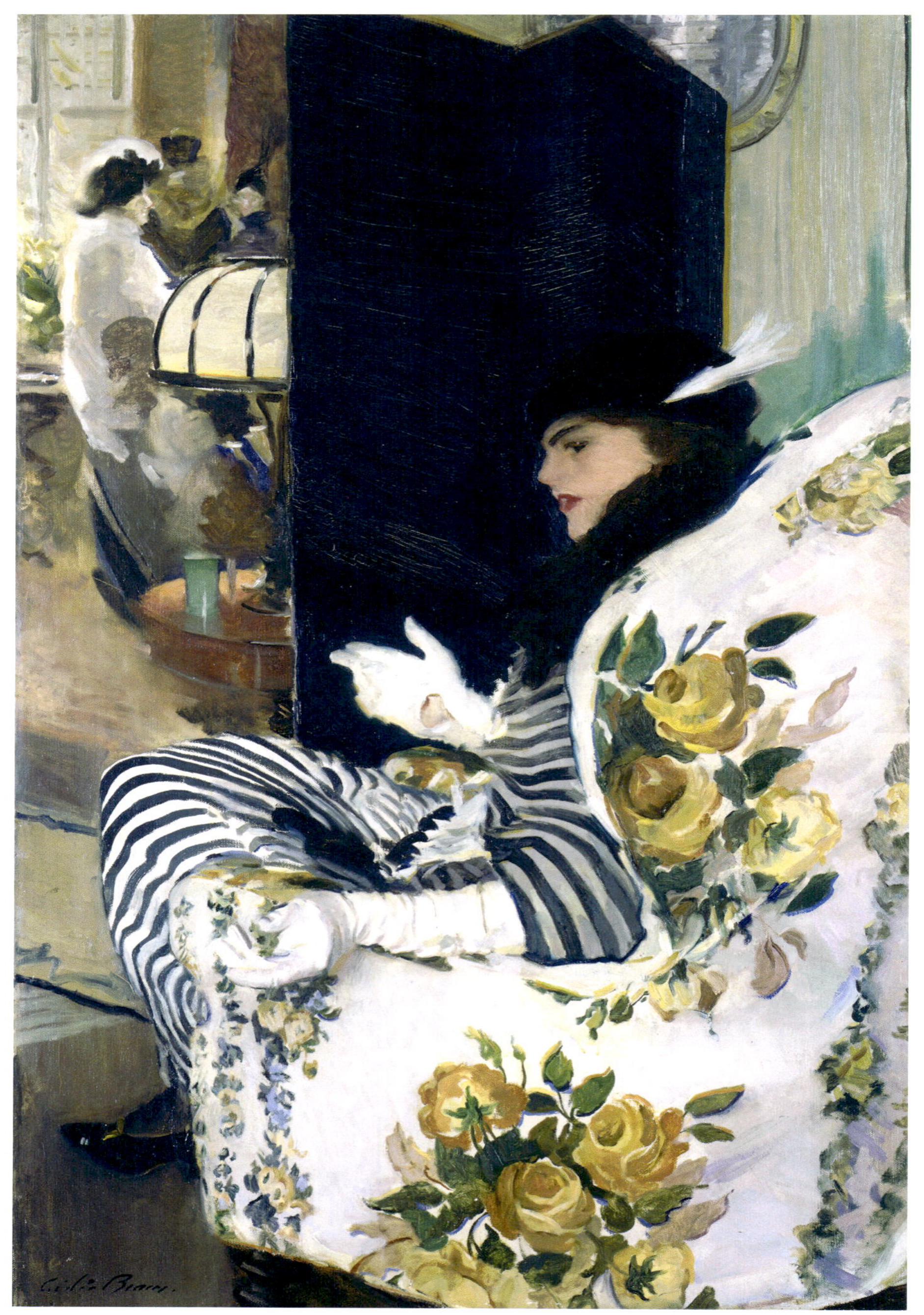

CECILIA BEAUX

I cannot see why they've adjourned the Meeting
When I have come all the way from Boston
And why, indeed, we cannot have it
In a more commodious hotel.
Why, just look at me in these loose chintz covers
With big blowsy yellow roses, swags –
Swags! – down the sides. I cannot see
Why they are not doing things my way. Rule 12.
Dammit it all, Cecilia Beaux, dammit all.
As I stated at the Meeting, Cecilia –
And you were in the front row, Cecilia,
Hiding behind your sketch-pad and crayons –
The only hope for Art in America and in Ohio
In the Open Doorway of War
And, in particular, Toledo, Ohio
Is not John Sloan – much less his mentor Robert Henri:
No, our sole hope is the Casino! The Hollywood Casino!
Where a woman can be solitary! And not only solitary
But most stern and most high and most conspiratorial
In the privacy of a black doorway –
In the lit-up gloom of the true confessional –
Can sharpen her eyes and her tongue as well as her mind –
On one dollar winning sixty dollars
Just-a like THAT

And practice her numbers
And wear her most impregnable white kid gloves
          buttoned-up to the elbow!
And her most understated mink collar!
How many thousands of hours day and night
In my most chic black-and-white striped ankle-length dress
And my black velvet astrakhan beret with its –
Oh but how it breaks my heart to utter it –
With its solitary two egret wings just like poor Mercury –
How many thousands of hours day and night
Have I crouched in front of the roulette table of art, life and death
Or with one-armed bandits either side of me
Stealing glances at my little anthology of French poetry
Discovering the meaning of life and death and art!
What do you think I have got in my little black leather pouch of a purse?
Cheddar!
Un coup de dés jamais n'abolira le hasard.
'A throw of the dice never abolishes chance'.

LA SALLE CLARAC

1922

---

to Paula Reich

I can't believe I am standing alone
On this exhilarating – I can't believe it –
April morning in Paris – alone –
Near, yet far from home
In poor old Chartres –
Alone in the Museum of the Louvre –

Husband and children gone to Caen for the day –
No, I simply can't believe it –
In the most exciting gallery in the whole wide world –
The Clarac Gallery! –
Am I dreaming? Alone at the gilded glass case
Of three glass shelves of Greek antiquities,
All pitchers and vases and figurines,
Feeling like the young mother I really am –
The real, the true maternal seer –
Yes, young – I am NOT – yet – middle-aged!

How re-assuring it is to be a part of the French bourgeoisie!
Early this morning my husband went fishing in Normandy
And he took the children with him – the three of them.

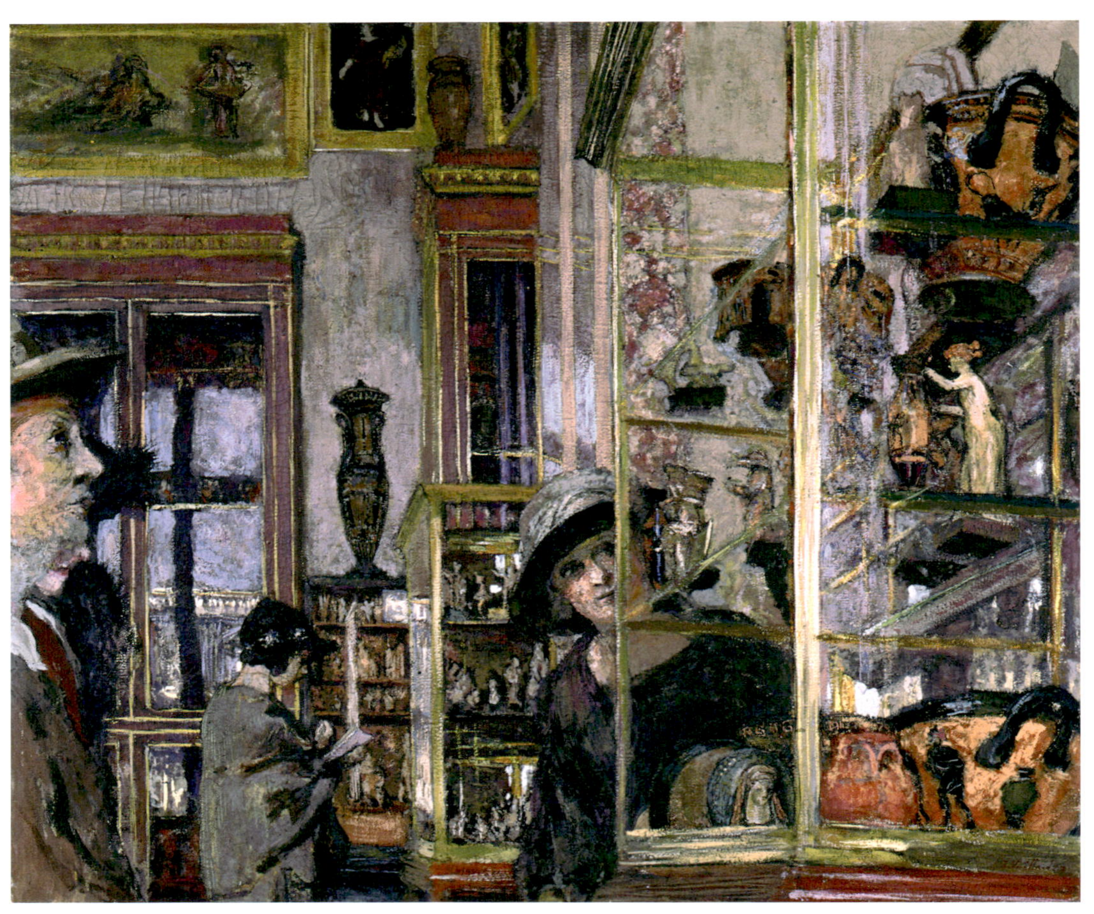

ÉDOUARD VUILLARD

I am free! Today I am free!
A lovely lady like me!
Perforce, therefore, I must wear my fur hat with tulle –
It's a fur-and-tulle day, *ma chérie!*
What kind of person could have created this sensational gallery?
All pink, blue and gold and Ancient Greek art of pure, utter beauty.
Am I dreaming?
Before he left, my darling, difficult husband
Kissed me twice on both cheeks and once full on the lips –
Oh dear – and I knew – I knew he meant it. I am free.

I brought myself up breakfast in bed:
A bowl of coffee, a croissant, demi-baguette with butter and jam
And I dozed between the sheets for a whole extra 45 minutes,
Soaked in the bath, took out my purple dress
Which I haven't worn since before the War
And my wide-brimmed hat
Purchased in *Au Bon Marché* in 1913
After the birth of our first. Am I dreaming?
Yes, I am dreaming but – for real! Have you ever
Let reality dream inside your flesh and your blood
Flooding into your entire body as well as your mind?
Supreme happiness, supreme contentment and
I am only 42! That I am slightly overweight – *un peu envelopée* –

Is of no matter for I am in the pink
And I have a heart of gold or so my husband always tells me
Or nearly always tells me.

Here I am in a tiny corner of Paradise in 1922!
If the after-life as distinct from Paradise really exists
It will look like the Clarac Gallery in the Louvre after the War:
On the middle shelf a terracotta figurine dancing!
On the top shelf an *exaleiptron* –
Every girl must have her *exaleiptron*!
Exaleiptrons are mandatory for all ladies:
The ultimate receptacle for a woman's toilette,
Particularly perfumed unguents.
On the bottom shelf a terracotta head – terracotta!

Up above me, over the window, behind me,
A fragment of a fresco from Pompeii:
Two nymphs flanking the River God.
My god but he is the spitting image of my spouse!
After luncheon – a not insubstantial late luncheon –
When I get back to our apartment in Chartres in the late afternoon
I will wrap up myself in my husband's wartime greatcoat
And lie down on our Persian carpet and in the last rays of the sun
Going down behind the Cathedral – close my eyes,
Dreaming of my children, of him, of Ancient Greece:
'The end of art is peace'.

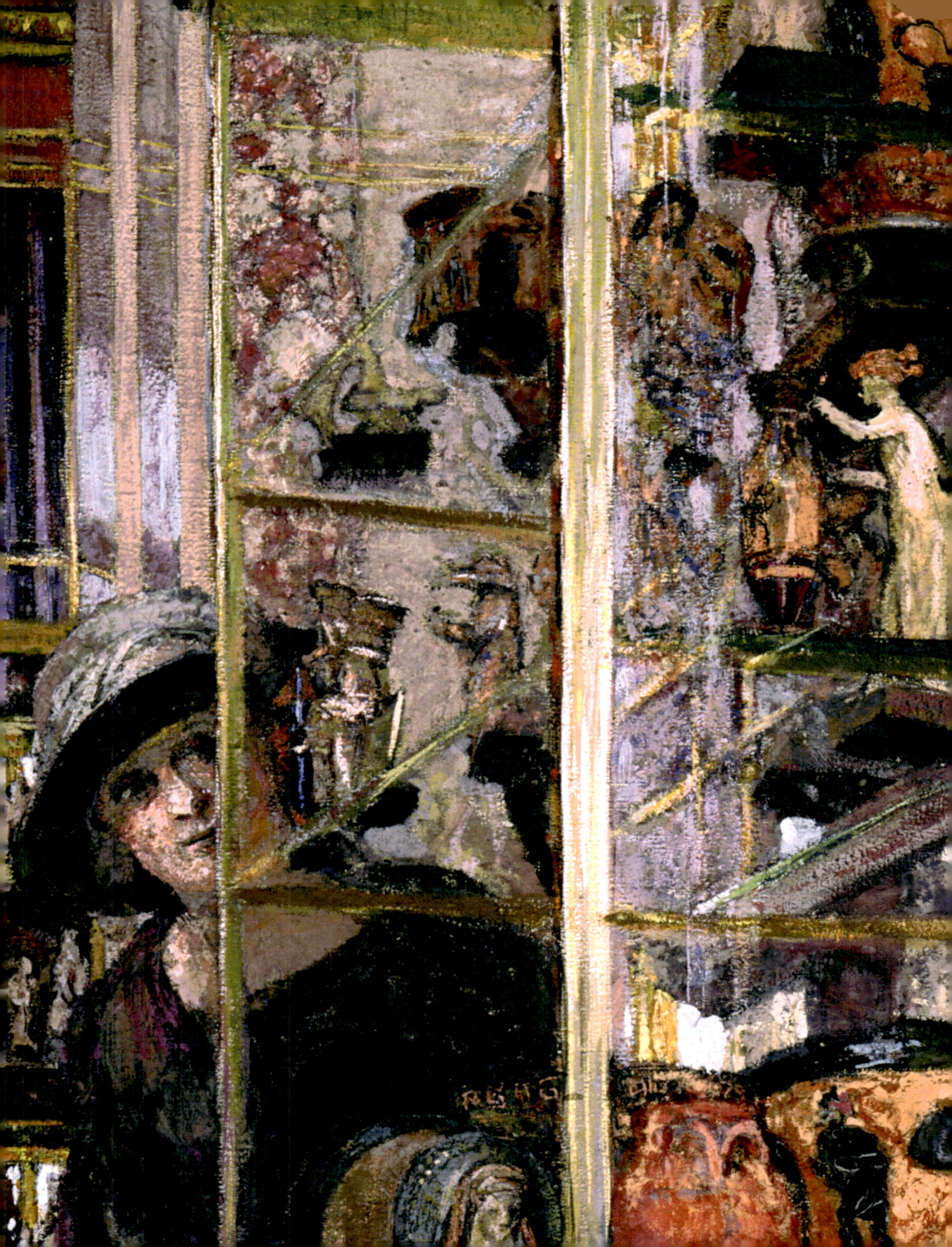

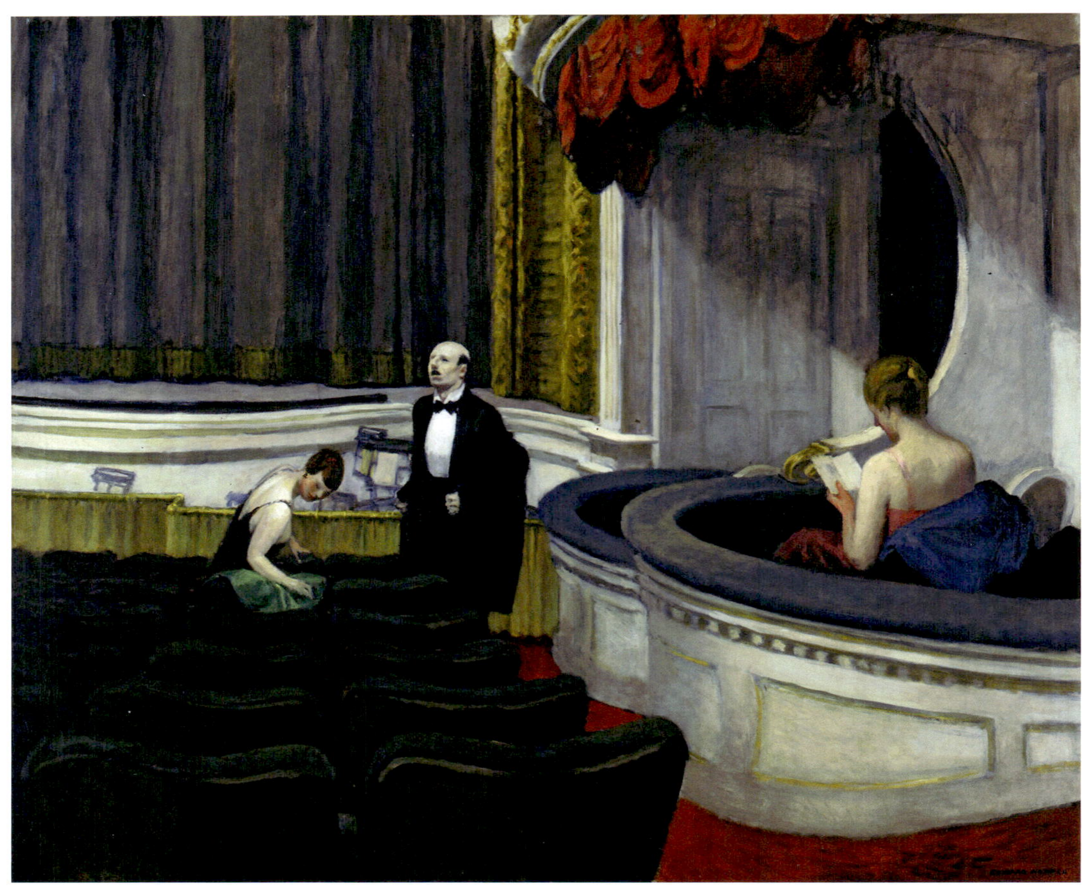

EDWARD HOPPER

I

I have rarely felt so lonely in my life
As I do here in the empty theatre with my wife.
O why did I marry into the Tribe of Early-Comers?
Where is Everybody?
So lonely, so helpless – like an ape in the zoo.
Yet only this morning I bought my first automobile!
An A-Model Ford, Tudor Sedan, Royal Maroon!
Why in the name of Henry Ford did I ever get married?
My boss says: "Because you need a cook."
But why on earth did I not hire a cook?

II

'Woman Alone in a Box of her Own' –
That was MY title – my original title.
What an embarrassing and crude predicament!
I reserved a box for myself
On the sunny side of the street
So that I could feel anonymous
In my discreet pink evening dress
As well as alone in the theatre.
What happens? Enter a married item,
Middle-aged, starchy who proceed to sit
On the aisle next to me – why, such is the excess

Baggage of their intrusion I cannot concentrate
On my printed programme. Immediately, the pair of them
Set about disturbing me, unnerving me:
She foostering with her green wrap on the back of her seat,
He pretending to look around the empty theatre
But, of course in reality stealing glances at me,
Baldy, moustachioed lecher.
What faithless beasts men are!
How glad I am to be a single woman
(And – I own my own beauty salon.)
Although I do take lovers from time to time
I live alone in a brownstone in Brooklyn.
I pity this married woman, shackled to such a cad,
So obviously full of himself, full of his own isolation,
A rain-barrel of self-pity and predatory lust.
Oh I cannot wait for the lights to go down;
For the theatre to go dark,
For Salome to whirl out from the wings in ecstasy.
O my Heart! O my Oscar Wilde!
Toujours la femme éternelle.

When in 1925 on a quiet evening in May in Paris, France
Mr and Mrs Adam and Eve were strolling along the Champs-Élysées
In their habitual garb – i.e. *nada, rien,* nothing, *keine, niente* –
And they chanced to poke their heads into the Théâtre des Champs-Élysées
They were so outraged by what they saw
They wanted to see it all, more and more:
An African-American female dancer on her elegant tippy-toes
Gyrating, kicking, jiving, swinging with nothing on –
Nothing on! –
Except for a string of yellow bananas around her wasp waist
Mrs Eve solemnly whispered to her pompous little husband Adam:
We must tell HIMSELF about this!

No sooner uttered than another bare-bottomed black woman
Came creeping across the stage again with nothing on
Except for a few leaves of palm sprouting from her behind
And tracked by the wildest black dame in Paris
Laughing her crazy head off, baring her teeth,
Under a plumed, cerise turban,
In a bullfinch-pink short dress – *Olé! Olé! Olé!* –
Saucy stockings, crimson gamp in hand.

But what indubitably took the biscuit – hissed old Mrs Eve –
Was the eruption onstage of a lone couple

Performing the Charleston – *Le Charleston, Mon Dieu!* –
Not any lone couple
But the black Prince of New Orleans in clerical black Tuxedo
Dancing cheek to cheek with a white Flapper –
Jiving orgasmically – no knickers, no nothing –
Wearing nothing except a skimpy, short, emerald green petticoat
Showcasing her pink thighs to the audience –
Both cheeks – and lifting up her petticoat
To expose these two cheeks for our edification.

Maurice Chevalier, tuxedo and bow-tie
With trademark sea-blue boater and cane
Came on skipping his blue, blue waltz;
Not only did he not atone
But added insult to injury with his insolent insouciance
And all this malarkey advertised as 'the Charleston'
Backed up by the eleven-piece jazz band of Josephine Baker –
'La Baker' – as she was proclaimed from the altar of Nôtre Dame –
With a scenic backdrop of Paris with New York City skyline,
Seductive Negro Cats, mouths with Abundant Red Lips,
A grand piano to out-strip any grand piano,
The Pianist going all out bonkers, hell for leather,
Tuba, Drum, Trumpet with Plunger, and the Holy Saxophone
Off-camera behind the iconostasis of the Goddess of Sex.

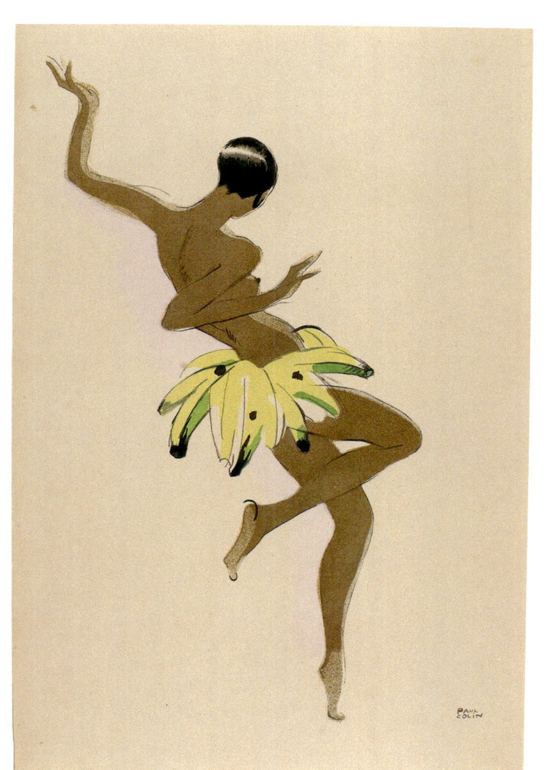 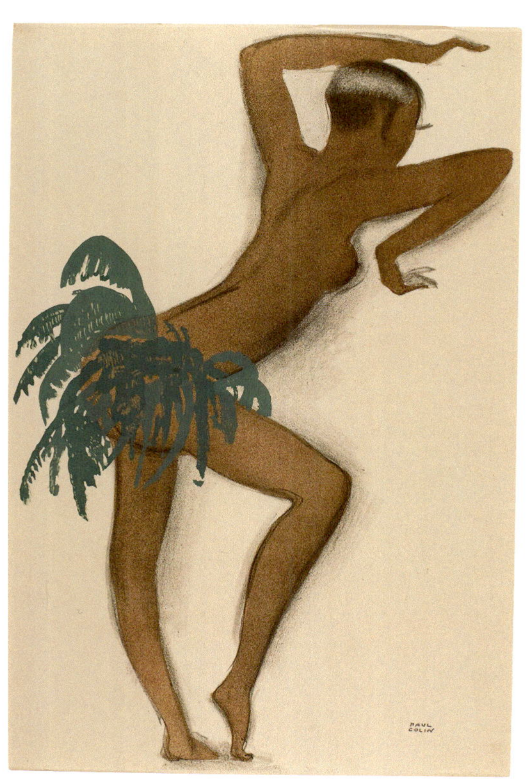

PAUL COLIN

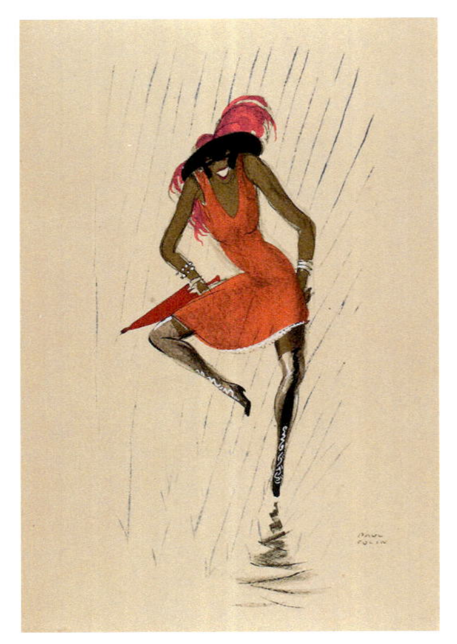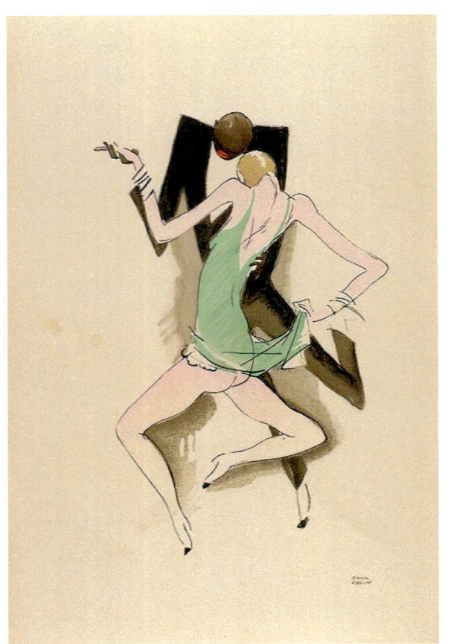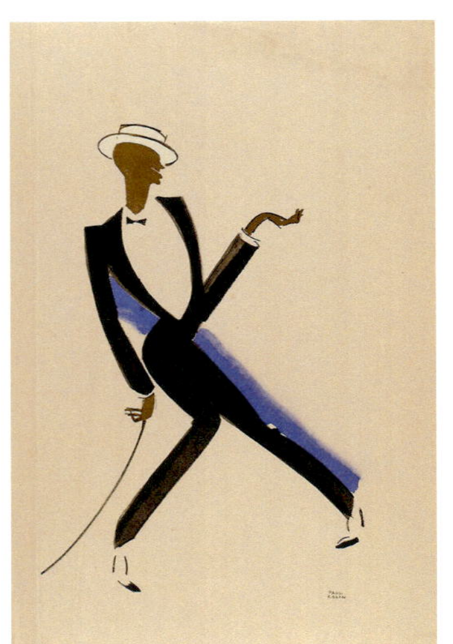

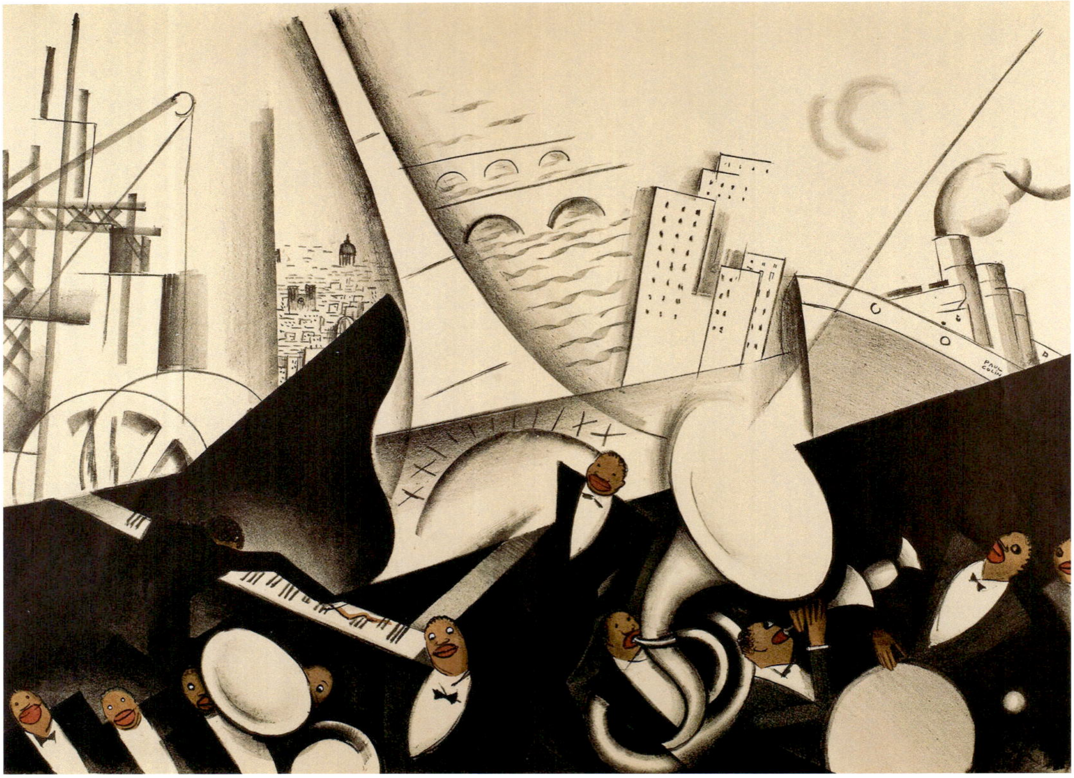

PAUL COLIN

Back outside in the fresh air of the Champs-Élysées
Mr Adam tweeted Mrs Eve:
"Hey! But you have to admit
They are better than we were in the Garden of Eden!
They are the last word in the mysticism of sexuality.
Jazz me, Eve, jazz me – let us soar again!"

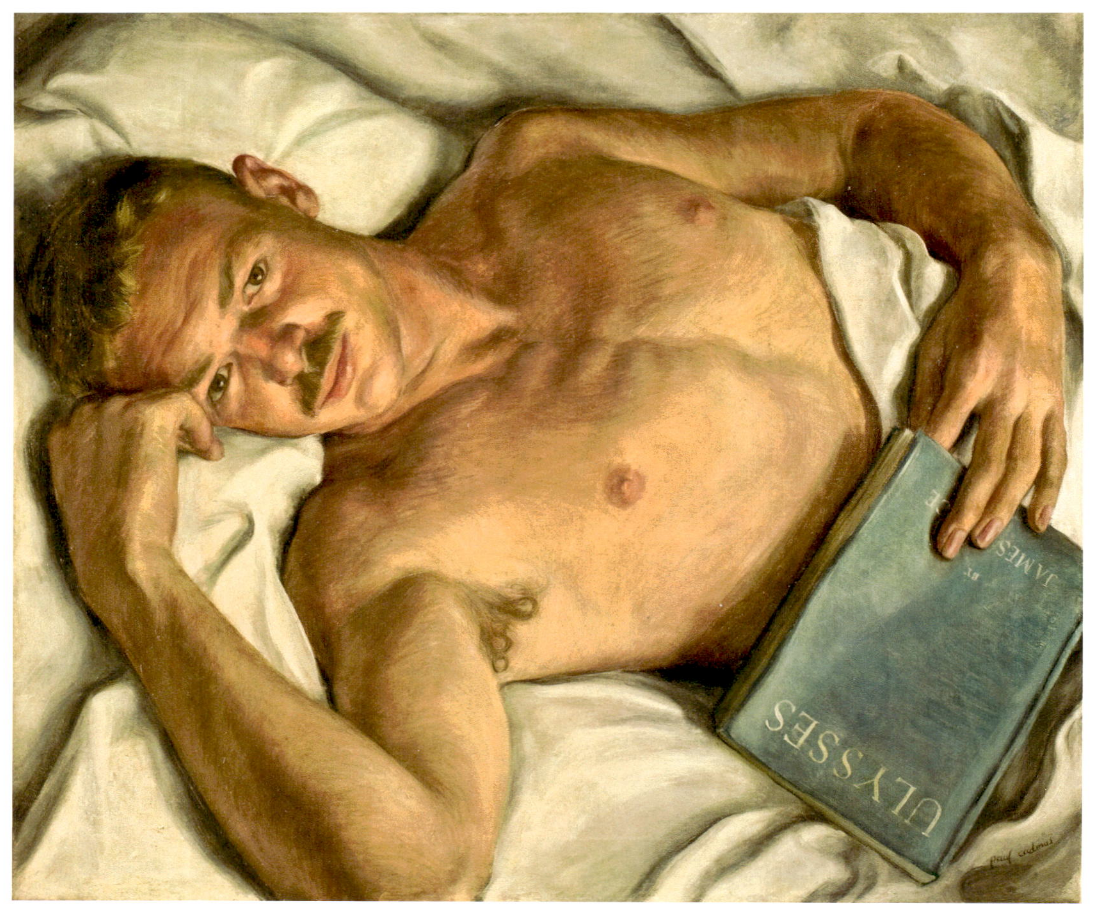

PAUL CADMUS

Paul, dear Paul, dear vast-hearted tender Paul
You knew, didn't you, that when you asked me
To pose for you between the sheets of our bed
With a copy of *Ulysses* – that pine-green edition
Of the Bible with gold lettering – you knew that what James Joyce's
Whopping great fabulous novel is all about is 'HOMECOMING'?

That's what you knew, isn't it, that's what
Lay behind your initiating your portrait of me,
Your strong, your stubborn, your own little Jerry French?
The homecoming of the beloved to his lover;
The homecoming of the boy to his mother and father.
"O such nipples, such armpits, such biceps,
Such fingers, such eyebrows, such elbows, such ribs . . ." you mumble
But all along it's really Joyce and his flaming *Ulysses*.

O Paul, dear Paul, dear vast-hearted, tender Paul
Your Jerry is plucky but sick with waiting for you;
Lying here between the sheets yearning for you.
Paul, PLEASE come home
To your sweetheart, your true love, please, please, please, PLEASE.

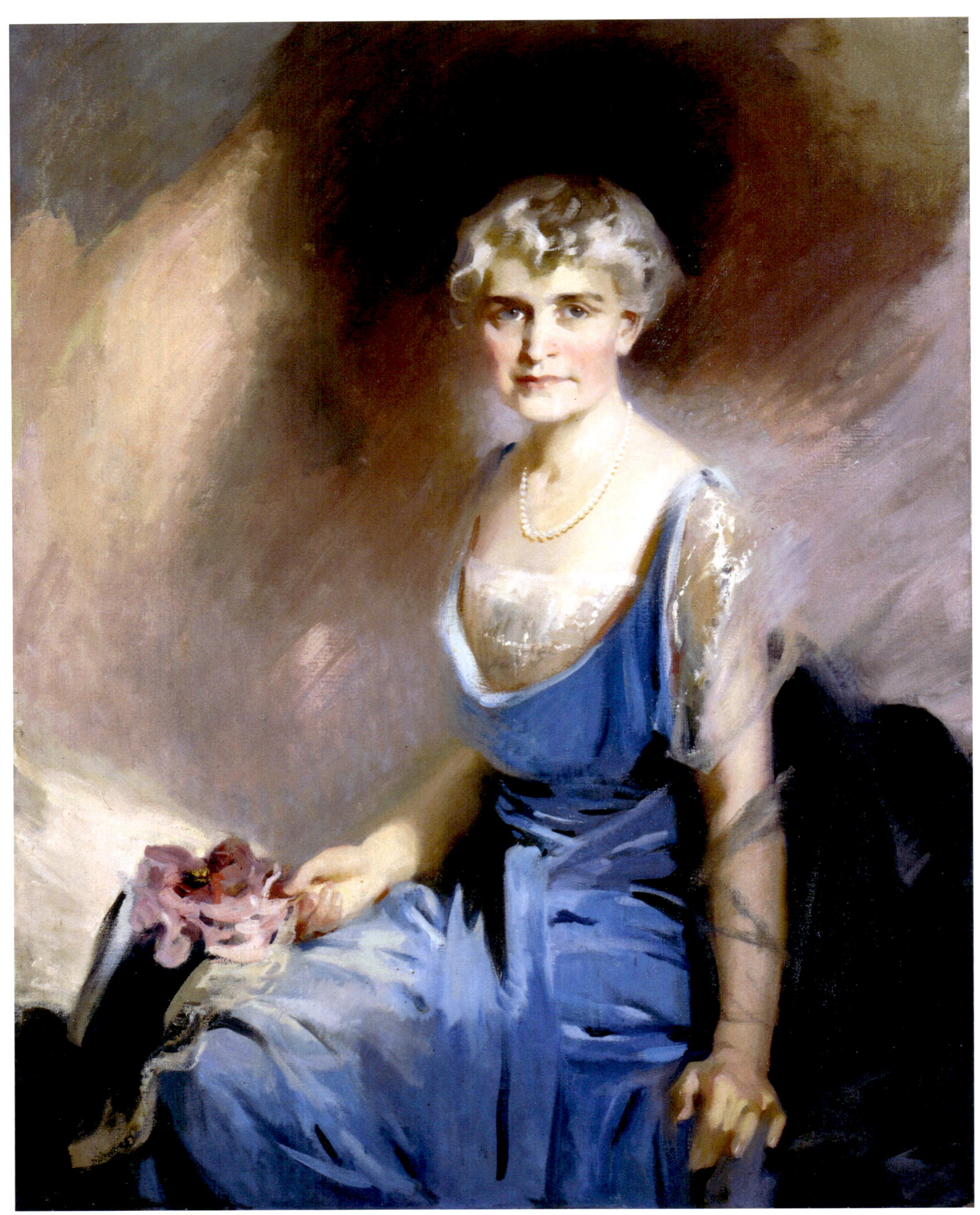

JEAN MACLANE

FLORENCE SCOTT LIBBEY

ABOUT 1933

I

To be bright as well as beautiful – a girlish fancy –
But so in spite of everything it came to pass.
I sit to my portrait by Mrs Jean MacLane late in life
Simply attired – plainly, gracefully, although I say it myself.
I do not require the layers of over-fed self-important hens in their fifties
Who cannot see their own feet over their own belly-buttons –
Yards of scarves, collars, frills, ruffs, tucks, capes –
I do not require to be a walking jewellery shop-window display
All ear-rings, brooches, bracelets – I have no need.
Why should I wear any accessory except for my wedding-ring
(My large husband, poor dear, died eight years ago)
And a single – a single – strand of pearls.
In late middle age I lead a full, happy, above all exciting life
Of Music and Ballet and Opera in my Peristyle Theater
And – as you may know – 'twinkle, twinkle little star' –
A few artworks scattered about our great Toledo Museum of Art.
However I do confess to a tincture, a smidgeon, of vanity!
If you are visiting my portrait you will always find
A handsome young middle-aged man sitting in front of me
(I stipulated the Museum provided an arm-chair.)

II

I enjoy and rejoice in the simple elegance of my beauty.
Well, say, not exceedingly beautiful but simply good-looking!
My jaw means I am good-looking but not 100% beautiful.
I have kept my own teeth – I mean to say
My lips are still filled with my own teeth.
My red cheeks are my own – merely a thin veneer of rouge.
My lipstick is subdued – subdued strawberry.
I am confident in my status
But I have no need to rub it in.
I am sensitive to other people's needs and desires.
I have allowed myself to go elegantly grey. No dye.
(Of course, once upon a time I was young Mrs Scott Libbey
With dark, curly hair. Nowadays – just natural, curly, grey hair.)
And – as for my concessions to haute couture – there are none!
A blue velvet dress, gauze bodice, chiffon sleeve,
White hat in hand with a broad blue band with a pink peony.
Do I lighten your black Ohio winter sky? Tell the truth! I do!

DANCER RESTING

1940

Matisse – O my Matisse – my very own Matisse!

I had only to look him in the eye and –

My inner wolf howling at the moon –

His nose was inside my blouse before you could say 'Delectorskaya'.

O my poor Matisse, my poor, poor Matisse!

What he would not do for me!

'Your BODY LANGUAGE' he used cry 'your BODY LANGUAGE'

And resting his *tête* between my knees –

His poor, brilliant, competitive, tormented brain-box –

I'd whisper: *Mais oui, mon pauvre, mais oui!*

Je sais, je sais, je sais!

How devout you are! The most devotional male

In Villefranche-sur-Mer –

A *vrai* Provençal pilgrim kneeling at the feet of your Russian

       Competition –

Desiring one thing, and desiring one thing only

And knowing I will give it to him in Onion Domes

Provided that first he washes my feet

Being the one true dog of a man that he is,

Being the one true Orthodox dog in the Alps Maritimes;

Secondly, that he vows with all his soul

To wash and iron all my blouses, sashes and knickers and all my lingerie;

Thirdly that along with all bed sheets and pillow cases

He hangs it all out to dry on the Quays of Vieux Nice;

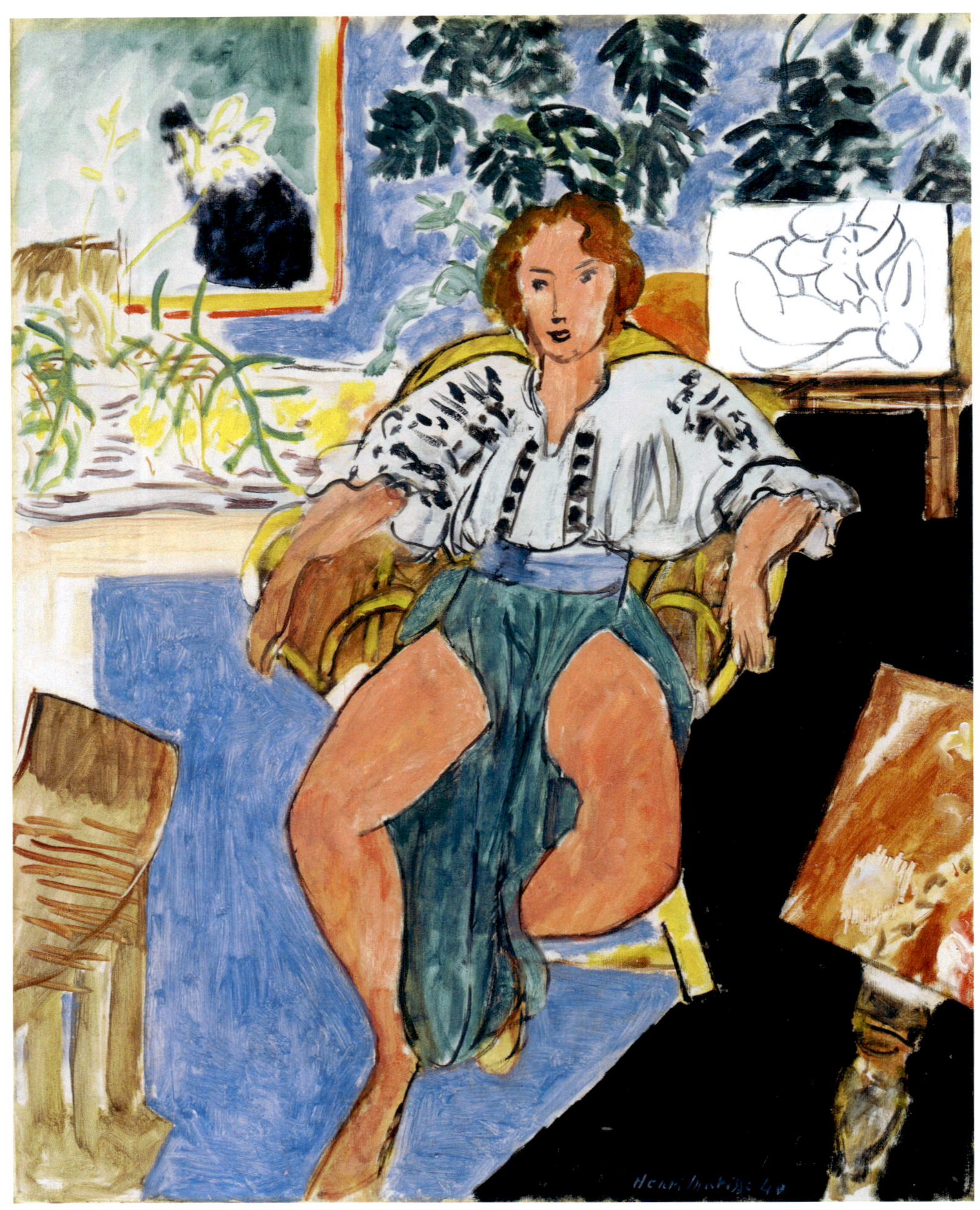

HENRI MATISSE

Fourthly and, *naturellement*, most crucially of all
That he pulls all the necessary strings
To have me appointed Director of the *Musée du Louvre*:
This being the aptest moment in contemporary history,
Year Two of World War II,
Being the Prima Donna Russian Dancer that I am *je crois*
I have no interest in anybody but *moi*.
O my poor Matisse, my poor, poor Matisse,
There now, come now, *maintenant, ici*
On the floor, under the furniture, *ma chérie*.
Afterwards if you're an exceptionally good boy . . .
But only if you're a very, very, very exceptionally good boy . . .
We might – we just might – might . . .
Ride up in my jeep to the peaks of our mountains
And have a . . . well, a . . . a summit *conférence*
Before yet another liturgical season of contemplation!

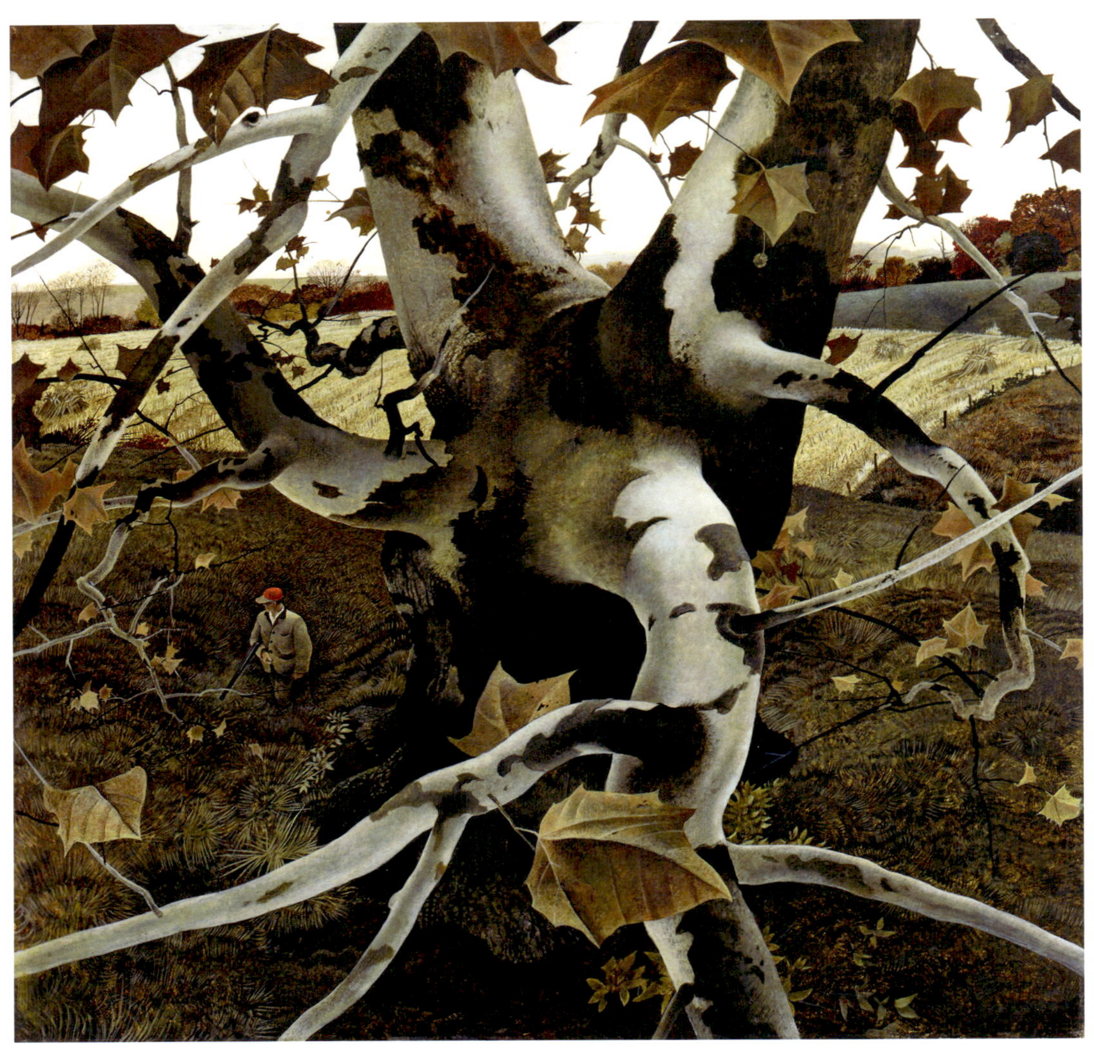

ANDREW NEWELL WYETH

to Jeff Boyer

Despite the pre-eminent, golden-cheeked, buttoned-up
Professor Horace Litotes B. O'Brown of Columbia
Croaking that "Andrew Wyeth lacks sociological data"
When I see a lone Friesian bull high in the bare treetops of October
I know that it is the artist who is telling us the truth.
Next year – the war having gored the world – my young widow
Will give birth to a solitary, autistic son
And the 1950s! Buddy Holly, rave on!

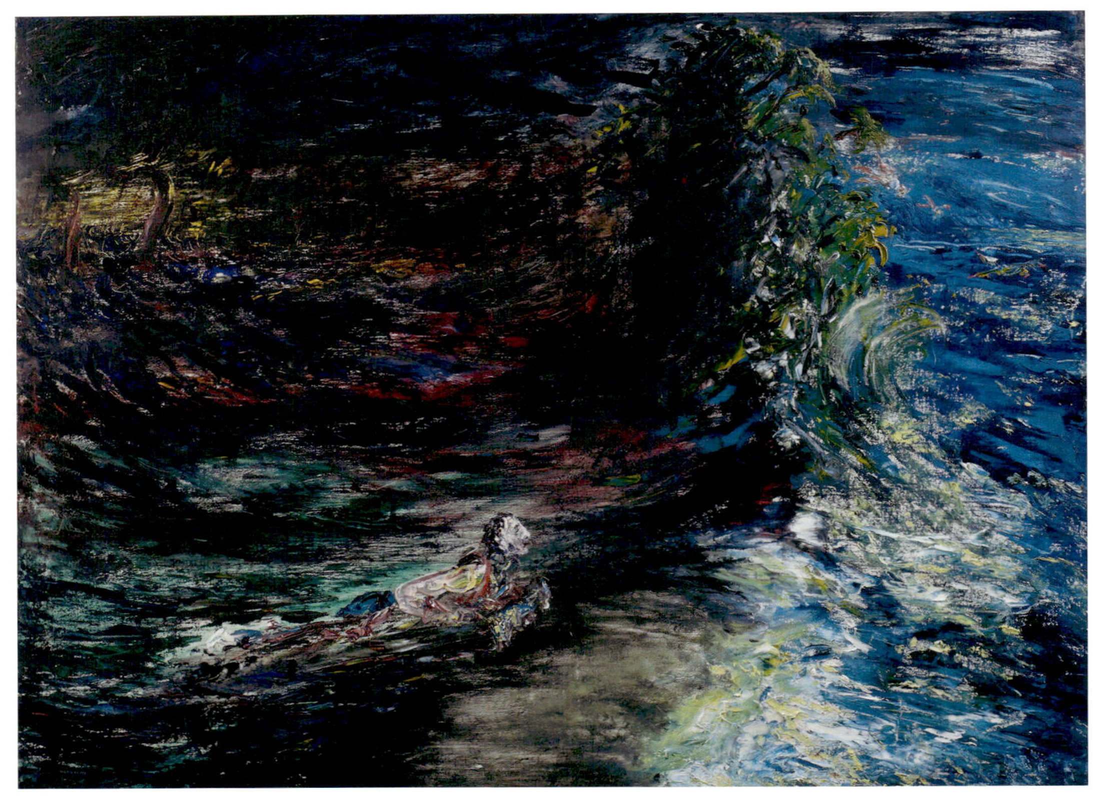

JACK B. YEATS

Going for a swim every day of my life – loping out across the city –
Off the steps at the Half-Moon half-way down along the mole
In Dublin Bay known as the Great South Wall,
By my early 70s I was fearless – you could say –
Although I myself would never make such a fatuous claim –
And so on an October morning in 1944 on a high tide –
(1944 – the Year that Changed the World)
The Sixteenth of October, 1944, it was –
Birthday of Oscar Wilde and also, Ye Gods, Michael Collins –
I commenced to drown and that was almost all right with me –
All my life I'd pondered actually what it would be like to drown –
Fare thee well to my long life as a serious clown –
Head-up, shoulders straight, freezing arms limply flailing, asphyxiating –
Glimpsing a two-storey cottage on the Hill of the Head of Howth:
When I realised I was on the last-gasp brink
A colossal wave – sheer out of Hokusai –
With a back-up second roller out of Hiroshige –
All the way from Japan – flabbergasted Dublin Bay
And I began to rise up again with these two dumpers –
I was being given Another Chance!
I could hear my dear wife Cottie applauding from her bed!
(Sir, but did I adore my wife!)
You could maintain – although of course I myself would not maintain –
That I was born again!

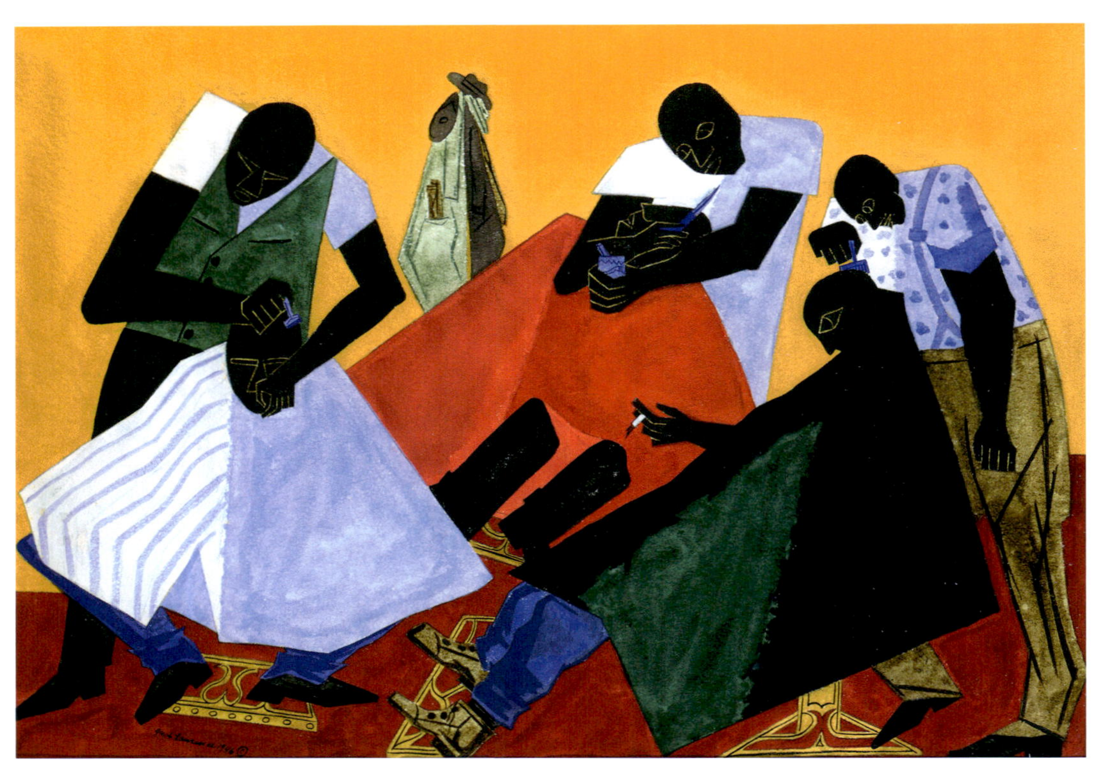

JACOB LAWRENCE

Go down to the Barber Shop, man, a-singing and a-weeping;
Come back up from the Barber Shop, man, a new-born-lamb;
A weaned boy-child on thy mother's breast,
Even so is your soul.

Going down to the Barber Shop, man, I am going down to my church
To be vested, robed, instructed in how to sit still in purdah;
To get sheared and to set my soul in silence, peace, chitter-chatter.
The great big barber man is my second mother –
O man but he has the Biggest Bosoms in Christendom.
He croons Basso Profundo to me: Bow down, man,
And let me see your neck – I SAYS 'all of your neck'.
Let my clippers and my brushes and my shears and my razors
Anoint and purify the nape of your neck.
I will rake up thy curls from my red-as-gold dust floor
For you to bring home to thy mothers, thy grandmothers, thy sisters.
The Barber Shop is where the Boy becomes the Man.

How good and how pleasant it is,
When brothers dwell in the Barber Shop!
It is like precious oil upon the head
Running down upon the beard,
Running down upon Aaron's beard,
Upon the collar of his robes.

It is like the dew of Hermon which falls
On the heights of Zion.
For there the Barber gives his blessing,
Life for ever.

We call the haircut 'the Holy Communion' and we screech with laughter.
The Barber Shop is where men go to meditate, man:
Superior urination, man!
After having hung up our dungarees
And our hats and donned our gowns
The tangerine mirror wall is our sacristy door
Behind which the patriarch Barber intones
Before stepping out and processing around us –
Incensing each of us. Each of us clients is an icon –
An iconic head –
To whom he imparts his blessing and only then
When I am having my first smoke –
My first ciggy of the day, my first roll-up,
(And, man, how I dig smoking left-handed my first smoke) –
He shears our locks, our curls, our tresses and our beards.
While he snips and shaves and cuts we meditate.

Meditation is the Ceramic of the Barber Shop, man:
The Sacramental Craft –
Kick-wheel, brush, spirit-level, belt, tongs, sponge, bowl –
The Orthodox Medicine for an African-American Harlem cat.

At the get-go of a cut
The Barber sings the Jazz Vespers;
At the wind-up of a cut
The Barber sings the Compline.
Lord, Praise our Tools, our combs, our razors;
Lord, I give thee thanks for my braces;
Lord, let me make good sounds with my golden pedals.
Lord, I wanna boogie-woogie with my laundress in her white smock.
He leads us out into the street, shakes
Hands with each of us, towels
Each of us down, blesses
Each of us thrice for the last time and smiles
"You're sure gonna die man"
Before breaking into Eddie 'Lockjaw' laughter –
Into Satchmo winkings, blinkings and gleamings:
"The Party's at West 125th and 2nd and
Don't worry about the booze, man, and
Don't worry about your eyebrows, and the broads
Is just fine and – do you know, man? –
Last night summertime began!
The Corn is Orient and Immortal Wheat
Which never should be reaped, nor was ever sown."

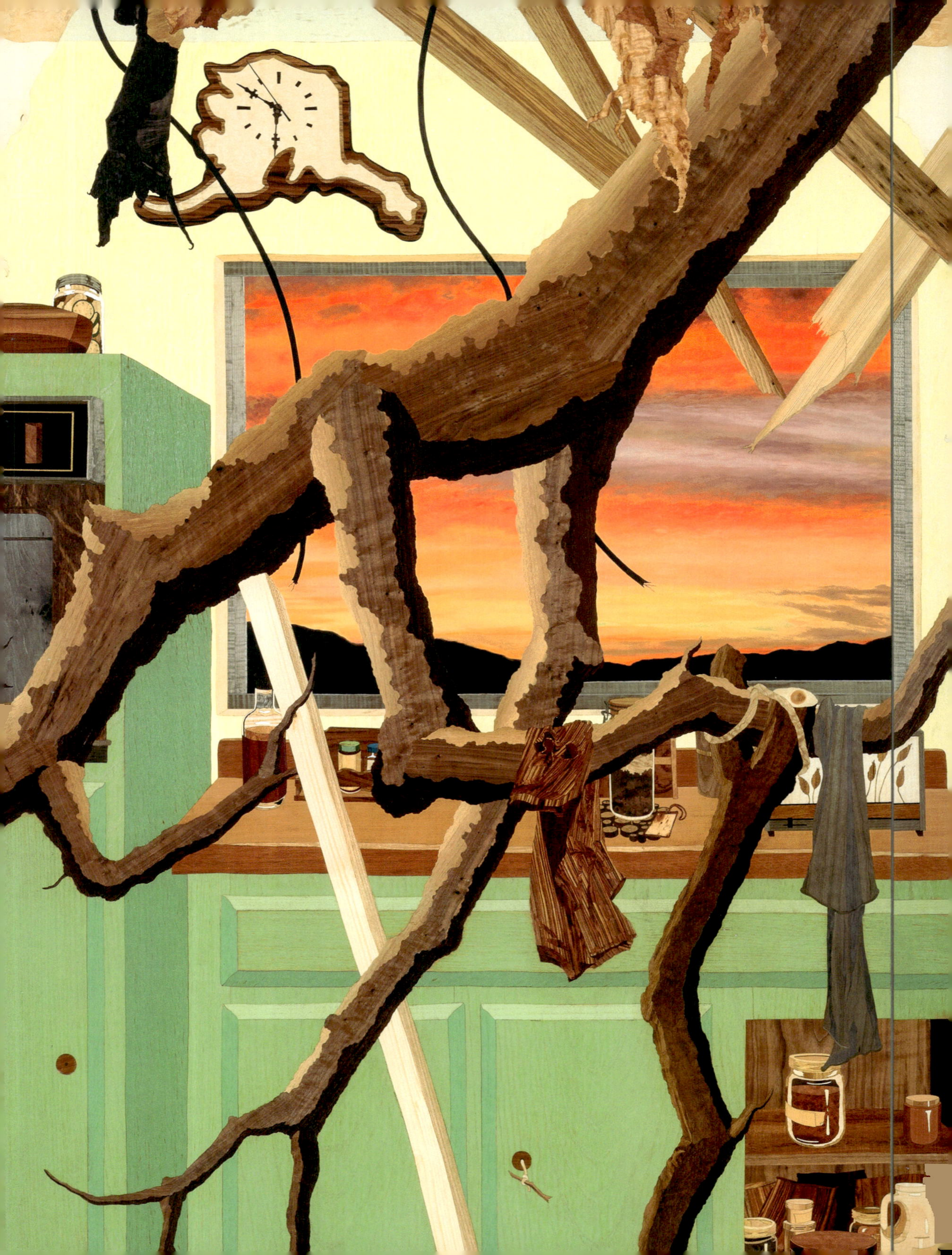

* * *

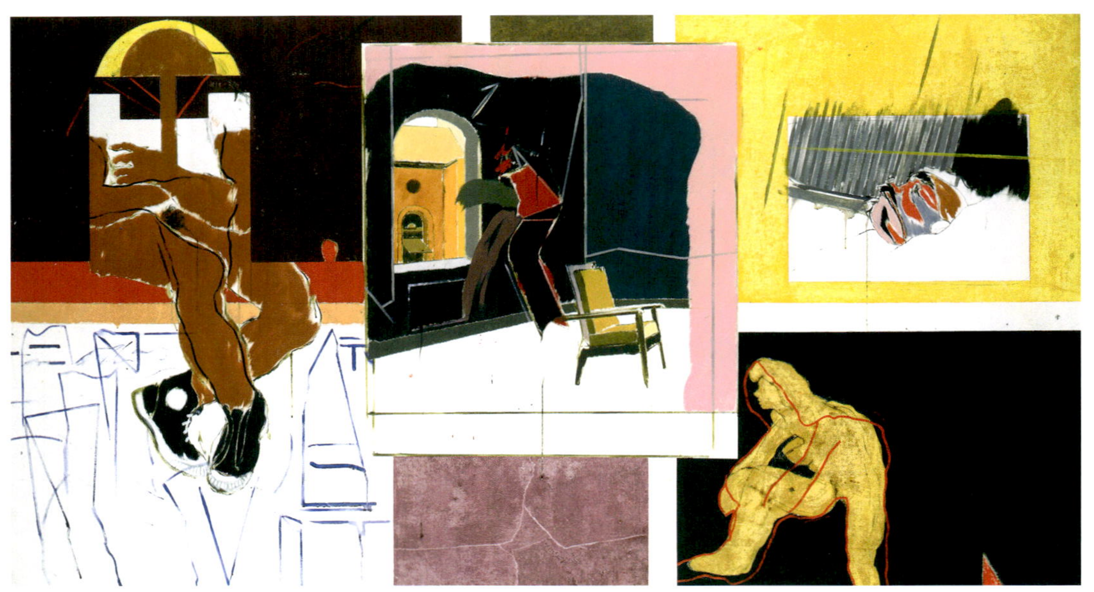

RONALD B. KITAJ

I was closest to my Mom.

Who in the name of God is R. B. Kitaj?
Who in the name of Yahweh (he was Jewish)?
How the hell do you say – do you pronounce his name?
'Kittage'? To rhyme with 'Cottage'?
Are we supposed to know?
What an ugly, ignorant, pile-up of an artwork!
Too much upward-mobility and mystique in art museums.
Too much hob-nobbing with mumbo-jumbo.
Too much zooming around galleries
Being nice and genteel and ignorant and pretentious.

Pronunciation: KITAJ: to rhyme with 'supply'
With stress on second syllable:
You will 'supply' Kitaj with – O My! – an apology
For your supercilious ignorance.
KITAJ rhymes also with HENRI (Robert)
And in the generation after Henri (Robert)
Kitaj is Ohio's first great post-modern painter.

Back in Toledo, Ohio in the 1970s, his widowed mom, Mrs Jeanne Kitaj –
Always dressed to kill – hair cut short and bobbed –
An elegant, petite, leading member of the Toledo Art Appreciation Society –
Oh how she loved to boast, in that sweet, meek, coy way of mothers, about
"O Ronnie, my only son in London, how proud I am of him!"

Kitaj was Ohio's first great 20th-century Nobody
Which is why after childhood and boyhood in Chagrin Falls
Following as closely as he could in the footsteps of Hart Crane –
That zany, gay poet also from Chagrin Falls –
At 17 Kitaj skedaddled after Hart Crane to New York City,
Joined-up for the duration of World War II,
Fell in love, discovered Paris
And finally London where for thirty-six years
He was the leading painter on the scene
Until a bunch of American-hating Jew-baiting London know-alls
In a rarefied orgy murdered Kitaj's young wife Sandra Fisher,
Herself also a painter,
And Kitaj took the next plane out of Gatwick
And pitched his last studio, made his final home
In Los Angeles. Aged 75, one afternoon
He committed suicide – lay down on his bed
And put a plastic bag over his head (straight out of Shakespeare).

And so now here this October afternoon in Ohio in the Toledo Museum of Art
We find ourselves shifting from foot to foot
In front of Kitaj's pictorial autobiography
Foretold prophetically in 1961 in London.
Like all true artists Kitaj wanted Fame
But – again like all artists who are true to their game –

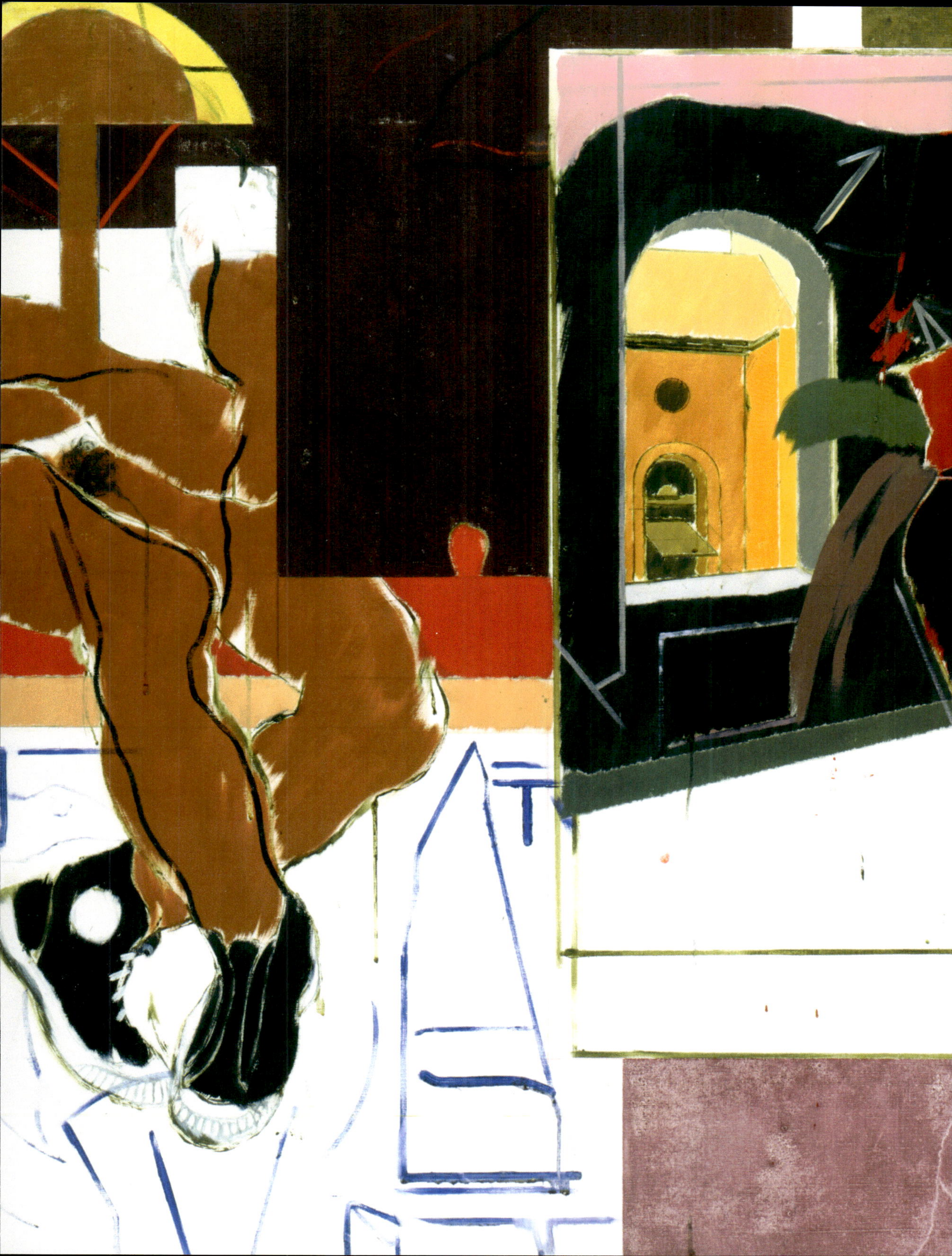

Shakespeare again, for example,
Kitaj wanted Oblivion.
And so after an omniscient, totally self-doubting life
In Ohio, Paris, London, L.A.
He stuffed his poor sore head into a plastic bag
And breathed his last.
Dreaming of womankind –
Of his almighty, petite mother and of his great-hearted painter wife.
Foretold it all pictorially 41 years earlier
In these five panels that you see before you.
Be silent now before you yourself in high-top sneakers –
A pair of CONVERSE GRIPPERS –
Jump out the window into the oven.
Beloved Nobody, better to jump than to creep.

I was closest to my Mom.

The most openly well-kept secret in the TMA
Is its moon landing painted-steel vehicle of 1962 –
The most ostentatiously, audaciously well-kept
Secret in all of the U.S.A:
2 Circle IV.

This is the ex-Studebaker car factory assembly worker
David Smith's aeronautic automobile
Named by him *2 Circle IV*
In memory of his mother and father
Which in 1962 having skirted the moon with it
He brought it back safely to land in Ohio
– Home of the Spaceman and the Aviator –
And landing it on the waters of Lake Erie
He parked it in the Toledo Museum of Art
Where now it gleams in the trees alongside Monroe Street.
'A side show at a country fair in Ohio' he called it.
David 'Melville' Smith – the Hart Crane of American Sculpture –
Painted-Steel Man!

Thirty years later when another Ohioan,
Ex-Moon Voyager Neil Armstrong from Wapakoneta
(Down Interstate 75 from Toledo in Northwest Ohio)
Visited *2 Circle IV* at the TMA

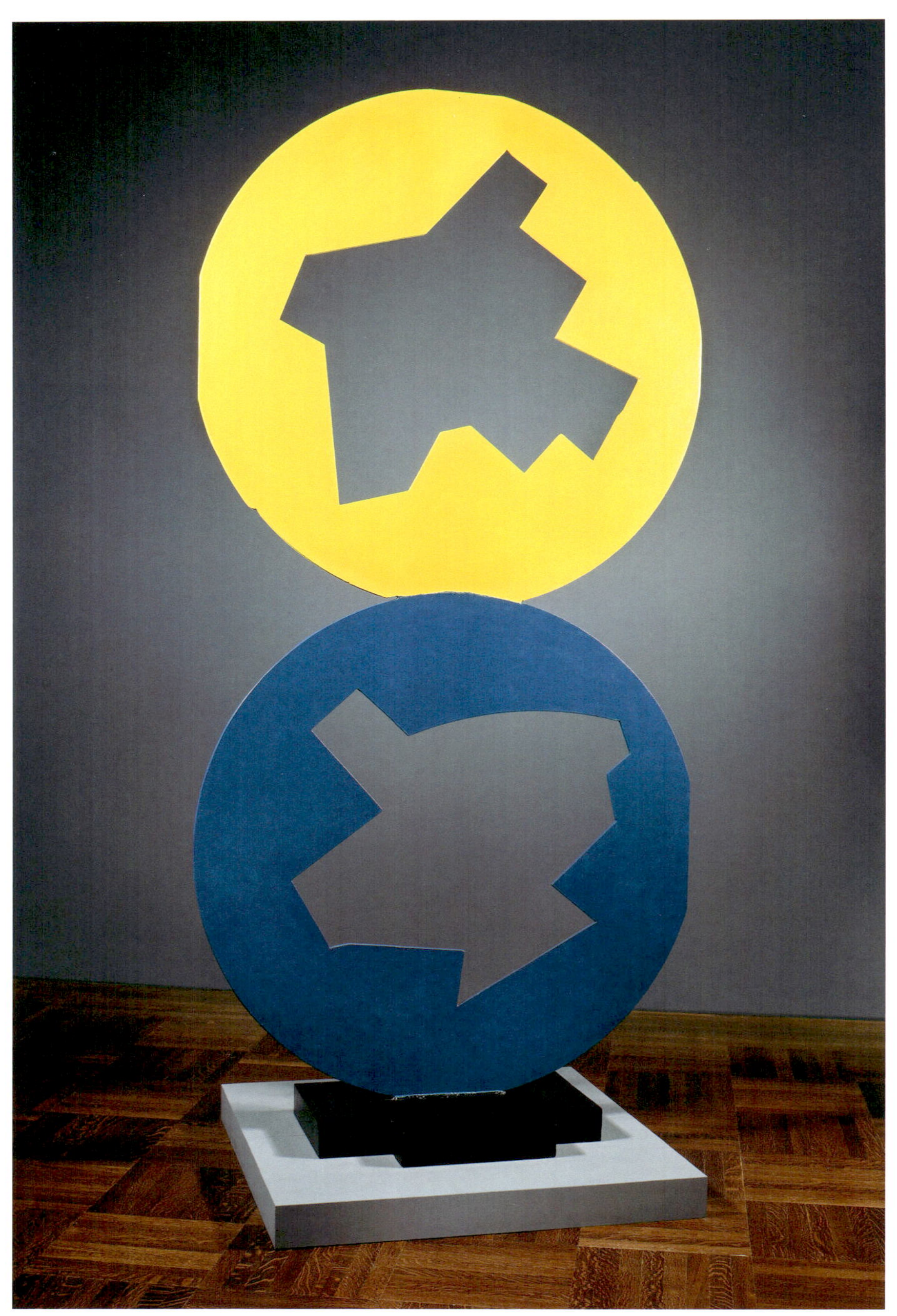

DAVID SMITH

He smiled a wry, wary, silent smile
Sighing: "*2 Circle IV* says it all
About Buzz Aldrin, Michael Collins and me
Much more than our words could ever say:
Let us now praise David Smith skidding off
          The rim of the cosmos
On a country road near Bennington, Vermont:
Welder, riveter, brush painter, sculptor, acetylene torch maestro,
          High flyer, aviator, groundsman, birdman.
In the written words of your closest mate Robert Motherwell:
'Oh David, you were as delicate as Vivaldi and as strong as a Mack truck'."

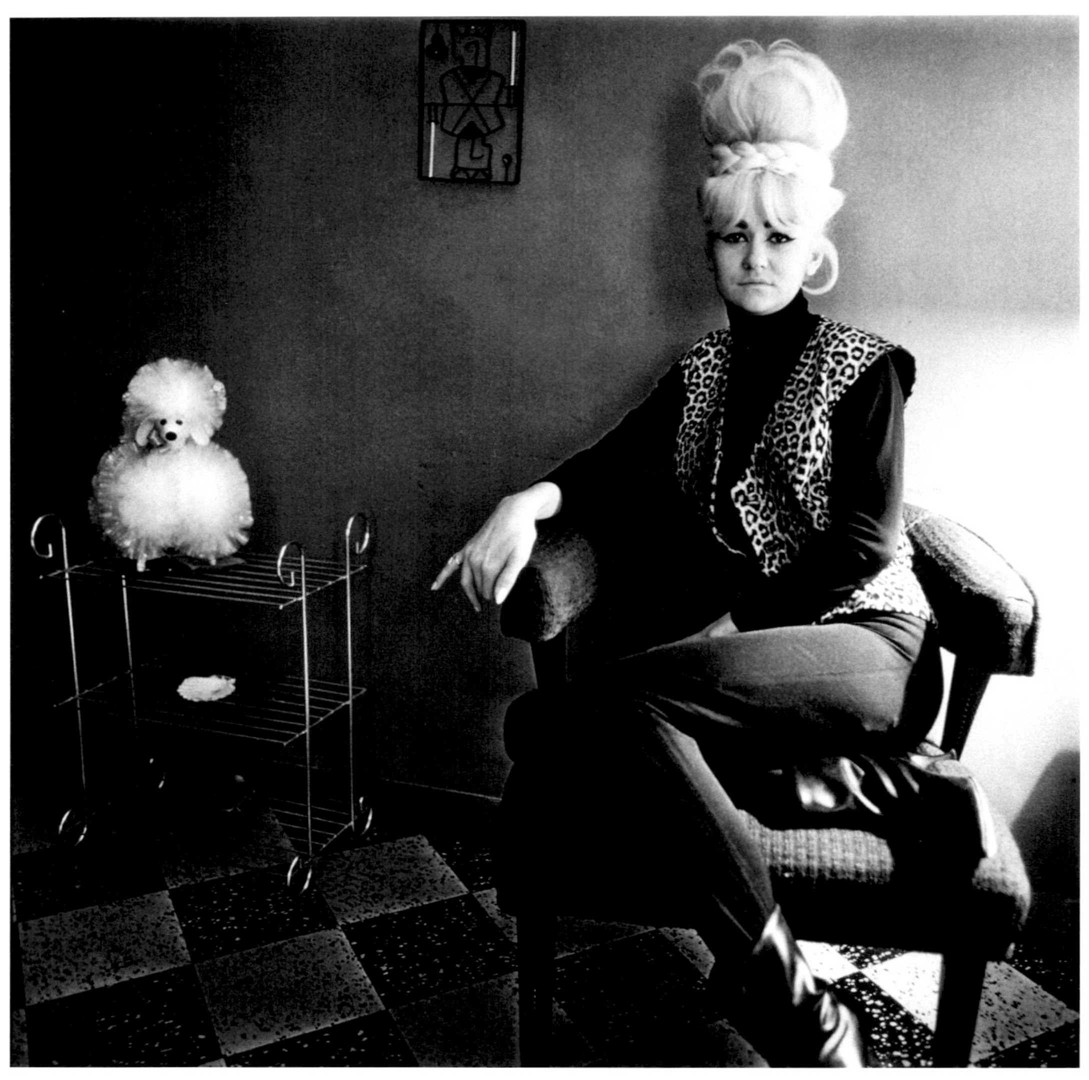

DIANE ARBUS

LADY BARTENDER AT HOME WITH A SOUVENIR DOG, NEW ORLEANS, LA., 1964

Honey I'm not kidding you!
With my charcoal eye-liner I'm not in my first youth –
Lonesome Lady Bartender at Home am I tonight –
A Manicured Poodle on a trolley is all well and good but . . .
What I need, what I demand, what I am going to devour
Are my old man's two German Shepherd Alsatian dogs
And then I'll be smiling-snarling like a tom-cat lording it over you!
My High German Roped-Up Bleached Poodle Hair-Do!
My 50-dollar nylon plait, my turtleneck,
My leopard-skin waistcoat, my leather boots,
My Jack of Hearts in Wrought-Iron – Bilateral Symmetry –
Cute, isn't it? SAY it's cute – 33 times after me!
I'm 33.
Honey I'm not kidding you!
And then I'll be smiling-snarling like a tom-cat lording it over you!

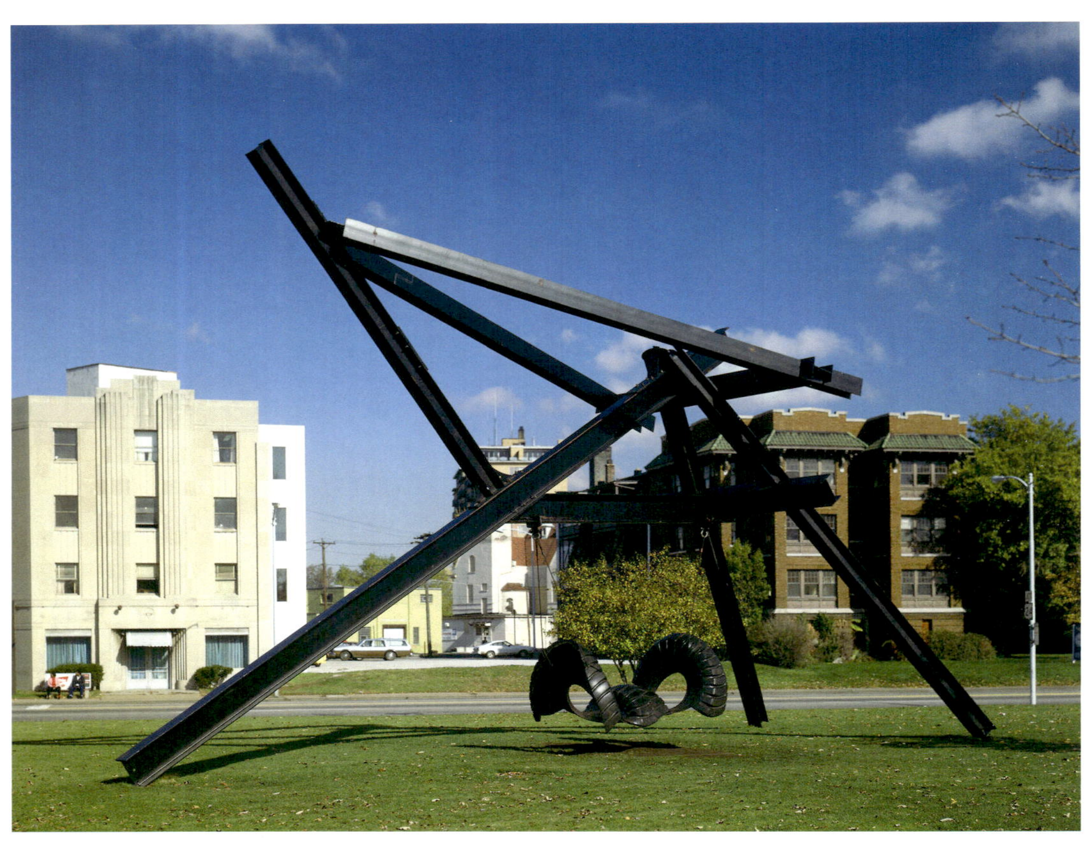

MARK DI SUVERO

Sure, sure, Lord, it ain't easy living on the Block –
No deprived area is easy existin' –
But I says to my man, Moby, when he won't get out of bunk –
Man, take the kid out – down over to the Big Swing.

The kid loves it, man, and so will you –
You dopey great hunk hugging your hangover –
Get out of the scratcher, rope up your pants,
And here's a brand-new white T-shirt I got uniquely for you.

What Big Swing? Come on, Lover-Boy, don't act ass with me,
The Big Swing the Museum Cats constructed on the corner
Of Monroe and Collingwood – the Big Swing
All the mamas and the papas bring their kids to and sing.

They call it 'Blubber' – whale 'Blubber' –
An old tractor-tire – the Great Big Swing.
Fact is, Big Ass, it's the biggest, grandest, slowest swing in Toledo, Ohio.
It's the biggest, greatest, grandest, slowest swing in all of the U.S. of A.

And I don't care if you've got the blues, Man,
I'm gonna whip you down to the Great Swing
Hand in Hand with your four-year old Princess
And you're gonna plant your great big fat ass on it

And between your knees your fabulous daughter
And she's gonna make you howl, Papa, she's gonna make
    you howl,
And you're gonna start howlin' her sweet lullaby
And the Great Lord's gonna rock you in his cradle!

If you're a good boy, Moby, and do as you're told,
Why – I'll be your Blubber tonight!
How about that, Baby?
And – I might even in the middle of the night - let you call me 'Blubber'!

'*Blub, blub, blub, blub, blub, blub, blub Belllllll-ubber!*'

I might even . . . I might even . . . I might even . . .
Didn't know it, Moby, didn't know it, did you. . . .
I might even . . . I might even . . . I might even . . .
Didn't know it, Moby, didn't know it, did you . . . SWING!

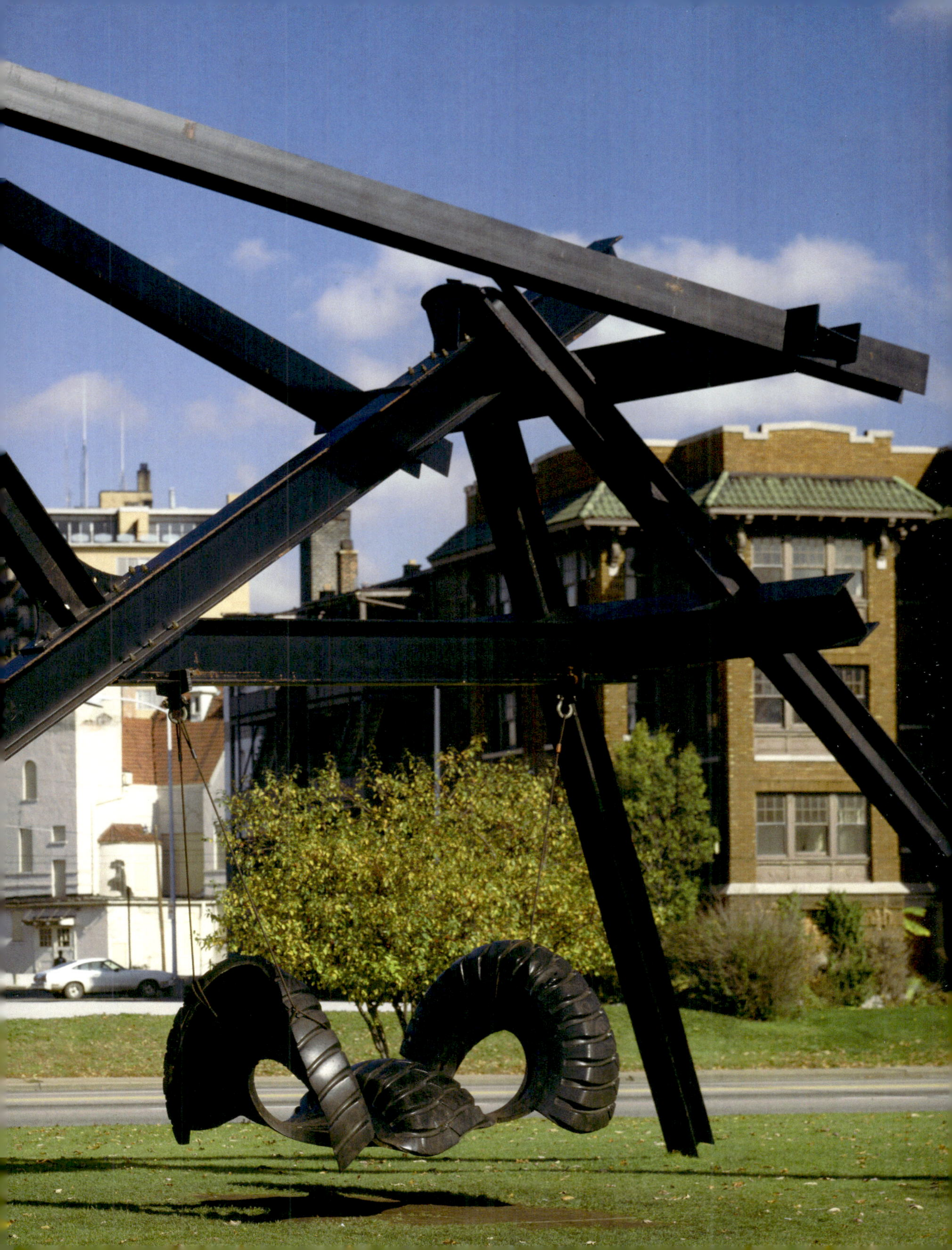

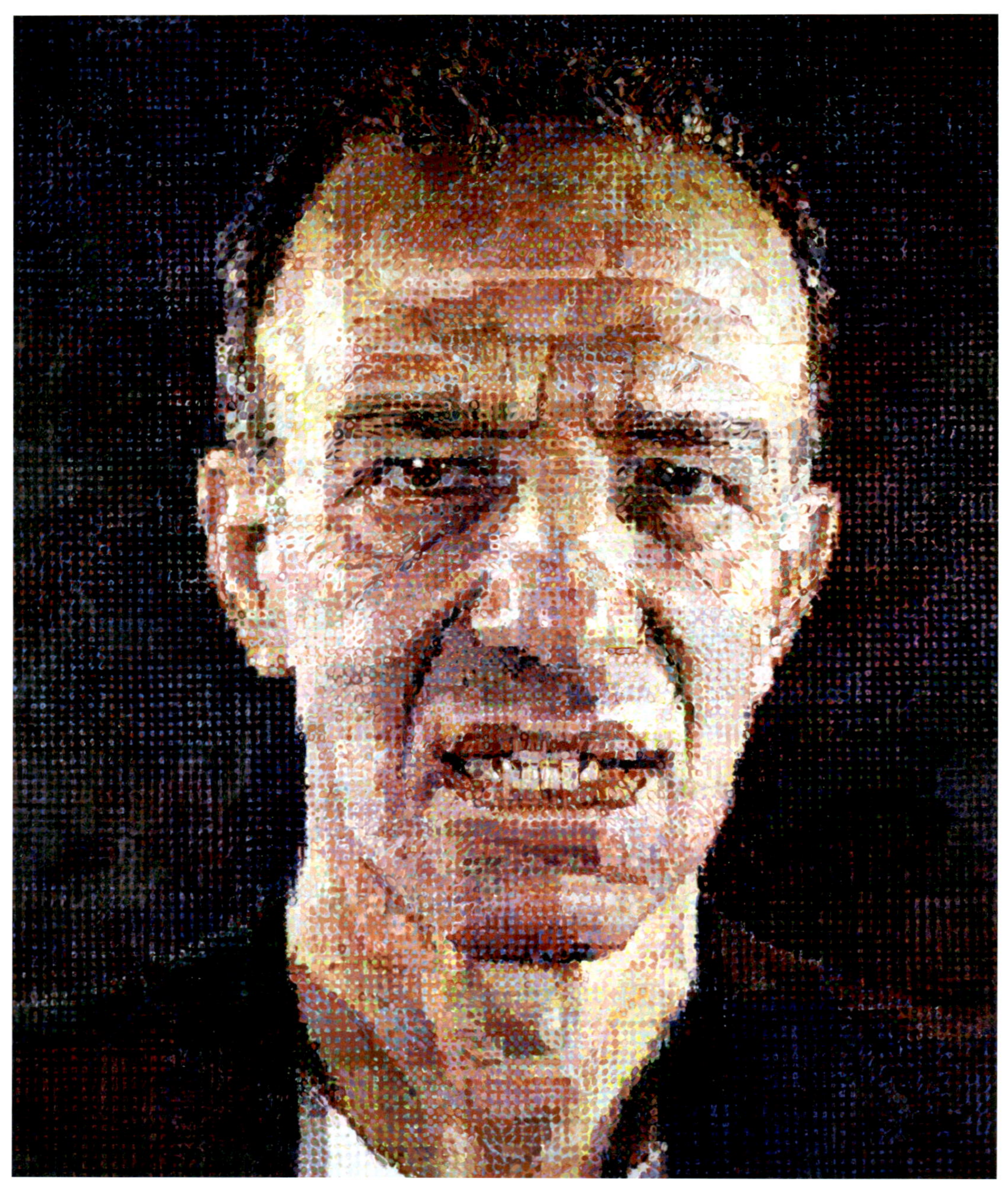

CHUCK CLOSE

Uh-huh . . . Uh-huh . . . Uh-huh . . . Uh-huh . . .
Am I up to doing a Sistine Chapel in Tiffin, Ohio?
I dunno, Chuck . . . I dunno . . . I just dunno . . .
What the Michael . . . to do. . . .

And here she is alone in the vast museum
Dancing a solo flamenco in front of OOKBAR,
A painting from the love-poetry of Sean Scully.
Long years ago she had gone with Sean Scully
To the seaweed baths, each to their cubicle,
And after he had draped his towel over the partition
She listened to him singing *Blood On The Tracks*:
"If you see her, say hello, she might be in Tangier."
Never in her life had she felt so sad, so happy!

           II
For evermore she would wear his colours,
She would be his secret sharer.
Back home in Akron, Ohio
She knitted a replica of his towel
Giving it a name of her own:
'Zipper Fly'.
At the foot of her double bed
She hung a vast reproduction of OOKBAR
Which she entitled voluptuously:
'Tiger Eating Zebra'; 'Crème Brûlée'; 'Sahara Sand',
Murmuring in her sleep in stripes of smiles:
"Something is entering me but I don't know what it is, Mr S."
In feminine energy alone is mortal delight.

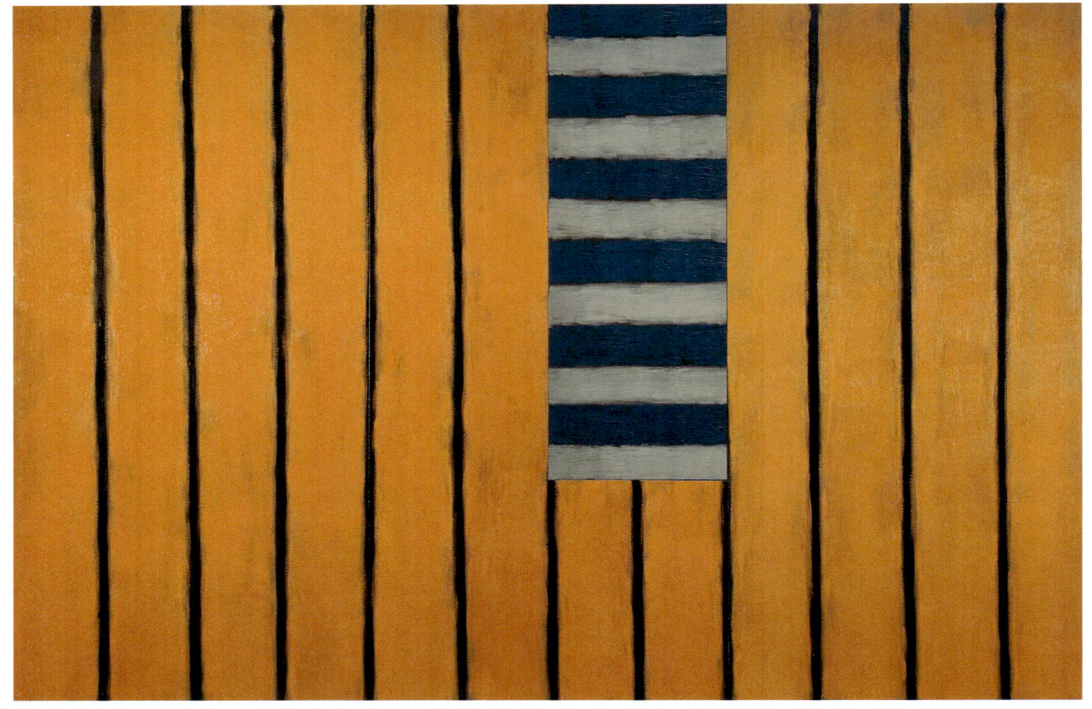

SEAN SCULLY

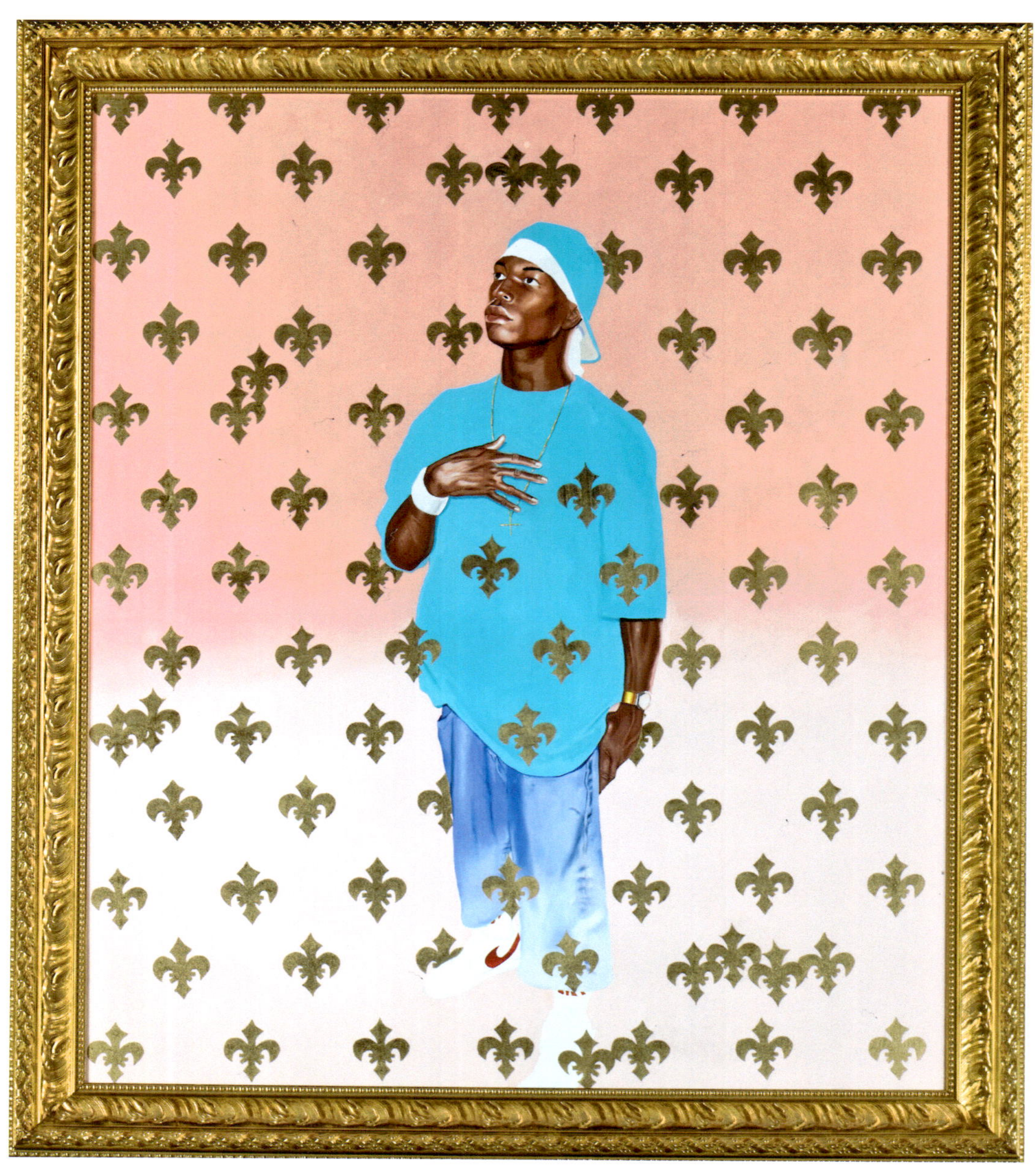

KEHINDE WILEY

"Frankie Paola" he cried out
When I inquired of him his name,
The guy beside me in the window seat
(I was in the aisle seat)
On the Delta commuter flight from Boston to Detroit.
"Pleased to meet you, sir" I said
"I am Veronique Mboya."
"Howdee, Veronique" he said, adding as if adding to my name
"I'm into religion, what are you into?"
"You won't believe it," I replied
"But I'm into religion too –
Well, sort of, I think.
Never quite sure what religion is.
But I was born Presbyterian –
Good Kenya stock –
Know what I mean?"

"Me too – never quite sure what religion is" he drawled
"Although I know I am a Saint –
Like Frankie of Assisi, you know the cat? –
I have a pet fish – a trout – Antonella, by name –
And a pet lamb, Martinello –
Being a Saint I am supposed to know
All about religion but I don't –
Like you know what I mean, Veronique?"

And he smiled this so serious, beginning-of-the-world smile
That his boney, coffee-beans young man's face
Looked not only humanly attractive but divinely attractive –
I mean, zoologically attractive
And I could feel this deep down consanguinity
'Cos I am thirty shades darker than he –
"I'm of good Kenyan stock" –
And he placed his right hand on his breast
Over his turquoise-blue chasuble-type T-shirt
Splaying the five exquisite long slender fingers
Of his right hand across his breast.

"Actually" he added "as you slid into your aisle seat
I had a dream!
I had a dream of myself as a priest – a smiling neighbourhood priest –
Old and sick and weary leaning on a stick
Corner of 23rd Street and Madison
Silently talking to himself: 'Pray thee for the good Kenya maid!'"

He wore his matching turquoise-blue baseball cap
Back-to-front and all across his T-shirt
Wild rose pink melting into ivory,
Fleurs-de-lis
Like Tomahawk airplanes flying up

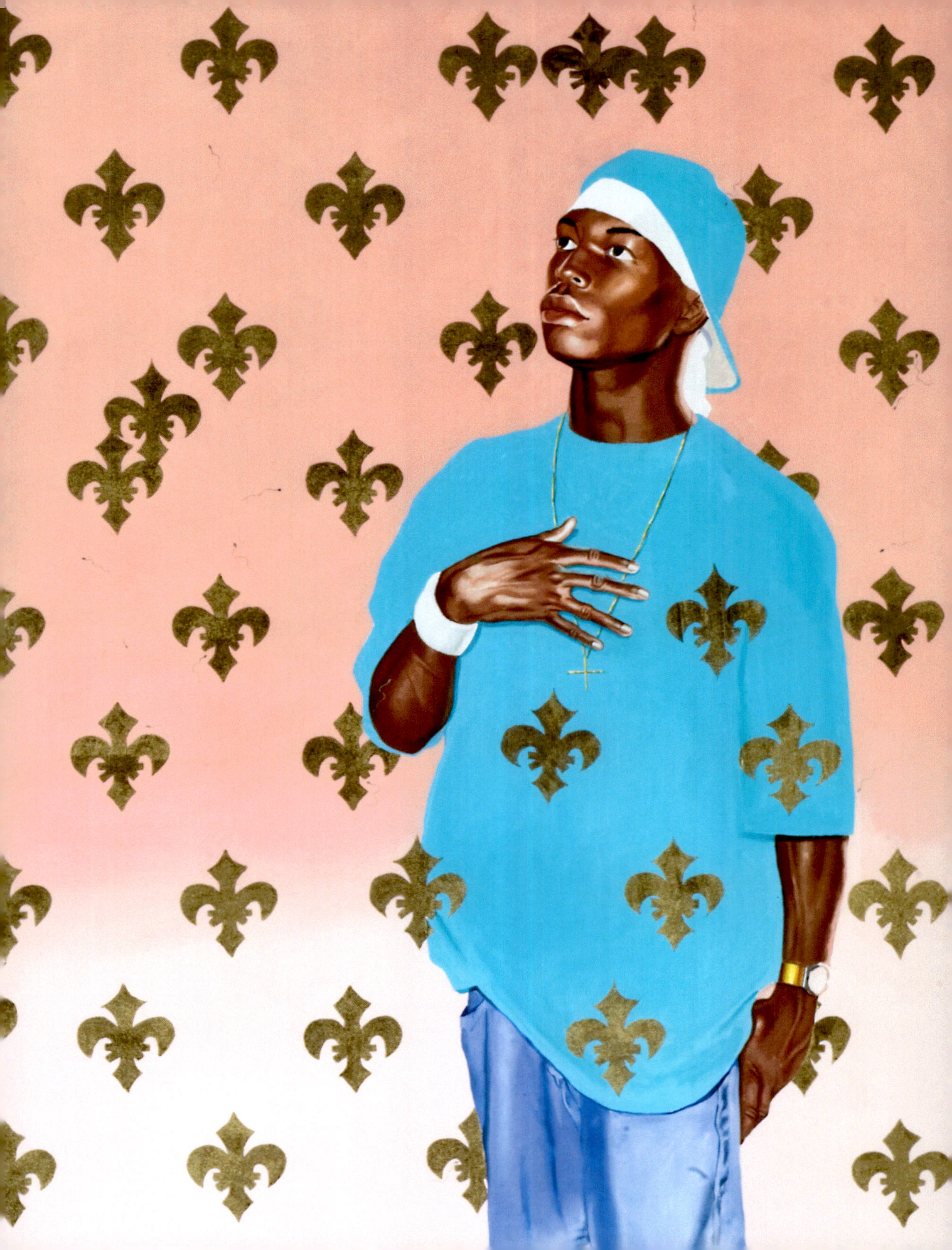

Out of his white Nike sneakers!
His baggy pale blue jeans
Pin-pricked in virtual spermatozoa.

He talked non-stop all the flight long
So that two-and-a-half hours flew by in five minutes.
"I live in a Cave in Brooklyn –
They call me a Minim –
All a gas –
I don't read newspapers – do you?" he shouted.
"Naw" I shouted back "nor me. Never.
What a waste of life – newspapers – their NEGATIVITY!
Crass!"
"Cool" he shouted
"Besides" I shouted
"I'm Kenyan Presbyterian."
"Cool, cool, cool, cool" he whispered
And exclaimed – with that mad saint's smile of his
And these blue eyes matching his gear –
"Veronique, what are you into with religion?"
And I said: "Genetics" and he loved that
And I said "And you, Frankie,
Along with religion and sainthood what are you into?"

"Painting paintings" he rejoined
And he laughed again his mad saint's smile
And as we began our descent into Detroit City
"Do you know what, Veronique?"
"No, Frankie, what?"
"We two loons together clinging –
We two should get together –
The painter and the geneticist!"
And he hugged me as we parted
And uproariously we both laughed –
All the other righteous passengers staring at us! –
And standing in front of me in the aisle
He spun around just one last time
Splaying his right hand across his breast
And he frowned affectionately at me
As if I was his young mother
And he said – "Oh, you know" – he said –
"I paint paintings and then I burn every one of them!"
And he was gone, my new golden-framed boy,
Saint Frankie Paola.

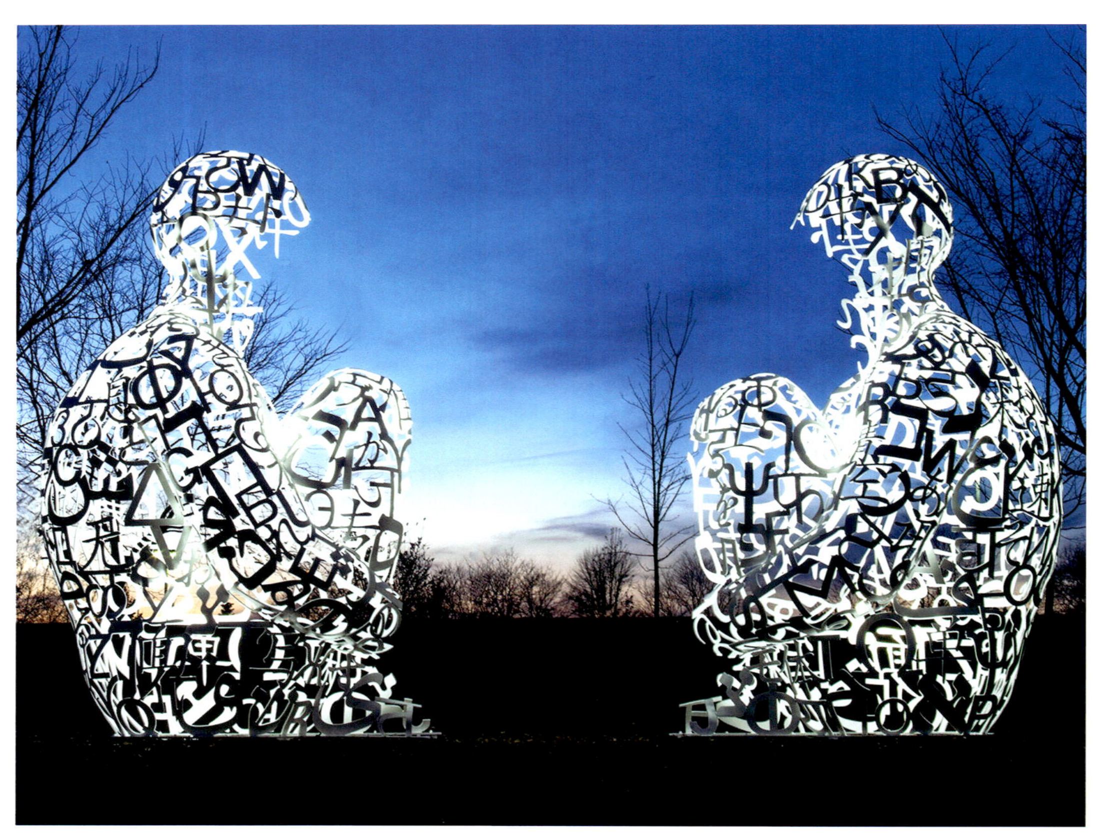

JAUME PLENSA

SPIEGEL (MIRROR)

2010

---

to Colm Tóibín

Sitting by the Grand Bassin in the Luxembourg Gardens in Paris
On a Sunday afternoon in late August
Among the children of God and Allah and Yahweh
Lapping up all the different languages traipsing past
Where really am I?
I am on the shores of Lake Erie – Wild, Wild Erie –
On the borderline of Michigan and Ohio
Among the Power Stations billowing white smoke,
Among the white egrets and the bald eagles,
Hand in hand with my true love
Who like me is a woman also –
Both of us welders in Toledo, Ohio
For a small automobile garage
Repairing, refitting Jeeps. Jeepers Creepers!
We are at peace with ourselves and the world.
The work is hard but we cherish our leisure
In late summer walking the marshes of Erie,
In early winter visiting the Toledo Museum of Art
Inside or outside or both.
I am a Christian-Muslim and she is a Jewish-Muslim.
We call ourselves the Arabian Knights of Ohio!

We dwell in the corner at the intersection
Of Monroe and Collingwood in the Mirror complex.
Of course we are a same-sex marriage
But we're also a two-sex marriage.
Mirror, mirror on the wall,
Who is the fairest one of all?

I

Satellite maps, Sat Nav maps, Ordnance Survey maps, Route maps, Naval Charts –
Michiganders, Ohioans, Detroiters, Toledoans,
New Yorkers, Pennsylvanians, Ontarians,
Where am I? With whom am I?
Lake Erie! Your tail, your spine, your hind-leg, your ears, your whiskers,
O my poor, little, recycled-silver, white-footed mouse –
I need to hug you so badly I could die.
Water? Give me some water and let me live a little.

II

I have seen Neil Armstrong and Chief Little Turtle
    Smoking a pipe – a pipe of peace –
        In Wild, Wild Erie.

I have seen Wild, Wild Erie smile
    And blow smoke-rings out of its nostrils
        At Sherwood Anderson and Hart Crane.

I have seen Lincoln, Roosevelt, Kennedy, Obama,
    On the lake-front at Ashtabula
Lined up on straight-backed chairs
    Listening to the wailing waters of Wild, Wild Erie.

I have seen Lake Erie decapitated
    And yet live to tell the tale.

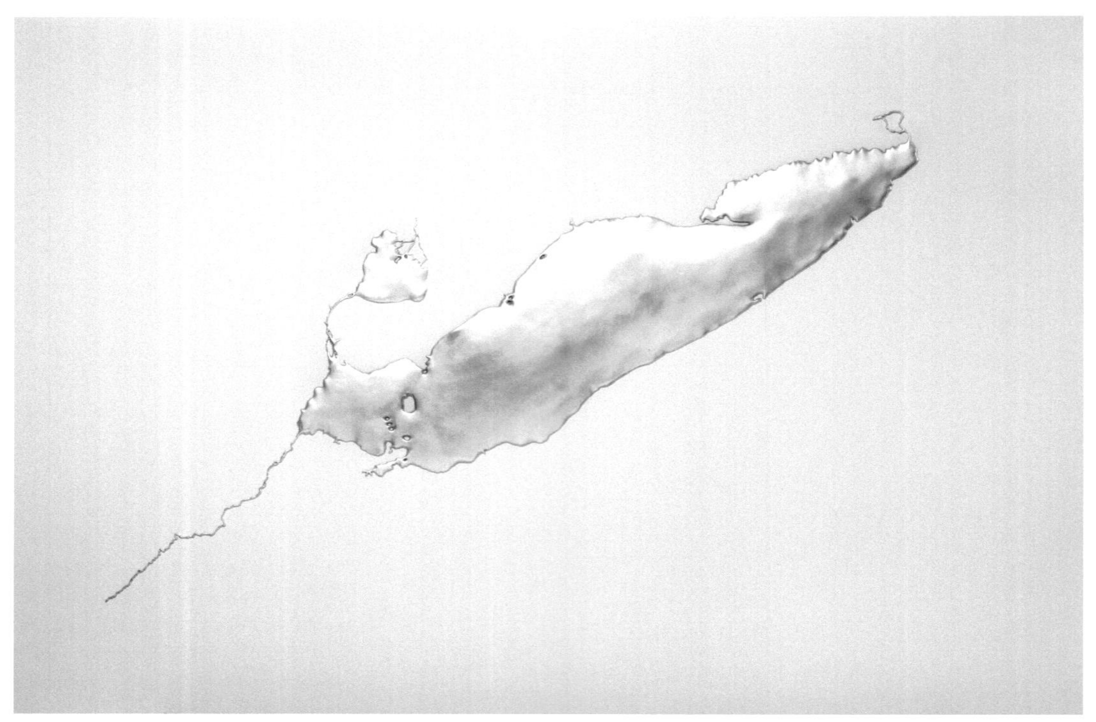

MAYA LIN

III

Sophisters, economists, calculators
Manipulate Lake Erie as Flesh-and-Blood
Who should both lie on her back
And yet lie on her stomach, simultaneously.
My Erie! Your Erie! Our Erie!
Homeless Huron Mouse!
Such theory! Such practice!
Such morality! Such immorality!

IV

I cannot sleep for thinking
Of Wild, Wild Erie and her silver tail –
O that silver tail – you have never
Seen a thing so long, so thin,
So elongated.

What is it, what is it? –
I cried out to my Mom
When first I could squawk.

My Mom cried: That's Wild, Wild Erie's tail
And its name is Maumee!
Which is why
My Mom named me Maumee.
          Erie:
I am your Maumee.

V

Here on Interstate 90 in the dead of night
Curled-up, an injured, silver animal:
Not a badger, not a fox, not a deer, not a cat, not a mink,
Not a squirrel, not a skunk, not a rabbit, not a moose,
But my darlingest silver mammal of all
With whom I have grown up since I was thirty-three seconds old – ERIE!
Wild, Wild Erie!
Water? Give me some water and let me live a little.

KITCHEN

I

If I hadn't a-been a woman
I'd a-been a tree

I stand at my kitchen sink bawling my ballad
In front of my tree
Whose tree-rings constitute my sole route-map
Of where I want to go in my life –
My very own personal dendrochronology
And every day I mop up my floor –
My beautifully exquisite linoleum indigenous floor
Marking every cross-roads in my life,
Every cross-roads past, present and to come:
How many cross-roads can a woman cross over
In one day between sun-up and sun-down?

If I hadn't a-been a woman
I'd a-been a tree.

II

I have lived alone for so long, long,
O so very long,
I have come to regard catastrophe as normal.

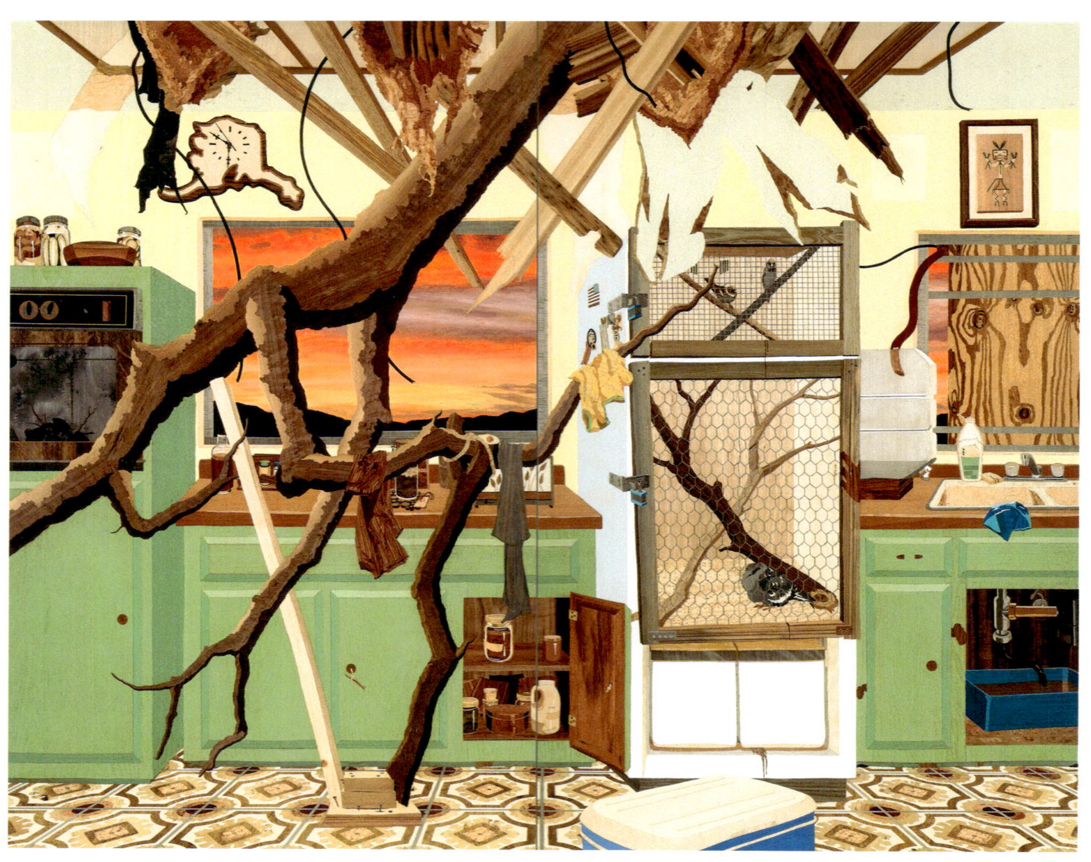

ALISON ELIZABETH TAYLOR

(I last met a friendly human in 2001
The day after 9/11:
A teenage African-American girl crossing the street asked me:
'May I hold your hand?')

Last year a tree – a sycamore – fell through my roof
But after I'd gotten over the surprise – indeed, the shock –
(After all, it near severed my head at the neck –
In fact, all I got out of it was a broken arm –
An elbow-fracture, to be precise)
I simply did not have enough dough to repair it
And a week passed and then a month passed
And, matter of fact, I grew quite to like it!
I grew to like living with half-a-tree in my kitchen.
In fact, now as I stare at it all, I recall saying to myself:
"At last, someone to live with again,
Someone to keep me company."

Oh I agree the whole shebang gives me a pain in the ass
From time to time, most of all the floor planks
Of my bedroom protruding down through my kitchen ceiling
But you get used to catastrophe, you get used to monsters,
Including the Paris, France Massacre of Friday the 13th
And my fallen tree is now the object of my affections.

So when my young middle-aged son drove down from Brandywine, Ohio
With armfuls of Balsa Wood and belly-bags of fretsaws and nails –
He's a Do-It-Yourself freak and he started hammering, blow-torching,
Sanding, staining my kitchen floor
Suddenly I cried out: O my son, O my son, enough, enough!
But Ma – he growls back at me – what about your electrics?
I said: in this day and age who wants electricity?
I admire all my beautiful loose ends, all my beautiful wires – dangling!
A bit more dangling in our lives would not go amiss!
And I am a demon for the washing-up liquid
And the native Indian girl doing her bird-dance in front of my eyes
And my little Sean Johns fridge magnet – or is he called Jasper Scully? –
What matter? It's the STRIPE I go for, not the man.
Fact is my tree has proved useful.

At twilight I stand at my kitchen window
Watching the red sunset on the black hills –
On the black hills of – where is it I do dwell?
I can smell dementia – my own and the world's –
Crawling all over me
And I cannot say that I do not like it.
It's a comfortable, comforting smell.
It's what we are, after all. What we all are.
It's like shit.

The falling-down world is my home
And my home is my resting-place.
Lonely? No, no – no, no, no –
I have everything, as you can see
And besides – I have two sparrows and one pigeon!

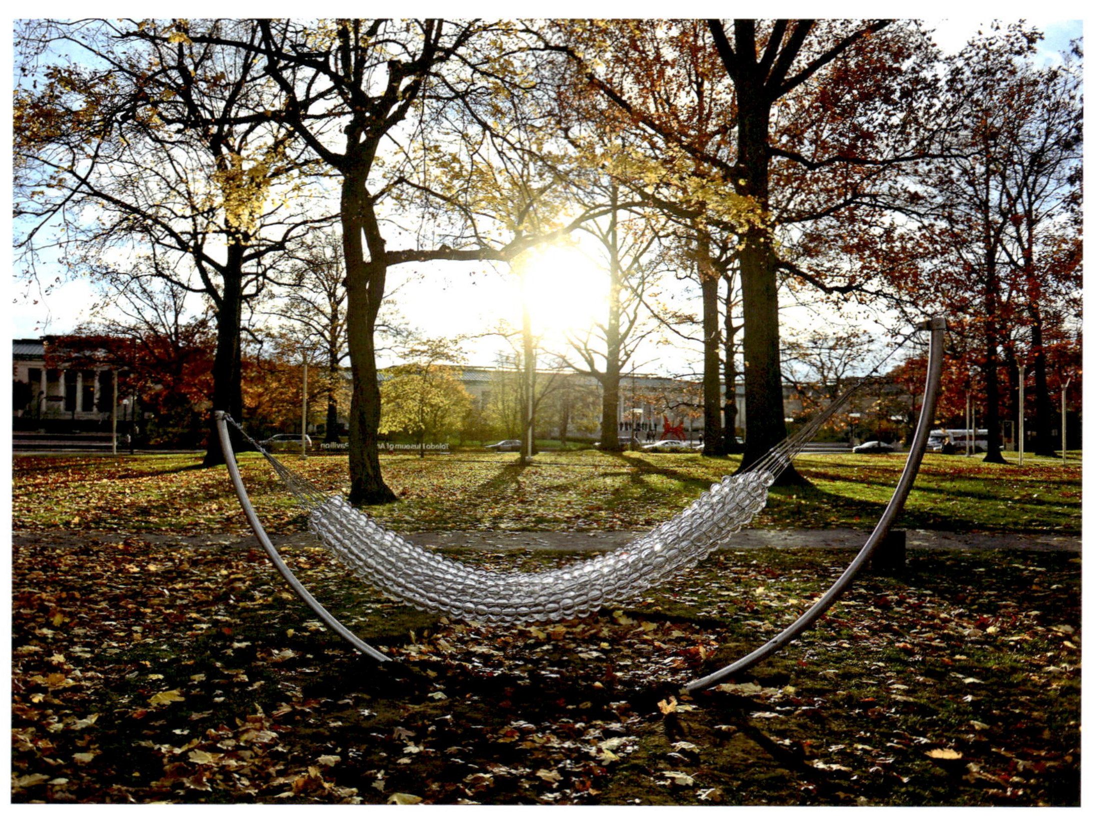

PINAREE SANPITAK

to Jutta Page

Like any self-respecting, horizontal hobo
Or upright, vertical citizen of the Union
I am a connoisseur of public seating
Than which there is no more conspicuous embodiment of civilisation.
From Paris, France to Paris, Texas;
From Westport, Ireland to Invercargill, New Zealand;
From Alice Springs to Kyoto to Barcelona to Novosibirsk
I have savoured the art of the public seat
But it was not until one hot August morning
Under blue skies brushed lightly with cloud,
Strolling the main drag of Toledo, Ohio
On the north side of Monroe through a splash of parkland
I stumbled – no, I swayed – hot, hot the day –
Into a glass hammock by the sidewalk.
Gingerly I lay down, painstakingly stretching out
And, gal, it was Hawaii boutique-style, the Côte d'Azur!
Composed of 260 wired glass balls, strung up between steel posts,
A hammock made for the portliest poet in port –
O great Wallace Stevens, eat your heart out! –
Or for a stag on the skyline of the prairie.
Here I am reposing like a stag tilting in full flight,
Swaying in the breeze under oak tree and maple,
My carefree dangled fingers wine-tasting uncut grass
In urban parkland, watching the auto traffic –

Semis, arctics, flatbacks, limos, taxis, coaches, buses, tankers, Buicks, police cars
And Cadillacs, Cadillacs, and more Cadillacs
Of every hue and colour in the palette –
What a choreographed procession to amuse my reclining torso!
And across Monroe Street the façade of the Toledo Museum of Art –
That scintillating flight of steps, the Ionic Columns,
Alexander Calder's scarlet *Stegosaurus* stalking the redbrick terrace.
I closed my eyes and smiled! O Memory!
O Robert Henri, O Kitaj, O Sherwood Anderson, O Hart Crane, O Ohio!
This hammock is a thing of perfect balance and, therefore, beauty.
'I balance all, bring all to mind'.
'O commemorate me where there is water'.
I opened my eyes and smiled.
I crossed my feet and played with my prayer beads
With my hands in my pockets. Once I was a minor Football Star . . .
O yes! And later . . . well . . . later . . . later . . .
I had appointments for this morning but I'm going nowhere.
LIBRA OK.
I'm gonna snooze in my hammock all morning – in my glass
        Hammock on Monroe.
For an hour or two, know, live and inhale, exhale Peace.

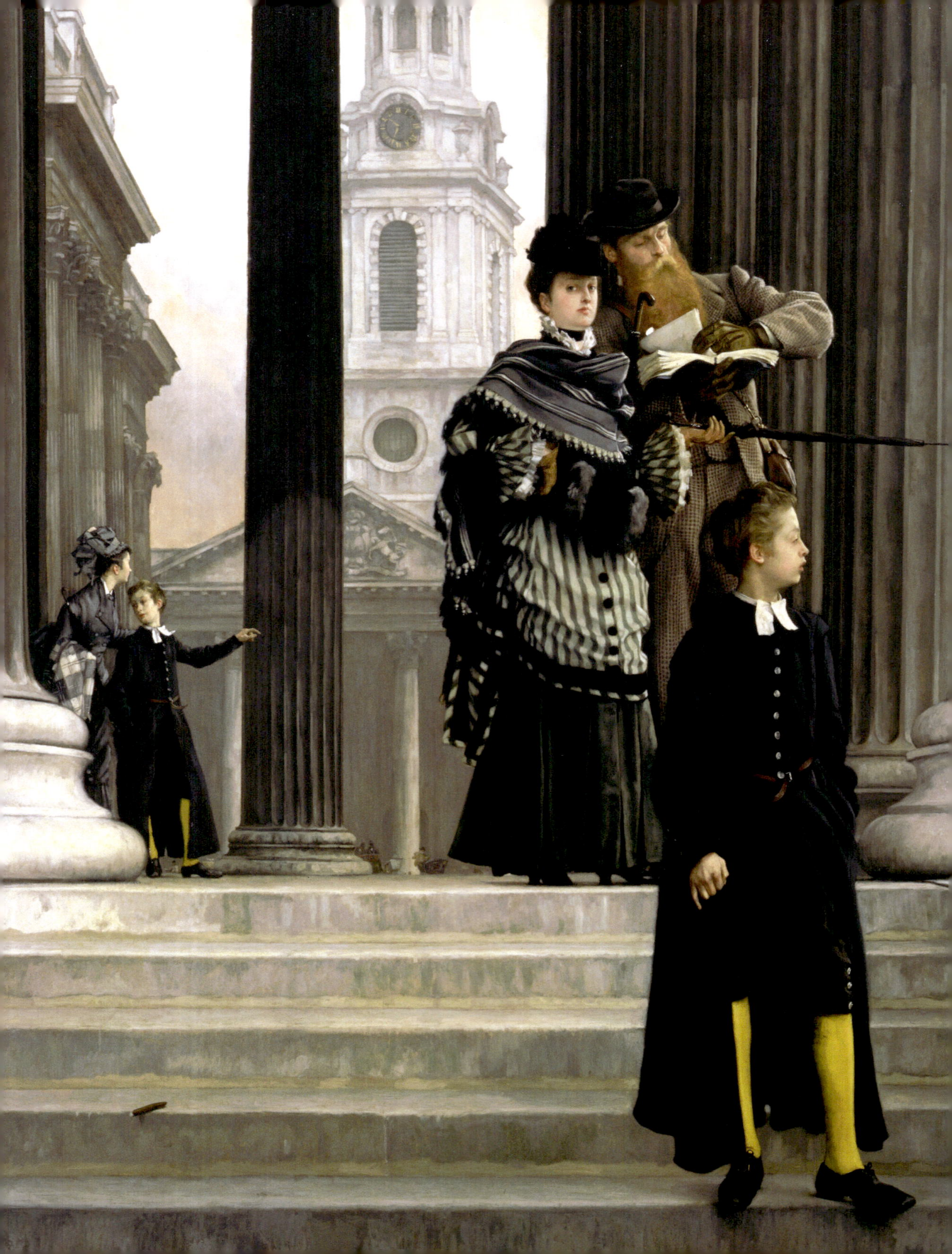

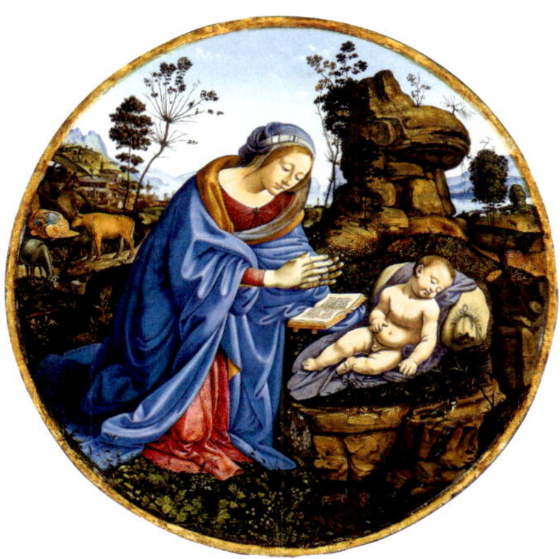

Piero di Cosimo (Italian, Florence, 1462–1521),
The Adoration of the Child, oil on wood panel, about
1495–1500. Diam. 63 in. (160 cm). Purchased with
funds from the Libbey Endowment, Gift of Edward
Drummond Libbey, 1937.1

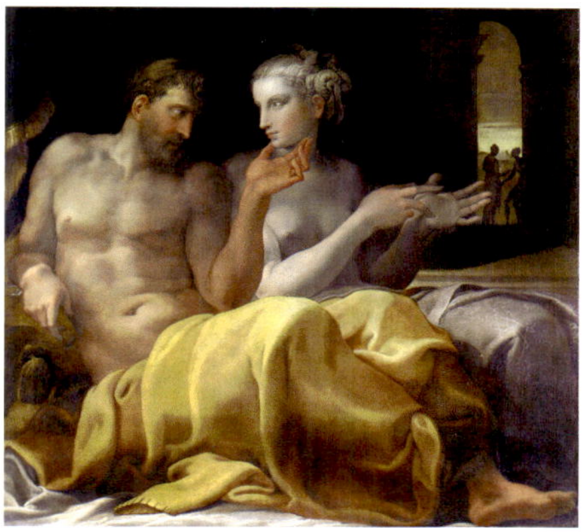

Francesco Primaticcio (Italian, Mantua, active
France, 1504–1570), *Ulysses and Penelope*, oil
on canvas, about 1560. 44¾ × 48¾ in. (113.6 ×
123.8 cm). Purchased with funds from the Libbey
Endowment, Gift of Edward Drummond Libbey,
1964.60

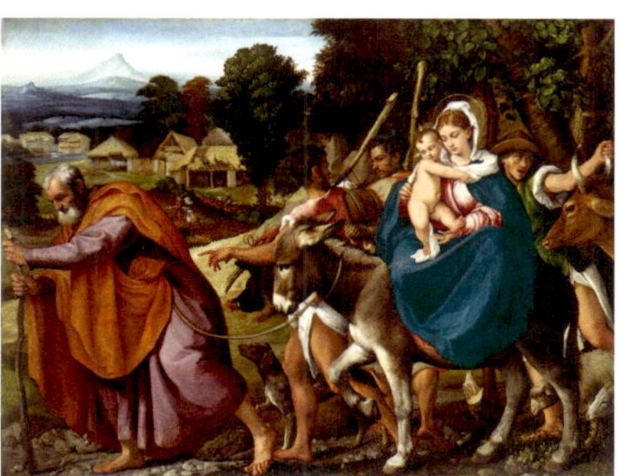

Jacopo dal Ponte, called Jacopo Bassano (Italian,
Venice, about 1515–1592), *The Flight into Egypt*,
oil on canvas, about 1540–45. 62 × 80 in. (157.5 ×
203.2 cm). Purchased with funds from the Libbey
Endowment, Gift of Edward Drummond Libbey,
1977.41

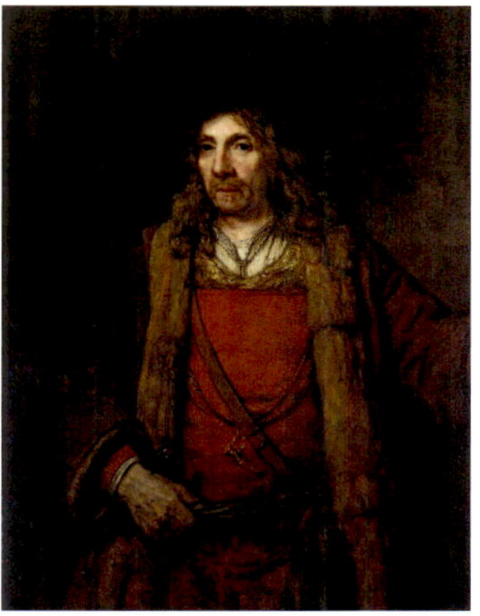

Rembrandt Harmensz. van Rijn (Dutch,
1606–1669), *Man in a Fur-Lined Coat*, oil
on canvas, about 1655–60. 45¼ × 34¾ in.
(114.9 × 88.3 cm). Clarence Brown Fund,
1977.50

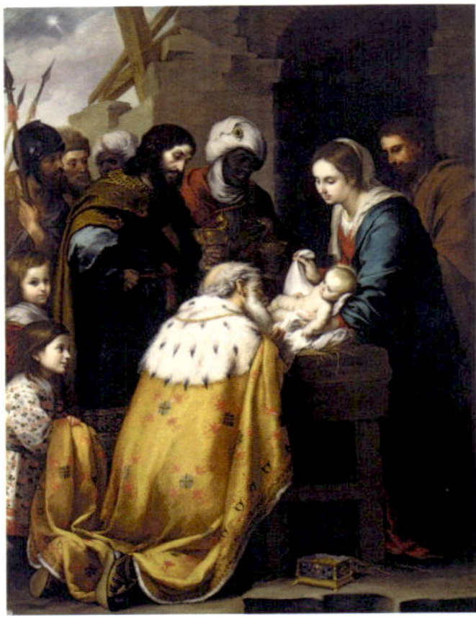

Bartolomé Esteban Murillo (Spanish, 1617–1682), *The Adoration of the Magi*, oil on canvas, about 1655–60. 75⅛ × 57½ in. (190.8 × 146.1 cm). Purchased with funds from the Libbey Endowment, Gift of Edward Drummond Libbey, 1975.84

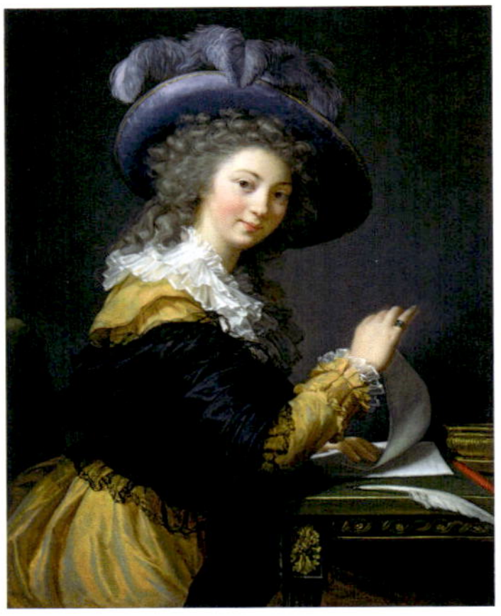

Élisabeth-Louise Vigée-Le Brun (French, 1755–1842), *The Comtesse de Cérès*, oil on canvas, 1784. 36 × 29 in. (91.4 × 73.7 cm). Purchased with funds from the Libbey Endowment, Gift of Edward Drummond Libbey, 1963.33

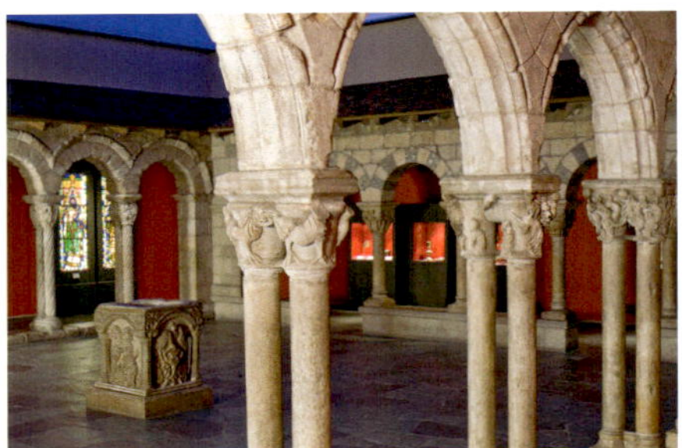

French, The Cloister Gallery, sections of three arcades, marble, mid-12th to early 15th century. Purchased with funds from the Libbey Endowment, Gift of Edward Drummond Libbey, 1929.203–208; 1931.81–99; 1934.93A–E

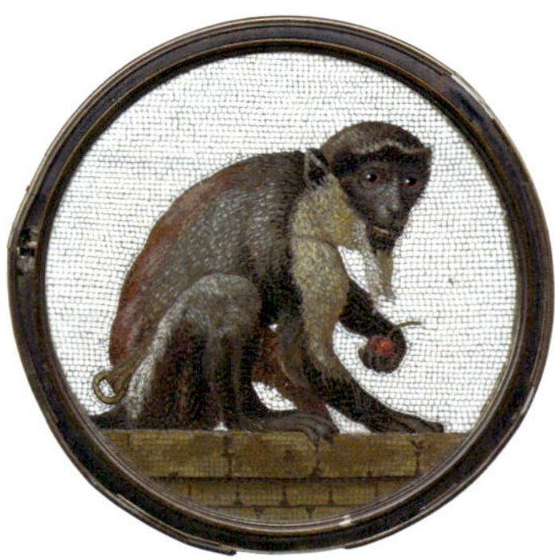

Giacomo Raffaelli (Italian, Rome, 1743–1836), *Micromosaic Box with Monkey*, polychrome opaque glass; cut, assembled on copper; tortoiseshell frame, 1794. Rim diam. 3 in. (7.9 cm); H. (box) 1 in. (2.54 cm). Mr. and Mrs. George M. Jones, Jr. Fund, 2004.67

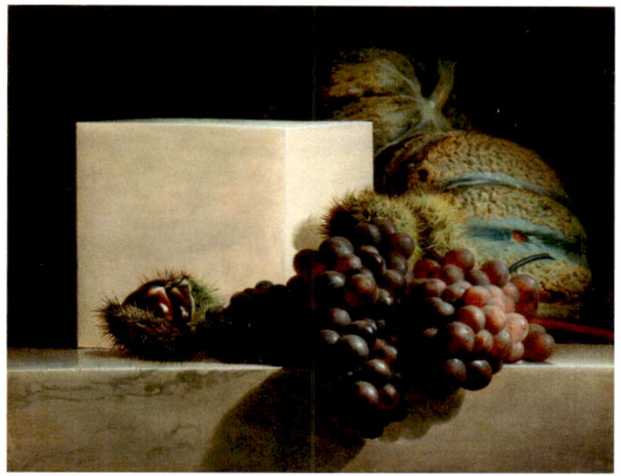

Antoine Berjon (French, 1754–1843), *Still Life with Grapes, Chestnuts, Melons, and a Marble Cube*, oil on canvas, about 1800–10. 12¹⁵⁄₁₆ × 16⅝ in. (32.8 × 41.4 cm). Purchased with funds given by Dr. and Mrs. James G. Ravin, 2015.4

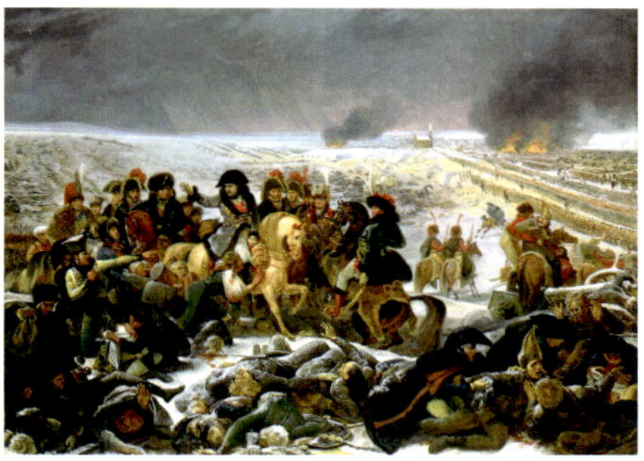

Antoine-Jean Gros (French, 1771–1835), *Napoleon on the Battlefield of Eylau*, oil on canvas, 1807. 41¼ × 57⅛ in. (104.9 × 145.1 cm). Purchased with funds from the Libbey Endowment, Gift of Edward Drummond Libbey, 1988.54

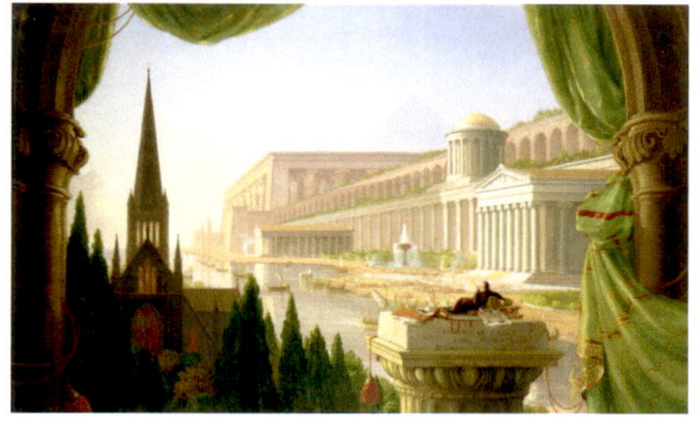

Thomas Cole (American, born England, 1801–1848), *The Architect's Dream*, oil on canvas, 1840. 53 × 84¹⁄₁₆ in. (134.7 × 213.6 cm). Purchased with funds from the Florence Scott Libbey Bequest in Memory of her Father, Maurice A. Scott, 1949.162

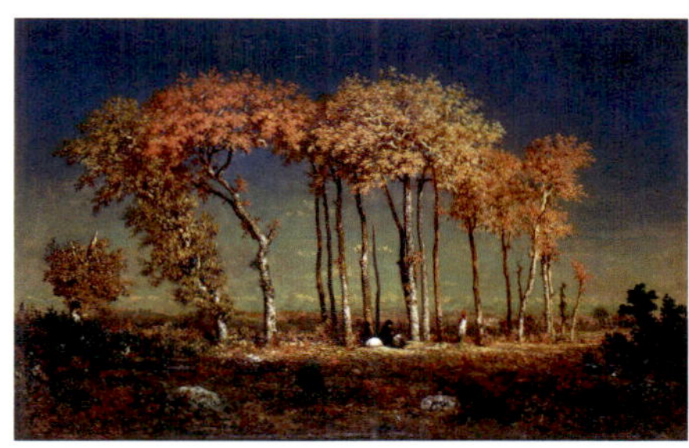

Pierre-Étienne-Théodore Rousseau (French, 1812–1867), *Under the Birches, Evening*, oil on wood panel, 1842–43. 16⅝ × 25⅜ in. (42.2 × 64.5 cm). Gift of Arthur J. Secor, 1933.37

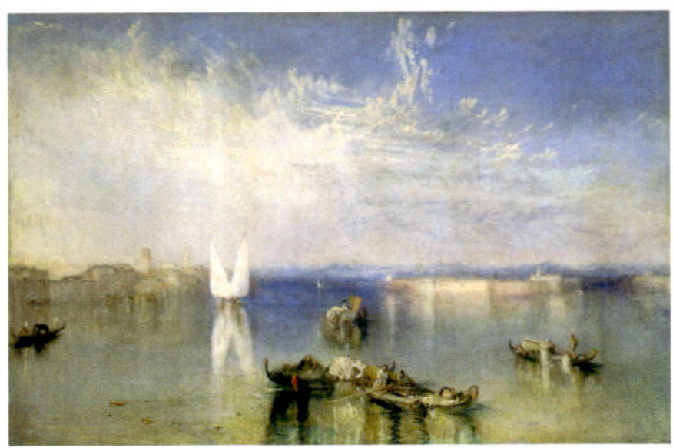

Joseph Mallord William Turner (British, 1775–1851), *The Campo Santo, Venice*, oil on canvas, 1842. 24½ × 36½ in. (62.2 × 92.7 cm). Gift of Edward Drummond Libbey, 1926.63

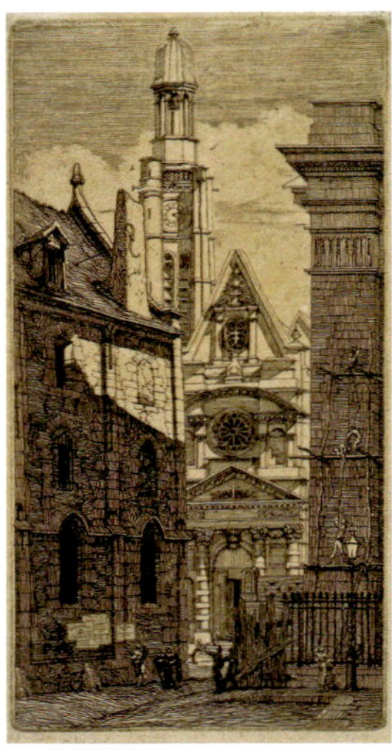

Charles Méryon (French, 1821–1868), *Saint-Étienne-du-Mont, Paris*, from *Eaux-fortes sur Paris (Etchings of Paris)*, etching, 1852. 9⅞ × 5⅛ in. (25 × 13 cm). Winthrop H. Perry Fund, 1948.7

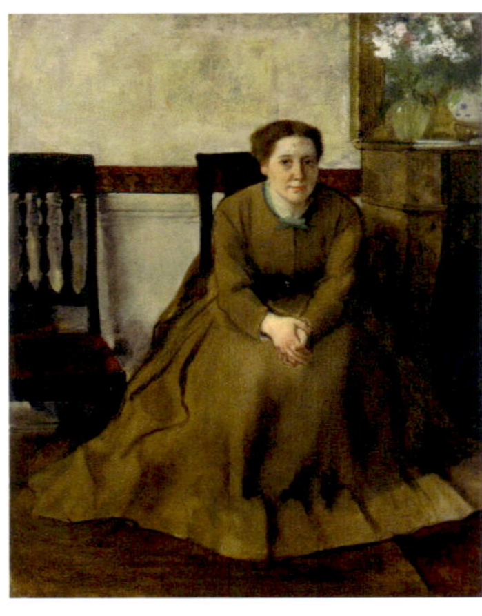

Edgar Degas (French, 1834–1917), *Victoria Dubourg*, oil on canvas, about 1868–69. 32 × 25½ in. (81.3 × 64.8 cm). Gift of Mr. and Mrs. William E. Levis, 1963.45

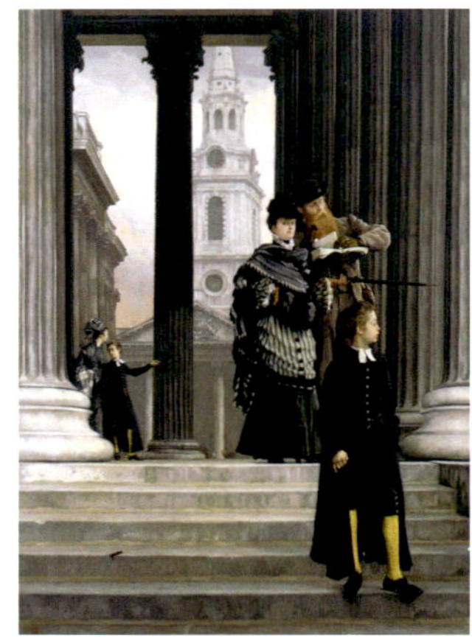

James Tissot (French, 1836–1902), *London Visitors*, oil on canvas, about 1874. 63 × 45 in. (160 × 114.2 cm). Purchased with funds from the Libbey Endowment, Gift of Edward Drummond Libbey, 1951.409

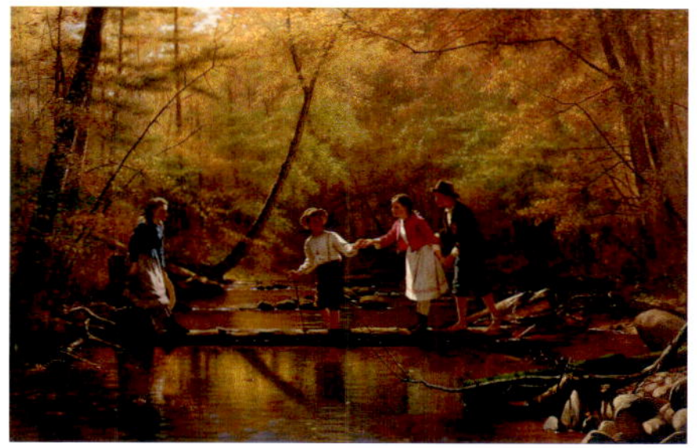

John George Brown (American, 1831–1913), *The Country Gallants*, oil on canvas, 1876. 30¹⁄₁₆ × 46 in. (76.4 × 116.8 cm). Purchased with funds from the Florence Scott Libbey Bequest in Memory of her Father, Maurice A. Scott, 1949.23

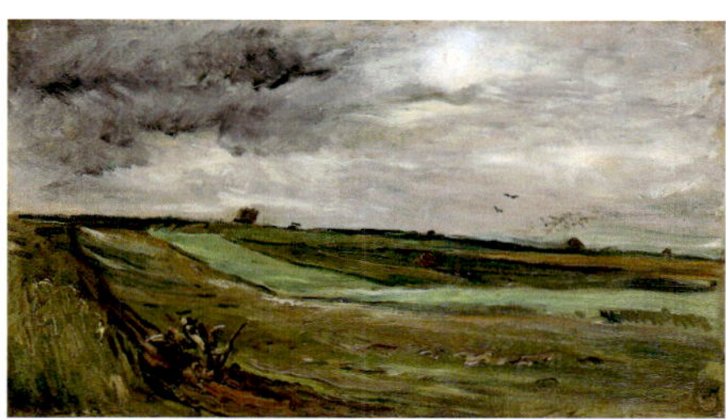

Charles-François Daubigny (French, 1817–1877), *Auvers, Landscape with Plough*, oil on canvas, about 1877. 18⁵⁄₁₆ × 32¹⁄₁₆ in. (46.5 × 81.5 cm). Purchased with funds from the Florence Scott Libbey Bequest in Memory of her Father, Maurice A. Scott, 2015.18

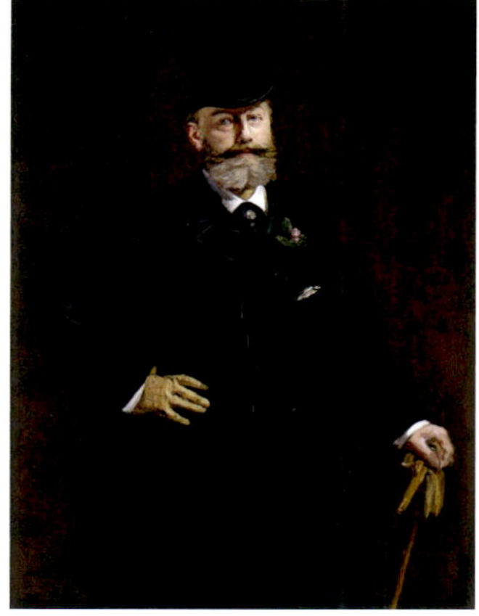

Édouard Manet (French, 1832–1883), *Antonin Proust*, oil on canvas, 1880. 51 × 37¾ in. (129.5 × 95.9 cm). Gift of Edward Drummond Libbey, 1925.108

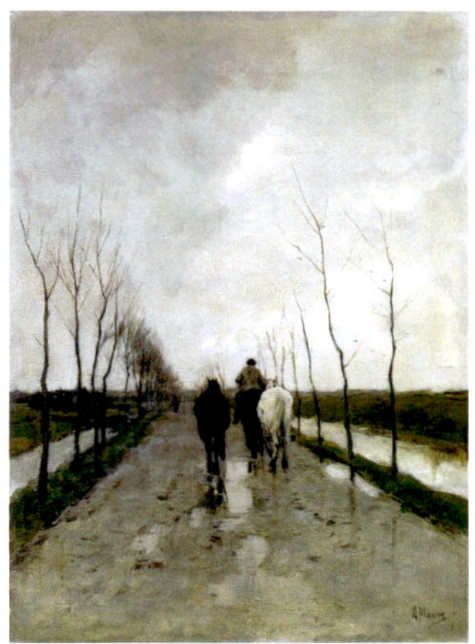

Anton Mauve (Dutch, 1838–1888), *A Dutch Road*, oil on canvas, about 1880. 20 × 14½ in. (50.5 × 36.8 cm). Gift of Arthur J. Secor, 1922.22

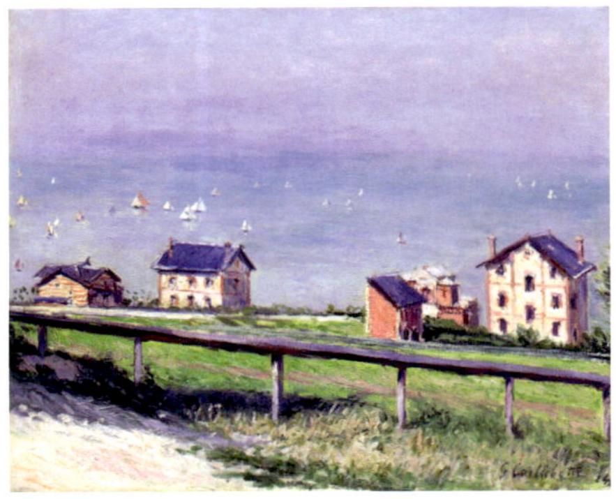

Gustave Caillebotte (French, 1848–1894), *Regatta at Trouville*, oil on canvas, 1884. 23¾ × 28¾ in. (60.3 × 73 cm). Gift of The Wildenstein Foundation, 1953.69

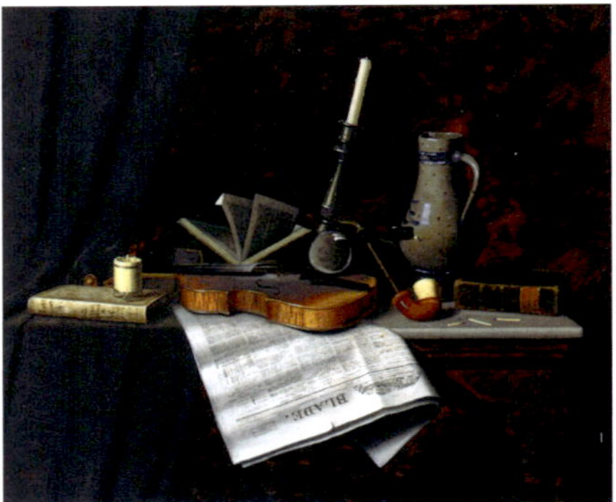

William Harnett (American, born Ireland, 1848–1892), *Still Life with the Toledo Blade*, oil on canvas, 1886. 22⅛ × 26³⁄₁₆ in. (56.1 × 66.5 cm). Gift of Mr. and Mrs. Roy Rike, 1962.2

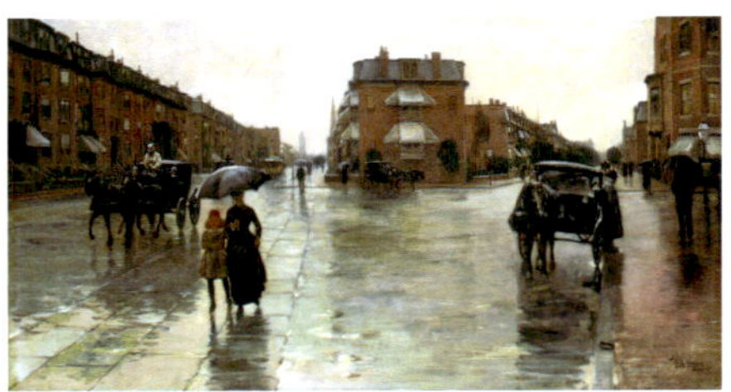

Childe Hassam (American, 1859–1935), *Rainy Day, Boston*, oil on canvas, 1885. 26⅛ × 48 in. (66.3 × 122 cm). Purchased with funds from the Florence Scott Libbey Bequest in Memory of her Father, Maurice A. Scott, 1956.53

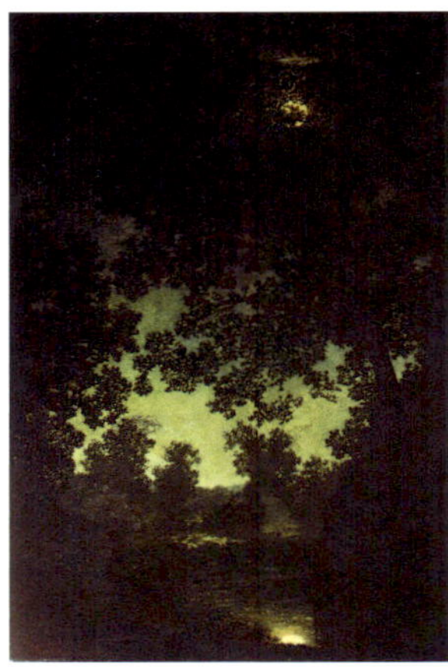

Ralph Albert Blakelock (American, 1847–1919), *Brook by Moonlight*, oil on canvas, before 1891. 72⅛ × 48¹⁄₁₆ in. (183.2 × 122.1 cm). Gift of Mr. and Mrs. Edward Drummond Libbey, 1916.4

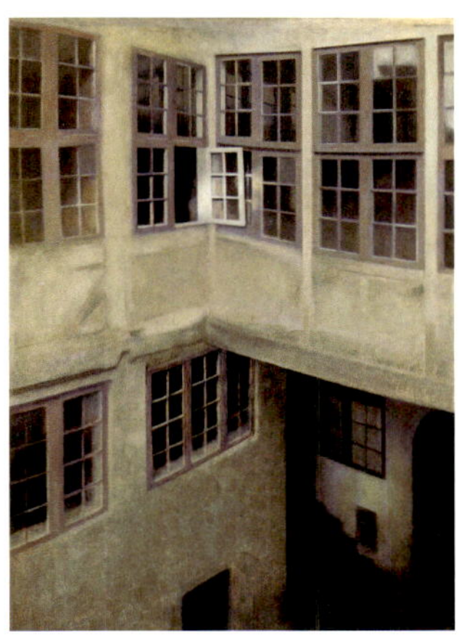

Vilhelm Hammershøi (Danish, 1864–1916),
Interior of Courtyard, Strandgade 30, oil on
canvas, 1899. 25⅞ × 18⅝ in. (66 × 47 cm).
Gift of The Apollo Society, 2000.30

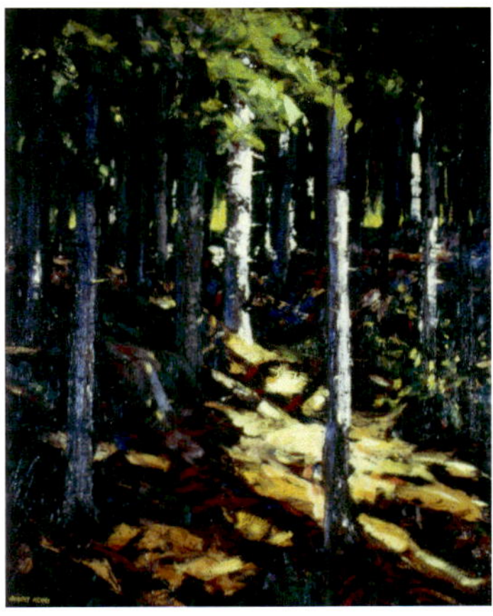

Robert Henri (American, 1865–1929), *Cathedral
Woods, Monhegan Island*, oil on canvas, 1911.
31⅞ × 25⅞ in. (81 × 65.7 cm). Frederick B. and
Kate L. Shoemaker Fund, 1919.47

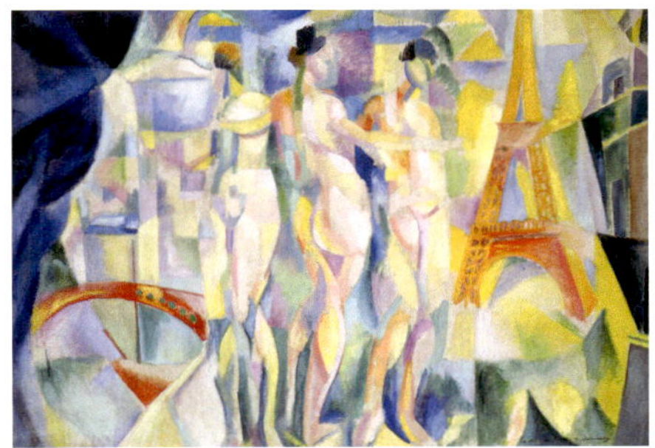

Robert Delaunay (French, 1885–1941), *The City of
Paris (La ville de Paris)*, oil on canvas, about 1911.
47¹/₁₆ × 67¹³/₁₆ in. (119.5 × 172.2 cm). Purchased
with funds from the Libbey Endowment, Gift of
Edward Drummond Libbey, 1955.38

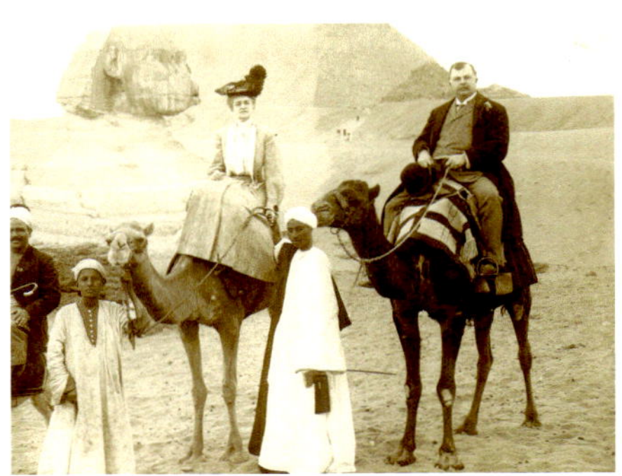

Edward Drummond Libbey and Florence Scott
Libbey (Toledo Museum of Art founders),
Camel-back, Egypt, 1906

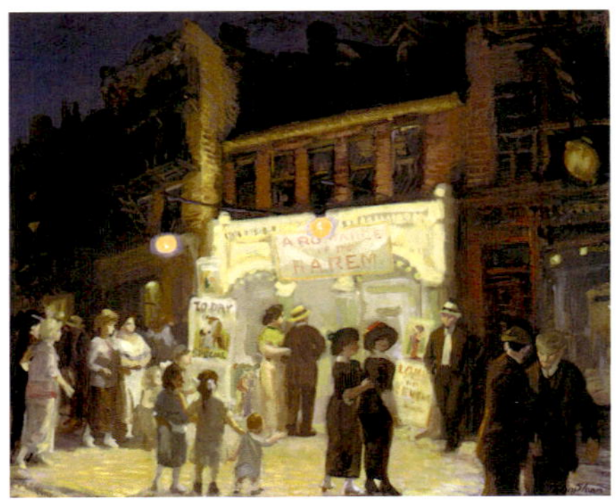

John Sloan (American, 1871–1951), *Movies*, oil on canvas, 1913. 19⅞ × 24 in. (50.5 × 61 cm). Museum Purchase, 1940.16
© 2016 Delaware Art Museum / Artists Rights Society (ARS), New York

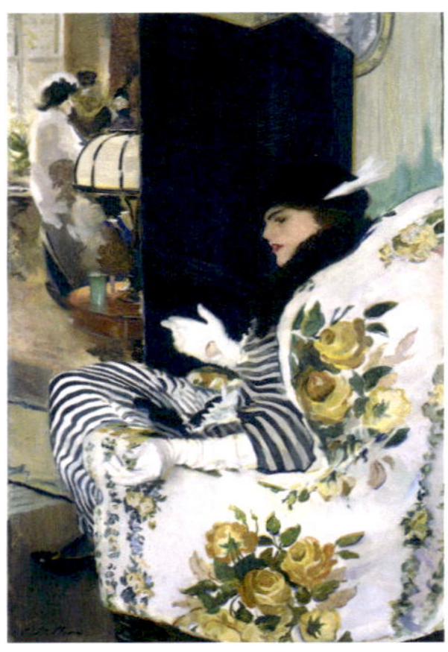

Cecilia Beaux (American, 1855–1942), *After the Meeting*, oil on canvas, 1914. 40¹⁵⁄₁₆ × 28⅛ in. (104 × 71.5 cm). Gift of Florence Scott Libbey, 1915.163

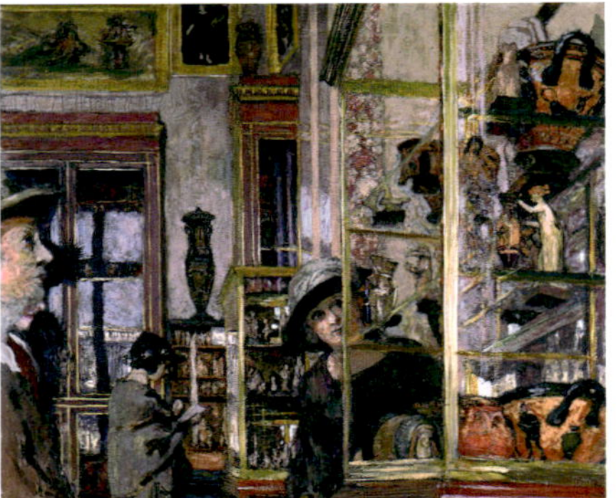

Édouard Vuillard (French, 1868–1940), *La Salle Clarac*, oil with distemper on canvas, 1922. 38⅝ × 45⅝ in. (98.1 × 115.9 cm). Purchased with funds from the Libbey Endowment, Gift of Edward Drummond Libbey, 1999.2
© 2016 Artists Rights Society (ARS), New York / ADAGP, Paris

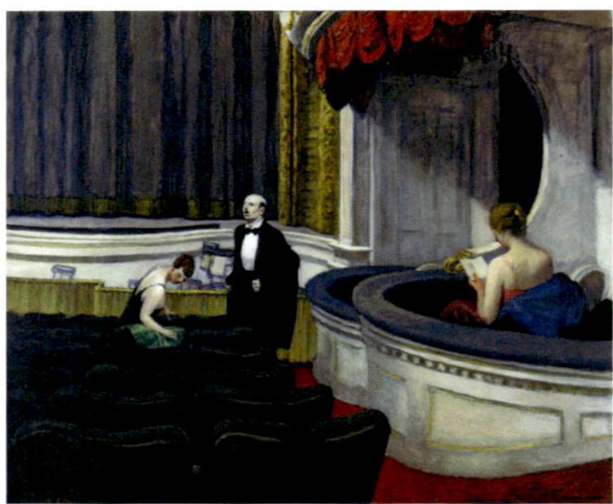

Edward Hopper (American, 1882–1967), *Two on the Aisle*, oil on canvas, 1927. 40⅛ × 48¼ in. (102 × 122.5 cm). Purchased with funds from the Libbey Endowment, Gift of Edward Drummond Libbey, 1935.49
© Heirs of Josephine N. Hopper, Licensed by the Whitney Museum of American Art

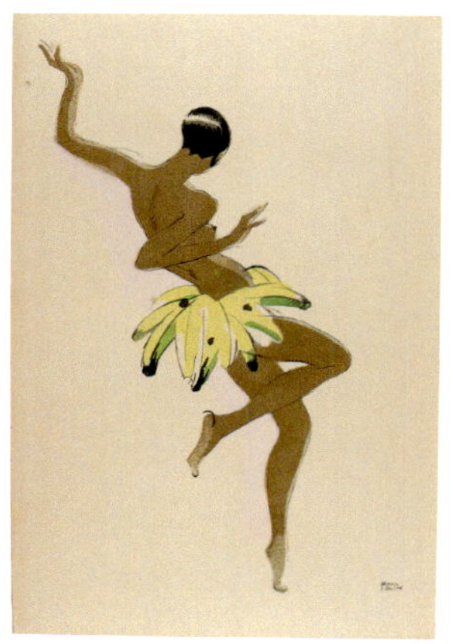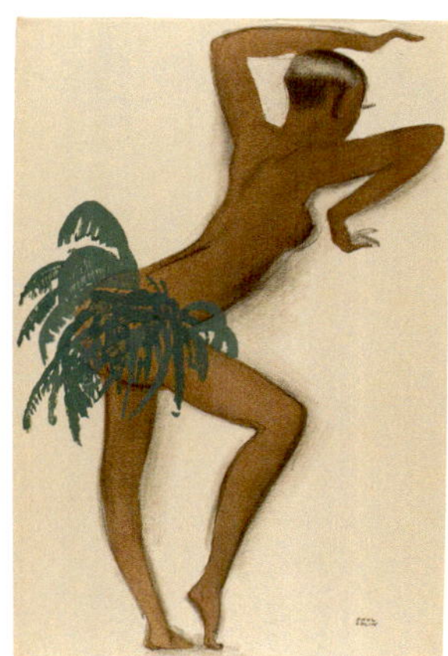

Paul Colin (French, 1892–1985),
The Black Craze (Le tumulte noir),
portfolio of lithographs with pochoir
color, 1927. 20 × 13 in. (50.8 × 33 cm).
Gift of The Apollo Society, 2009.24.
Top, left to right: "Josephine Baker
(Banana Skirt)," "Josephine Baker (Palm
Skirt)," "Dancer in the Rain," "Couple
Dancing the Charleston (Green Dress),"
"Dancer in Tuxedo with Cane (Maurice
Chevalier)," "Jazz Band."
© 2016 Artists Rights Society (ARS),
New York / ADAGP, Paris

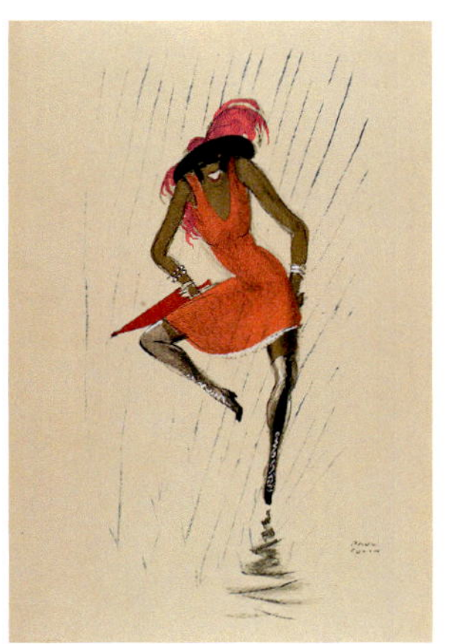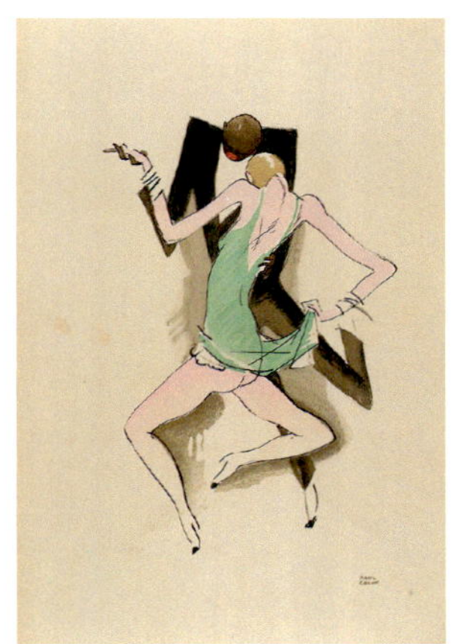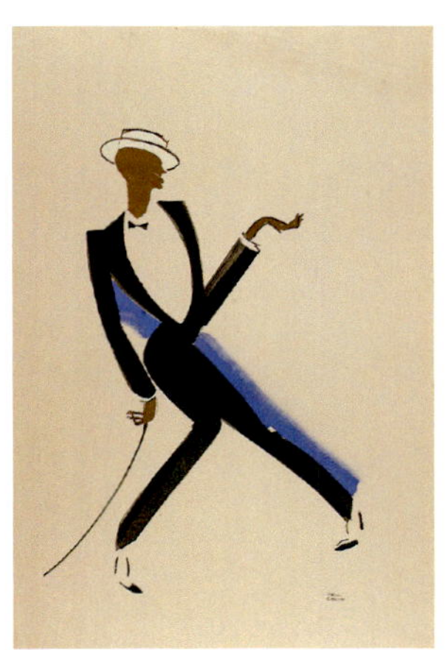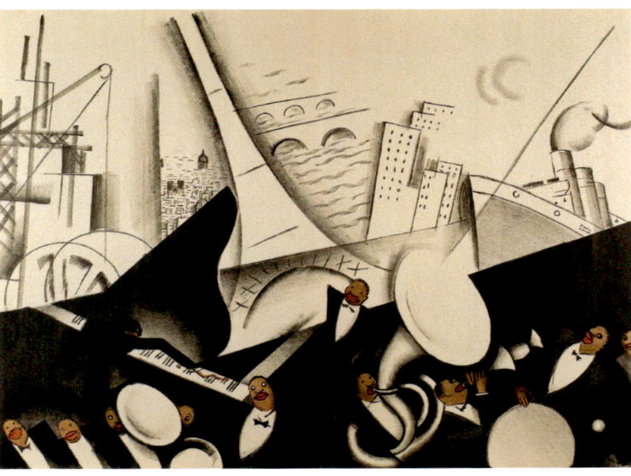

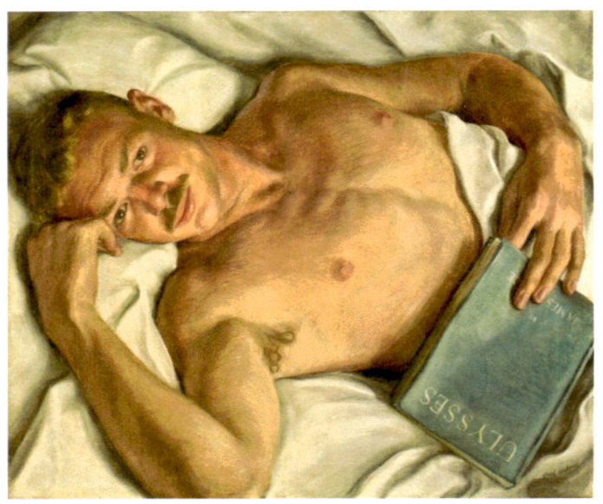

Paul Cadmus (American, 1904–1999), *Jerry*, oil on canvas, 1931. 20 × 24 in. (50.8 × 60.9 cm). Purchased with funds from the Libbey Endowment, Gift of Edward Drummond Libbey, by exchange, 2008.140 Art © Jon F. Anderson, Estate of Paul Cadmus / Licensed by VAGA, New York, NY

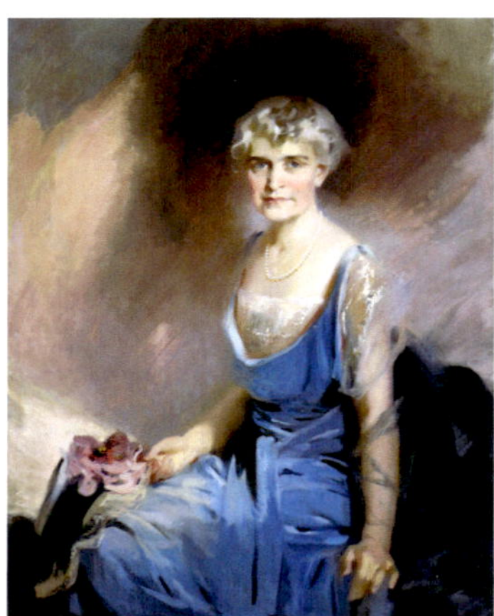

Jean MacLane (American, 1878–1964), *Florence Scott Libbey*, oil on canvas, about 1933. 49¾ × 39¹⁵⁄₁₆ in. (126.5 × 101.5 cm). Gift of Florence Scott Libbey, 1938.22

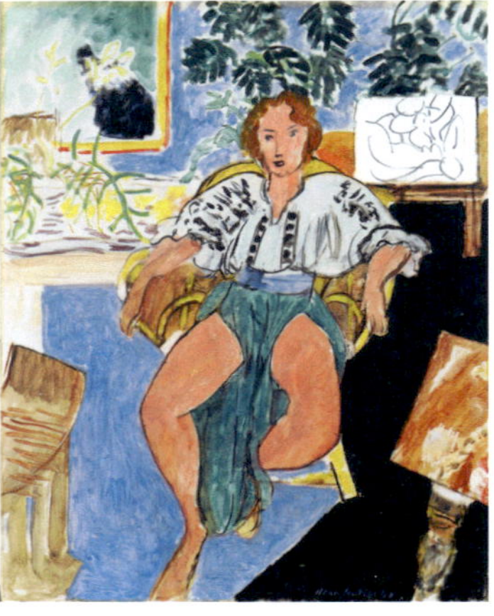

Henri Matisse (French, 1869–1954), *Dancer Resting*, oil on canvas, 1940. 32 × 25½ in. (81.3 × 64.8 cm). Gift of Mrs. C. Lockhart McKelvy, 1947.54 © 2016 Succession H. Matisse / Artists Rights Society (ARS), New York

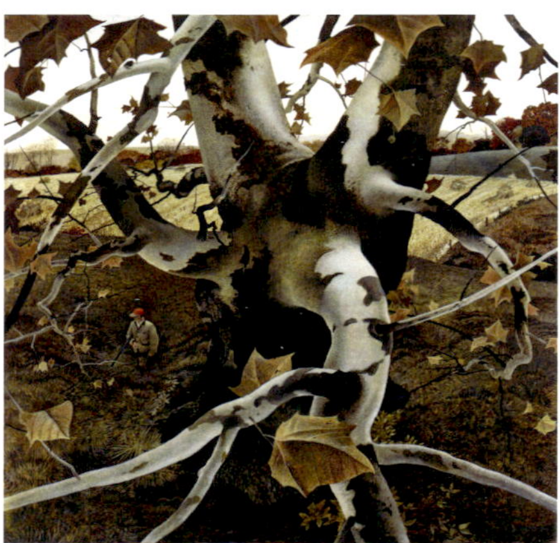

Andrew Newell Wyeth (American, 1917–2009), *The Hunter*, tempera on Masonite, 1943. 33 × 33⅞ in. (83.8 × 86 cm). Elizabeth C. Mau Bequest Fund, 1946.25 © 2016 Artists Rights Society (ARS), New York

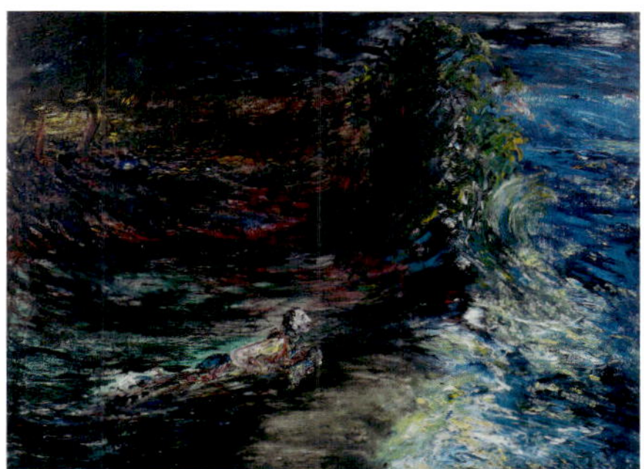

Jack B. Yeats (Irish, 1871–1957), *Another Chance*,
oil on canvas, 1944. 36 × 48 in. (91.4 × 121.8 cm).
Purchased with funds from the Libbey Endowment,
Gift of Edward Drummond Libbey, 1949.15
© 2016 Artists Rights Society (ARS), New York

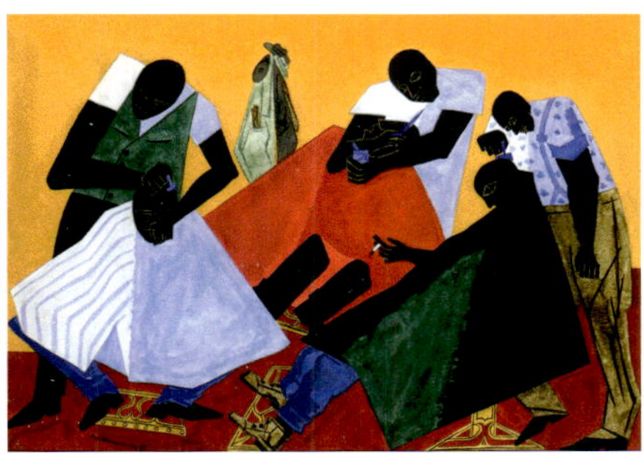

Jacob Lawrence (American, 1917–2000), *Barber
Shop*, 1946. 21⅛ × 29⅜ in. (53.6 × 74.6 cm).
Purchased with funds from the Libbey Endowment,
Gift of Edward Drummond Libbey, 1975.15
© 2016 The Jacob and Gwendolyn Lawrence
Foundation, Seattle / Artists Rights Society (ARS),
New York

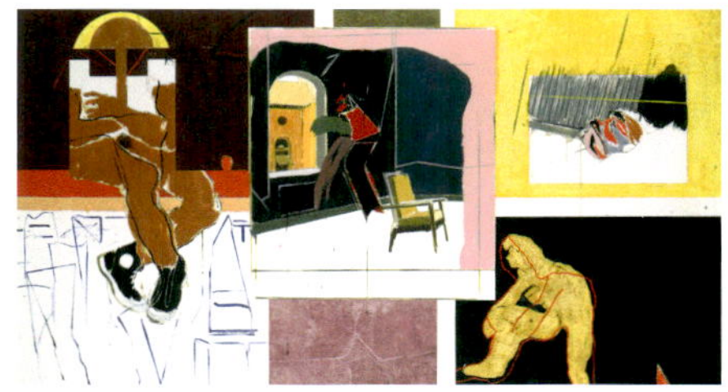

Ronald B. Kitaj (American, 1932–2007), *Notes
Toward a Definition of Nobody—A Reverie*, oil on
canvas, 1961. 48 × 88 in. (122 × 223.5 cm). Gift of
Dr. and Mrs. Joseph A. Gosman, 1973.42
© Estate of R. B. Kitaj

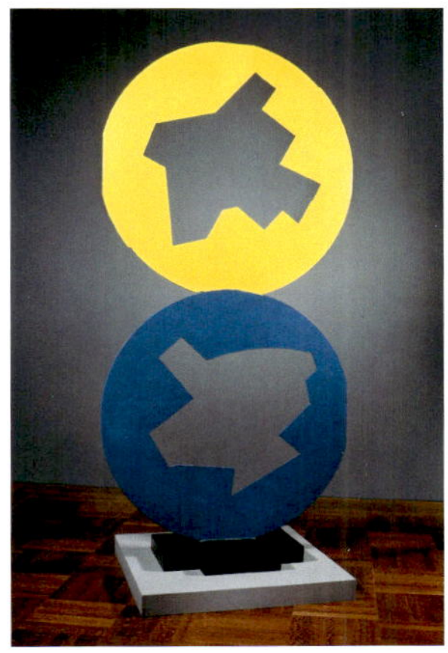

David Smith (American, 1906–1965), *2 Circle IV*,
painted steel, 1962. H. (with base) 9ft., 11 in. (3 m);
W. 65 in. (165.1 cm); Depth 28 in. (71.1 cm).
Purchased with funds from the Libbey Endowment,
Gift of Edward Drummond Libbey, 2001.3
Art © Estate of David Smith / Licensed by VAGA,
New York, NY

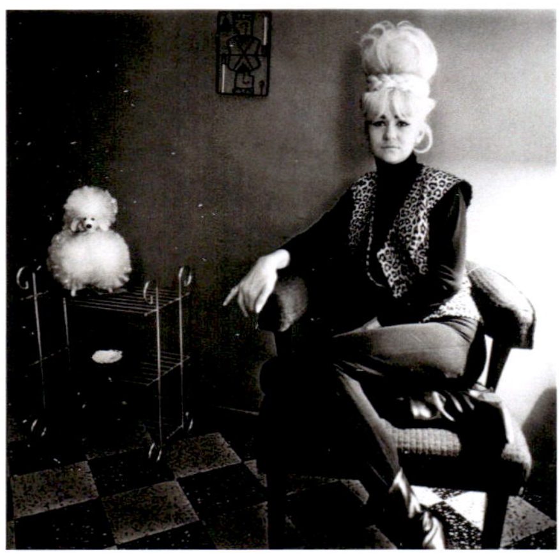

Diane Arbus (American, 1923–1971), *Lady Bartender at Home with a Souvenir Dog, New Orleans, La., 1964*, gelatin-silver print, 1964 (printed later). Image: 14½ × 14½ in. (36.8 × 36.8 cm). Gift of Florence Scott Libbey, by exchange, 2006.147
© The Estate of Diane Arbus

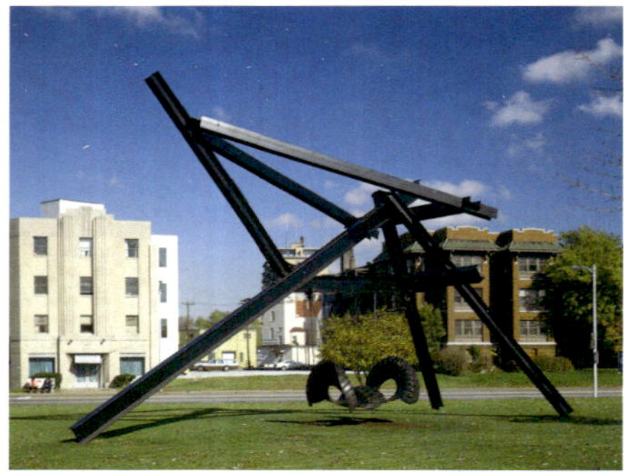

Mark di Suvero (American, born 1933), *Blubber*, painted steel and rubber, 1979–80. H. 35 ft. (10.67 m); W. 25 ft. (7.62 m); Depth: 60 ft. (18.29 m). Purchased with funds from the Libbey Endowment, Gift of Edward Drummond Libbey, 1984.76
© Mark di Suvero

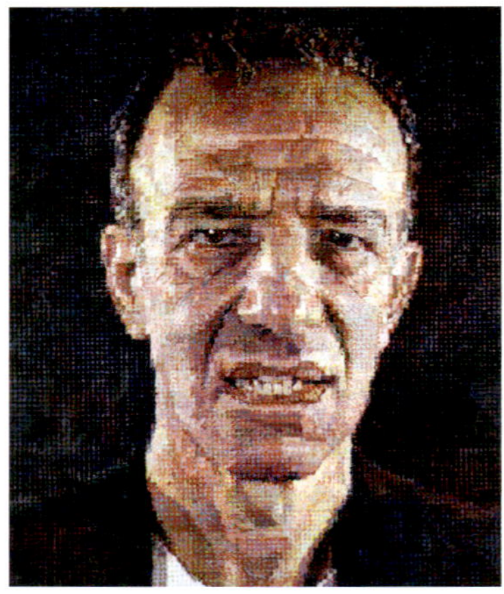

Chuck Close (American, born 1940), *Alex*, oil on canvas, 1987. 100¼ × 84 in. (254.6 × 213 cm). Gift of The Apollo Society, 1987.218
© Chuck Close / Courtesy PaceWildenstein, New York

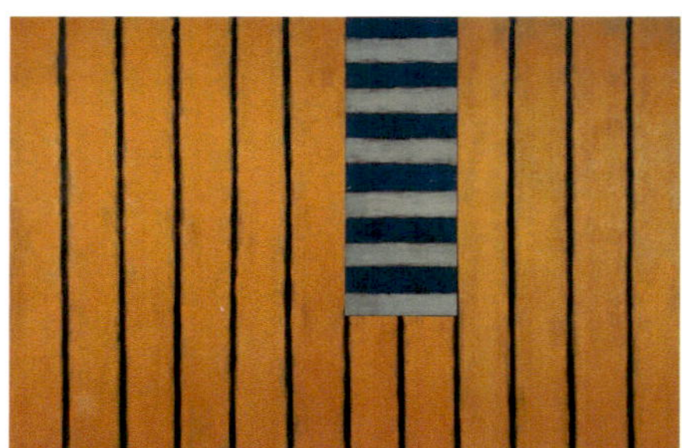

Sean Scully (American, born Ireland, 1945), *Ookbar*, oil on linen, 1993–94. 96 × 114 in. (243.8 × 289.6 cm). Gift of Edward Drummond Libbey, Dr. and Mrs. Joseph A. Gosman, Felix Wildenstein, and Paul Reinhardt, in memory of his father, Henry Reinhardt, by exchange, 2012.101A–C
© Sean Scully

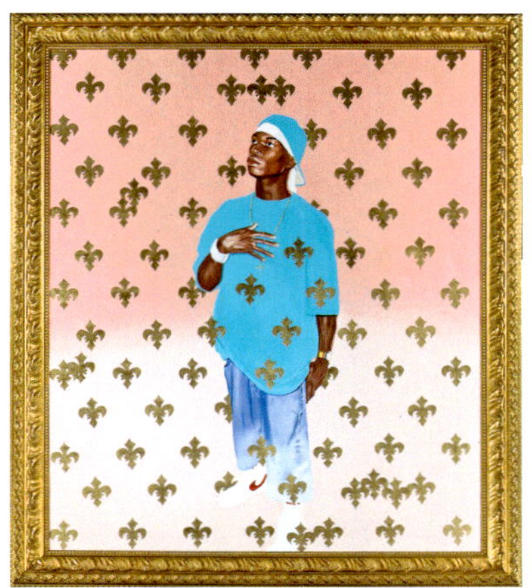

Kehinde Wiley (American, born 1977), *Saint Francis
of Paola*, oil on canvas with artist's frame, 2003.
82 × 70 in. (208.3 × 177.8 cm). Gift of Charles L.
Borgmeyer, Mrs. Webster Plass, and C. W.
Kraushaar, by exchange, 2005.290
Saint Francis of Paola © 2003 Kehinde Wiley,
used by permission.

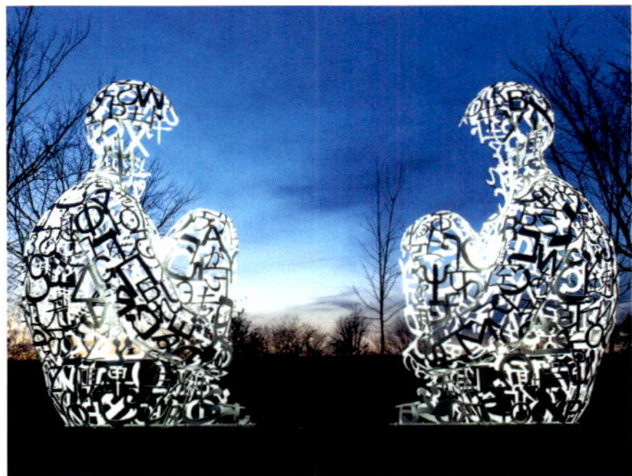

Jaume Plensa (Spanish, born 1955), *Spiegel*, painted
stainless steel, 2010. Two identical figures: H. 12 ft.,
4½ in· (3.77 m); W. 92½ in. (235 cm); Depth:
96½ in. (245 cm). Purchased with funds given by
Rita Barbour Kern and Gift of Mrs. George M.
Jones, Jr., by exchange, 2012.84A–B.
© 2016 Artists Rights Society (ARS), New York

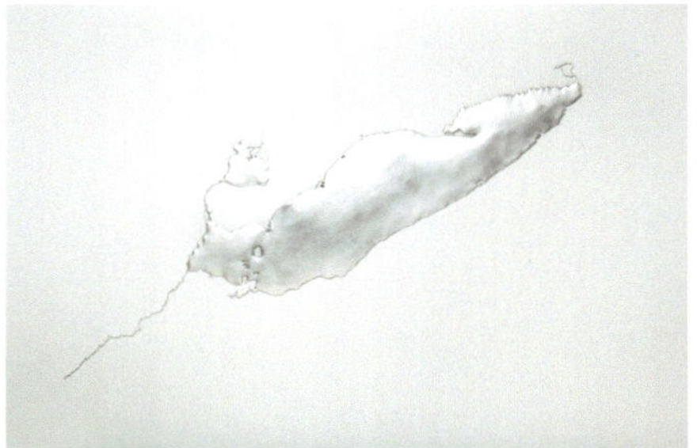

Maya Lin (American, born 1959), *Silver Erie*,
recycled silver, 2012. H. 24¾ in. (62.9 cm);
W. 54 in. (137.2 cm); Depth ½ in. (1.3 cm). Gift of
Mr. & Mrs. William E. Levis, by exchange, 2012.103
© Maya Lin Studio, courtesy Pace Gallery

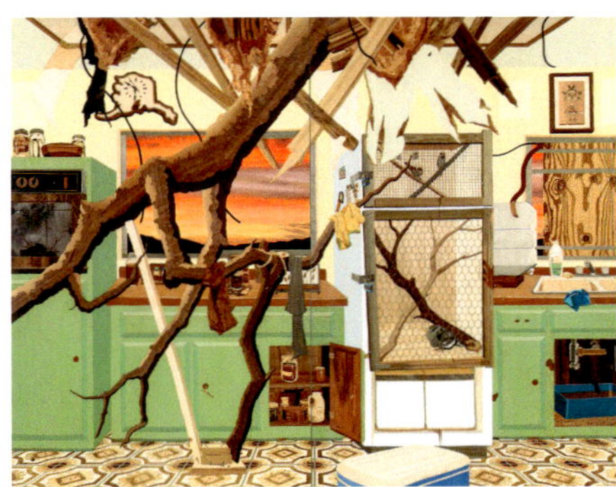

Alison Elizabeth Taylor (American, born 1973),
Kitchen, wood veneer, oil, acrylic, and shellac, 2014.
92 × 116 in. (233.7 × 294.6 cm). Purchased with
funds given in memory of Larry Thompson by his
children and grandchildren, 2014.22
© Alison Elizabeth Taylor, courtesy James Cohan
Gallery

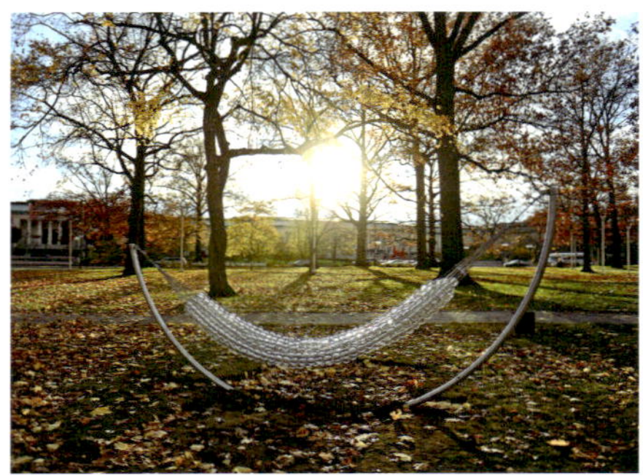

Pinaree Sanpitak (Thai, born 1961), *The Hammock*, blown glass and steel, 2014. Purchased with funds from the Libbey Endowment, Gift of Edward Drummond Libbey, 2015.54
© Pinaree Sanpitak

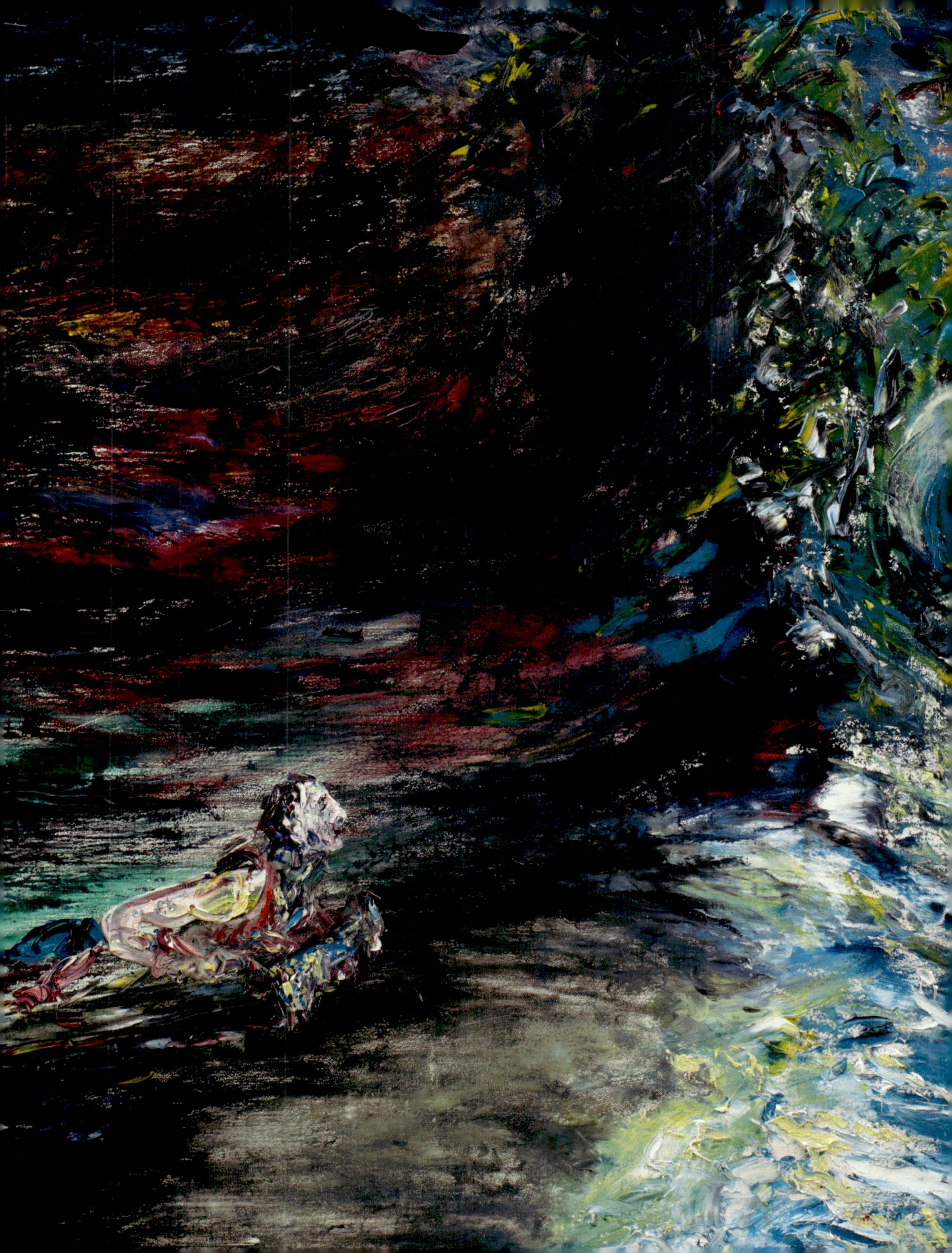

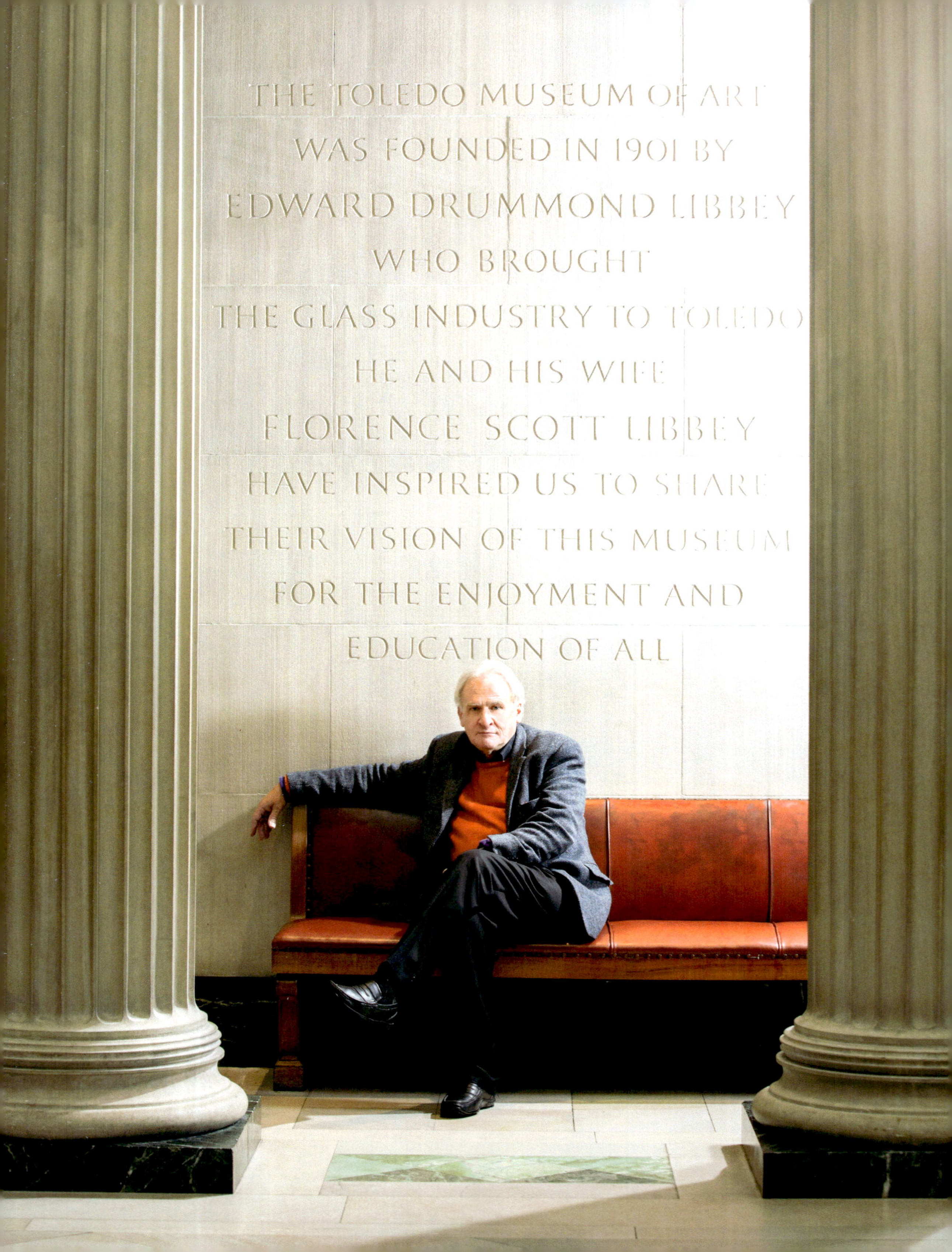
THE TOLEDO MUSEUM OF ART
WAS FOUNDED IN 1901 BY
EDWARD DRUMMOND LIBBEY
WHO BROUGHT
THE GLASS INDUSTRY TO TOLEDO
HE AND HIS WIFE
FLORENCE SCOTT LIBBEY
HAVE INSPIRED US TO SHARE
THEIR VISION OF THIS MUSEUM
FOR THE ENJOYMENT AND
EDUCATION OF ALL

Born in Dublin in 1944, Paul Durcan is celebrated as one of the most original voices in modern Irish literature. In 1981 he was appointed to Aosdána, the Irish equivalent of the American Academy of Arts and Letters. He is a Whitbread Prize–winning poet for the collection *Daddy, Daddy* (1990), was conferred an honorary Doctor of Literature degree by Trinity College, Dublin in 2009 and by University College, Dublin in 2011, and received the Lifetime Achievement Irish Book Award in 2014. He was Ireland Professor of Poetry from 2004 to 2007. He is the author of twenty-five collections of poems, including *The Art of Life* (2004), *The Laughter of Mothers* (2007), *Praise in Which I Live and Move and Have My Being* (2012), and *The Days of Surprise* (2015).

This Toledo Museum of Art publication was made possible with support from Mr. and Mrs. David K. Welles Jr. and the Stephen D. Taylor Family Foundation. Our sincere thanks to Hope and Deke Welles and to Julie and Steve Taylor for supporting the Museum's strategic initiatives to work with artists and teach visual literacy.

Published by the Toledo Museum of Art
2445 Monroe Street
Toledo, Ohio USA 43620
www.toledomuseum.org

Distributed by The Ohio State University Press
180 Pressey Hall
1070 Carmack Road
Columbus, Ohio 43210-1002
www.ohiostatepress.org

Library of Congress Cataloging-in-Publication Data
Names: Durcan, Paul, 1944- author. | Toledo Museum of Art.
Title: Wild, wild erie : poems inspired by works of art in the Toledo Museum of Art, Ohio / Paul Durcan.
Description: First edition. | Toledo, Ohio : Toledo Museum of Art, 2016.
Identifiers: LCCN 2016015499 (print) | LCCN 2016021618 (ebook) | ISBN 9780935172577 (hardcover) | ISBN 9780935172584
Subjects: LCSH: Art—Poetry | BISAC: POETRY / General. | ART / General.
Classification: LCC PR6054.U72 A6 2016 (print) | LCC PR6054.U72 (ebook) | DDC 821/.914—dc23
LC record available at https://lccn.loc.gov/2016015499

ISBN 978-0-935172-57-7

Toledo Museum of Art
Managing Editor: Paula Reich
Rights and Reproduction: Julia Hayes

Produced by Lucia|Marquand, Seattle
www.luciamarquand.com

Designed and typeset by Susan E. Kelly
Typeset in Adobe Garamond
Proofread by Barbara Bowen
Printed and bound in China by Artron Art Group

Cover illustration: Jaume Plensa (Spanish, born 1955), *Spiegel (Mirror)*, painted stainless steel, 2010. Photo: Richard Goodbody.

Frontispiece: Anton Mauve (Dutch, 1838–1888), *A Dutch Road*, oil on canvas, about 1880.

Details: p. 6, Vilhelm Hammershøi, *Interior of Courtyard, Strandgade 30*; p. 10, Edgar Degas, *Victoria Dubourg*; p. 25, Francesco Primaticcio, *Ulysses and Penelope*; p. 38, Thomas Cole, *The Architect's Dream*; p. 52, Pierre-Étienne-Théodore Rousseau, *Under the Birches, Evening*; p. 57, Joseph Mallord William Turner, *The Campo Santo, Venice*; p. 76, Charles-François Daubigny, *Auvers, Landscape with Plough*; p. 93, Childe Hassam, *Rainy Day, Boston*; p. 99, William Harnett, *Still Life with the Toledo Blade*; p. 100, Paul Colin, "Couple Dancing the Charleston (Green Dress)," from *The Black Craze (Le tumulte noir)*; p. 122, John Sloan, *Movies*; p. 131, Édouard Vuillard, *La Salle Clarac*; p. 156, Alison Elizabeth Taylor, *Kitchen*; p. 161, Ronald B. Kitaj, *Notes Toward a Definition of Nobody—A Reverie*; p. 171, Mark di Suvero, *Blubber*; p. 179, Kehinde Wiley, *Saint Francis of Paola*; p. 198, James Tissot, *London Visitors*; p. 213, Jack B. Yeats, *Another Chance*

Photography credits: Richard Goodbody, New York, p. 6, 40, 72, 76, 106, 164, 174, 182, 186, 190, 201, 203, 205, 209, 210, 211; Grand Lubell Photography, Sylvania, Ohio, p. 214; Image Source, Toledo, p. 38, 46, 96, 99, 108, 128, 131, 201, 204, 205, 206; Photography Incorporated (Ray Sess and Carl Schultz), Toledo, p. 2, 10, 20, 22, 25, 26, 28, 34, 44, 50, 52, 54, 57, 62, 66, 71, 80, 82, 84, 88, 93, 102, 110, 120, 122, 124, 132, 142, 146, 148, 152, 158, 161, 198, 199, 200, 201, 202, 203, 204, 205, 206, 208, 209; Christopher Ridgway, p. 150, 209, 213; Tim Thayer, Oak Park, Michigan, p. 172, 210; Toledo Museum of Art, p. 32, 36, 58, 100, 137, 138, 140, 166, 168, 171, 176, 179, 200, 202, 207, 208, 210, 211; Toledo Museum of Art Archives, p. 114, 205; Mark S. Tucker, Philadelphia, p. 16, 199; Andrew Weber, p. 194, 212